Oxford **BUSINESS** ENGLISH

GRAMMAR & PRACTICE

MICHAEL DUCKWORTH

Oxford University Press

Contents

Glossary of grammatical terms

Here is a short explanation of some of the grammatical terms used in this book.

Adjective A word like *large, cold, white, American*, etc. It helps to describe a noun or pronoun.
*I work in a **large, modern** office. It's **nice** and **spacious**.*

Adverb A word like *carefully, quickly, well, sometimes, yesterday, never*, etc. It is normally used to say how or when something happens.
*My father drives **slowly**. I'll see you **tomorrow**.*

Article A word that precedes a noun. *A* and *an* are called 'indefinite articles'; *the* is called the 'definite article'.

Auxiliary verb A verb like *be, do*, or *have* which is used with another (main) verb to form tenses, passives, negatives, and questions.

*The office **is** closed.*	*This **isn't** easy.*
*I **am** working.*	*How **are** you?*
*She **has** gone home.*	***Do** you like Germany?*

Conditional (or **conditional clause**) A clause or sentence constructed with *if, unless*, etc. It is normally used to discuss an event or situation in the future, present, or past, which may or may not be real.
***If** you are late, we'll start the meeting without you.*
***If** I were you, I would pay the bill now.*
***If** the roads hadn't been so busy, we would have arrived on time.*

Continuous form (see **Simple and continuous forms**)

Infinitive The infinitive is the basic form of the verb – *to see, to make, to like*, etc. If you look at the list of irregular verbs on pages 188–90 you will see the infinitive form in the first column. For example:

Infinitive	Past tense form	Past participle
to go	*went*	*gone*

The infinitive is usually introduced with the word *to*.
*I want **to leave**, but it's not so easy **to do**.*

Sometimes we use the 'bare infinitive' – this is the infinitive without the word *to*.
*You must **leave now**. You shouldn't **stay** any longer.*

-ing form
When the *-ing* form of the verb is used as a verb or an adjective, it is called the 'present participle'.
*I saw Peter **leaving**.*
*He's a very **annoying** person.*

The *-ing* form is also used as a noun (sometimes called a 'gerund').
***Travelling** light can help you get through customs quickly.*

Modal verb A word like *can, could, may, might, must, ought, shall, should, will, would*. A modal verb comes before the bare infinitive of another verb, and adds a certain kind of meaning: for example, ability, permission, obligation, probability, or certainty.
*I **can** speak Japanese, but I **can't** write it.*
*The problem **might** be to do with the computer system.*
*You **should** think about taking out a business loan.*
(Modal verbs are also called modal auxiliary verbs.)

Noun A word like *computer, accountant, information, Martin, America*. It is the name of an object, concept, place, or person. 'Concrete nouns' are things you can see or touch, like *a car, a table*, or *an office*. 'Abstract nouns' are things that you cannot see or touch, like *an idea, a decision*, or *an opinion*. Nouns can be countable: *one book, two pages, three ideas, four days*, etc.; or uncountable: *water, advice, freedom* (you cannot say *two waters, an advice*, etc.).

Object The object of a sentence (a noun or noun phrase) usually comes after the verb. In these sentences, *the report* and *a new telephone system* are the objects. They follow the verbs *wrote* and *installed*.
*Peter wrote **the report**.*
*We installed **a new telephone system** last week.*

Participle The *-ing* or *-ed* forms of verb endings. The *-ing* form is called the 'present participle'; the *-ed* form is called the 'past participle'.

Passive and active forms In an active sentence we say what people or things do, so we use active verb forms like *went, explain, is developing, will increase*. In this sentence, *The police* is the subject, *arrested* is the verb and *Alain* is the object. This is an active sentence.
*The police **arrested** Alain.*

In a passive sentence, we say what happens to people or things. The passive is formed by using the verb *to be* and a past participle. The object of the active sentence (*Alain*) becomes the subject. The subject of the active sentence (*the police*) is called the 'agent', and is introduced by the word *by*. This is a passive sentence.

*Alain **was arrested** by the police.*

Preposition A word like *to, in, behind, over, through, into, under*, etc. Prepositions are used to give information about things like place, time, direction, and manner.

*I telephoned our office **in** London **at** 7.00 this morning.*
*Last week we drove **through** the Alps **into** Switzerland.*
*We sent them the documents **by** fax.*

Pronoun A word like *it, me, you, she, they, him, her*, etc. which replaces a noun in a sentence, usually because we do not want to repeat the noun.

*I bought a new fax machine yesterday; **it** was very expensive.*
*Susan's car has been stolen, and **she** is very upset about **it**.*

Relative clause A clause beginning with a word like *who, where, which, whose*, or *that*. It is used to identify someone or something, or to give more information about them.

*These lenses, **which** cost only a few pence to produce, cost over $200 to buy.*
*Stefan Andersson is the consultant **that** we employed on our last project.*

Simple and continuous forms Tenses have both a simple and a continuous form. The simple form carries a sense of completion, or regularity of action. The continuous form carries a sense of continuity, or incompleteness of action. The continuous form ends in *-ing*.

	Simple	Continuous
Present	*he works*	*he is working*
Past	*he worked*	*he was working*
Present perfect	*he has worked*	*he has been working*

Subject The subject of a sentence (a noun or noun phrase) normally comes before the verb. It is usually the person or thing who does something, or is the main focus of attention. In the following sentences, the subjects are *My brother Peter* and *The sales conference*.

***My brother Peter** works in London.*
***The sales conference** will be held in September.*

Tenses The forms of a verb which help us to know the time of an action or event (past, present, or future). There are many different tenses. Here are two examples:

*I **work** in the centre of Munich. (simple present tense)*
*I **worked** in the centre of Munich. (simple past tense)*

Some tenses are formed with the main verb and an extra verb such as *be* or *have*. These extra verbs are called 'auxiliary verbs'.

*Antoinette **is working** late this evening. (present continuous tense)*
*Jan **has finished** his report. (present perfect tense)*

Transitive and intransitive verbs Some verbs are followed by an object, and some are not. If a verb is normally followed by an object, it is called a 'transitive verb'. The verb *to buy* has an object, so in this sentence, *bought* is the transitive verb, and *a car* is the object.

*I **bought** a car.*

If a verb is not normally followed by an object, it is called an 'intransitive verb'. The verb *to travel* does not have an object, so in this sentence, *travels* is an intransitive verb and there is no object.

*She **travels** frequently in Asia.*

Verb A word like *buy, sell, be, seem, think, break, decide*, etc. A verb describes an action, a state, or a process. In the following sentences, *competed, lies, buy*, and *sell* are the verbs.

*Five companies **competed** for the engineering contract.*
*La Défense **lies** to the west of Paris.*
*We **buy** and **sell** shares on the open market.*

1 Present simple

A Form

Look at the example of how to form the present simple tense of the verb **to work**. All verbs except **to be** and the modals (see Units 23–6) follow this pattern.

> I/you/we/they **work/do not** (**don't**) **work**.
> He/she/it **works/does not** (**doesn't**) **work**.
> **Do** I/you/we/they **work**? (**Yes**, I/you/we/they **do**./**No**, I/you/we/they **don't**.)
> **Does** he/she/it **work**? (**Yes**, he/she/it **does**./**No**, he/she/it **doesn't**.)

COMMON MISTAKES: A common mistake is to forget to put the **-s** ending on the he/she/it forms. All verbs except modals must end in **-s** in the third person singular affirmative:

WRONG: *Our new computer system* ~~work~~ *very efficiently.*

RIGHT: *Our new computer system* **works** *very efficiently.*

A second common mistake is to add the **-s** to the he/she/it forms of negatives and questions. We add the **-es** form to the auxiliary (do), and not to the main verb (**work**):

WRONG: *I know Karl* ~~doesn't works~~ *in Accounts.*

RIGHT: *I know Karl* **doesn't work** *in Accounts.*

B Permanent situations

The present simple is used to talk about actions and situations that are generally or permanently true:

IBM is the largest computer company in the world; it **manufactures** *mainframes and PCs and* **sells** *its products all over the world.*

C Routines and frequency

We use the present simple to talk about routines and things we do regularly:

I usually **get** *to the showroom at about 8.00 and I* **have** *a quick look at the post. The sales reps* **arrive** *at about 8.15 and we* **open** *at 8.30.*

D Facts

We use the present simple to talk about scientific or other facts:

Superconductors **are** *special materials that* **conduct** *electricity and* **do not create** *any electrical resistance.*

E Programmes and timetables

We use the present simple to talk about programmes and timetables. When we use the present simple like this, it can refer to the future:

There **are** *two flights to Tokyo next Thursday. There* **is** *a JAL flight that* **leaves** *Heathrow at 20.30 and* **gets** *in at 06.20, and there* **is** *a British Airways flight that* **departs** *at 22.00 and* **arrives** *at 08.50.*

Exercise 1
Form

Complete the dialogue using the verbs in brackets.

A: Where (1) *do you come* (come) from?
B: I (2)_____ (come) from Thailand. *come*
A: (3)_____ (you/live) in Bangkok? *Do you Live*
B: No, I (4)_____ (not/live) in Bangkok. I (5)_____ (live) in Chang Mai. *dont Live* *Live*
A: What (6)_____ (you/do)? *do you do?*
B: I'm an accountant. I (7)_____ (work) for Berli Jucker. *worKe*
A: How often (8)_____ (you/travel) to England? *do you travel.*
B: I (9)_____ (not/come) here very often.

Exercise 2
Permanent situations
(company activities)

Complete the information about the business activities of the Thai company Berli Jucker, using the verbs in the box.

operate	own	be

Berli Jucker Group (1) *is* one of Thailand's oldest trading organizations, and it (2)_____ a number of different companies that (3)_____ in four main business areas: manufacturing, engineering, marketing, and services.

export	have	produce

In our manufacturing division, we (4)____*have*____ factories that (5)__*produce*__ bottles, soap, and cosmetics for the local market, and we also (6)__*export*__ medical equipment to Europe.

install	do	manufacture

Our engineering division (7)_____ a great deal of work for Thailand's electricity authority; it (8)_____ Siemens power control systems, and our factory at Thai-Scandic Steel (9)_____ large steel structures for the electricity industry.

be	handle	import

There (10)_____ also a Marketing and Distribution division. This (11)_____ goods from our factories in Thailand, and also (12)_____ a wide range of products from overseas.

consist	be	sell

Our services division (13)_____ of a travel agency, Pacific Leisure, and an insurance group. There (14)_____ also a new Information Systems department which (15)_____ Informix products and FourGen applications.

1 Practice

Exercise 3
Routines and frequency

Complete the dialogue by putting the verbs into the correct form.

BRIAN: I need to speak to Gina about this new publicity brochure. [1]*Do you know* (you/know) where she is?

DIANA: She [2]_____ (not/work) on Fridays. She only [3]_____ (have) a part-time job now.

BRIAN: Right. When [4]_____ (she/come) to the office?

DIANA: Well, she [5]_____ (come) in from Monday to Thursday, but she [6]_____ (not/stay) all day. She usually [7]_____ (start) at 9.00 and [8]_____ (go) home at about 2.15.

Exercise 4
Scientific facts

Complete the passage using the verbs in the box.

go   have   make   rise

Cuts in interest rates [1]*have* a number of good effects on the economy. Firstly, they [2]_____ it easier for companies to make profits, because the cost of repaying loans [3]_____ down. As a result, share prices usually [4]_____.

feel   help   lead   spend

The second reason is that consumers [5]_____ more confident, so they [6]_____ more in the shops. This also [7]_____ manufacturers and retailers to increase their turnover. However, if interest rates are too low, this can sometimes [8]_____ to higher inflation.

Exercise 5
Programmes and timetables

Read the following dialogue. Make any necessary changes to the verbs in brackets.

LAURA: I need to be in Birmingham for a meeting tomorrow by 3.15. Have you got a train timetable?

CLAIRE: Yes, here it is. Right, there [1]*is* (be) a train at 12.47, and that [2]_____ (arrive) at 2.50, but it [3]_____ (stop) at most of the main stations on the way.

LAURA: Is there another one that [4]_____ (get) there before 3.00?

CLAIRE: No, but there [5]_____ (be) an Intercity Express that [6]_____ (get) in at five past.

LAURA: And when [7]_____ (it/leave)?

CLAIRE: It [8]_____ (go) at 1.15.

LAURA: [9]_____ (be) there any buses to East Street?

CLAIRE: Oh, yes, there's a bus that [10]_____ (run) every ten minutes and it only [11]_____ (take) about five minutes to East Street.

Choose a word from box A and a word from box B to describe what these people do, making any necessary changes to the verbs.

	A		B	
Personnel officers	Management consultants	invest	advise
An architect	A stockbroker	design	look after
A journalist	An air steward	write	arrange
Venture capitalists	Auditors	check	buy and sell

1 *An air steward looks after* passengers on a plane.
2 _____ stocks and shares.
3 _____ houses.
4 _____ in small, high-risk companies.
5 _____ the accounts of a company.
6 _____ companies on how they should be run.
7 _____ articles for a newspaper.
8 _____ interviews.

Look at the information about Berli Jucker on page 7, and write down some similar information about the business activities of your company.

_____
_____
_____
_____

Answer the following questions about your daily routine.

1 How do you get to work in the morning?
_____

2 How long does it take to get to work?
_____

3 What do you do in the mornings?
_____

4 What do you do for lunch?
_____

5 What do you do in the afternoons?
_____

6 What time do you usually finish?
_____

7 What do you do at the weekends?
_____

2 Present continuous

A Form

The present continuous is formed by using the present tense of the auxiliary verb **be** and the **-ing** form of the verb:

> I **am working/am not working.**
> He/she/it **is/is not (isn't)working.**
> You/we/they **are/are not (aren't) working.**
> **Am** I working? (**Yes, I am./No, I'm not.**)
> **Is** he/she/it **working**? (**Yes**, he/she/it **is./No**, he/she/it/ **isn't.**)
> **Are** you/we/they **working**? (**Yes**, you/we/they **are./No**, you/we/they **aren't.**)

(For spelling rules, see Appendix 1.)

B Moment of speaking

The present continuous is used to talk about an activity taking place at the moment of speaking:

*I'm afraid Mr Jackson's not available at the moment. He is **talking** to a customer on the other phone.*

C Current projects

The present continuous is used to talk about actions or activities and current projects that are taking place over a period of time (even if they are not taking place precisely at the moment of speaking):

*Barton's is one of the largest local construction companies. At the moment we **are building** a new estate with 200 houses and we **are negotiating** with the council for the sale of development land in Boxley Wood.*

D Temporary situations

The present continuous is used to indicate that an action or activity is temporary rather than permanent. Compare:

*Mrs Harding **organizes** our conferences and book launches.*
(The present simple is used because this is generally true.)

*Mrs Harding is away on maternity leave, so **I am organizing** them.*
(The present continuous is used because this is only true for a limited time.)

E Slow changes

The present continuous is used to describe current trends and slow changes that are taking place:

*The latest economic statistics show that both unemployment and inflation **are falling**, and that the economy **is growing** at an annual rate of 2.6%.*

(For information about how the present continuous is used to refer to the future, see Unit 13.)

Exercise 1
Moment of speaking

Put the verbs in brackets into the present continuous.

1 Could I ring you back in a few minutes? I *am talking* (talk) to someone
on the other line.
2 Jane's upstairs with Anne and Roy. They _____ (have) a meeting
about the catalogue.
3 What _____ (you/do) here? I thought you had gone to the airport.
4 Could you tell Mr Ford that Miss Lee is here? He _____ (expect) me.
5 Oh no, the printer _____ (not work). I'll call the Maintenance
Department.
6 This is a very bad line. _____ (you/call) from your car phone?
7 I _____ (phone) to tell you that your account is overdrawn by £326.

Exercise 2
Current projects

Read these newspaper extracts about various projects that different companies
are currently involved in. Match the extracts in column A with the extracts in
column B.

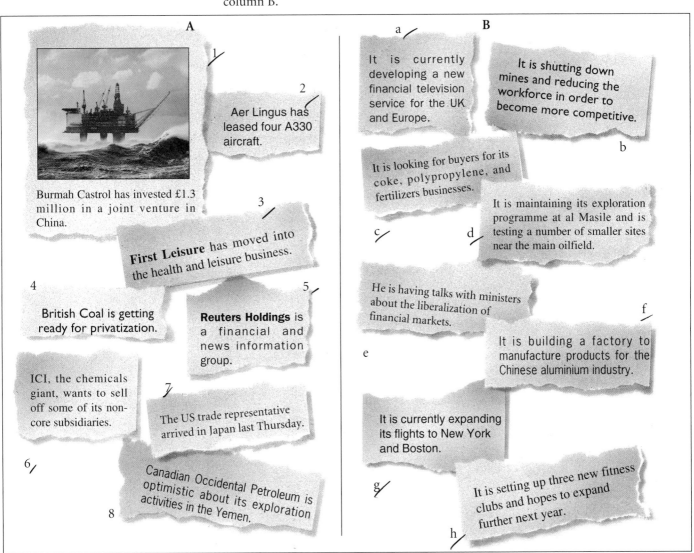

A

1

2 Aer Lingus has leased four A330 aircraft.

Burmah Castrol has invested £1.3 million in a joint venture in China.

3 **First Leisure** has moved into the health and leisure business.

4 British Coal is getting ready for privatization.

5 **Reuters Holdings** is a financial and news information group.

ICI, the chemicals giant, wants to sell off some of its non-core subsidiaries.

7 The US trade representative arrived in Japan last Thursday.

6

Canadian Occidental Petroleum is optimistic about its exploration activities in the Yemen.

8

B

a It is currently developing a new financial television service for the UK and Europe.

It is shutting down mines and reducing the workforce in order to become more competitive.

b

It is looking for buyers for its coke, polypropylene, and fertilizers businesses.

c

It is maintaining its exploration programme at al Masile and is testing a number of smaller sites near the main oilfield.

d

He is having talks with ministers about the liberalization of financial markets.

e

f It is building a factory to manufacture products for the Chinese aluminium industry.

It is currently expanding its flights to New York and Boston.

g

It is setting up three new fitness clubs and hopes to expand further next year.

h

Practice

Two friends meet in Paris. Read the dialogue and put the verbs into the present continuous.

PIERRE: Hello, Jason. What [1] *are you doing* (you/do) over here?

JASON: Hello, Pierre. I'm just here for a few days. I [2] _____ (attend) the conference at the Pompidou Centre.

PIERRE: Where [3] _____ (you/stay)?

JASON: At the Charles V.

PIERRE: Very nice. And how's business?

JASON: Not that good. The recession [4] _____ (affect) us. People [5] _____ (not/spend) very much and we [6] _____ (not/get) many new orders, but it could be worse. How about you?

PIERRE: It's much the same over here. Interest rates are still very high, so everyone [7] _____ (try) to cut down on expenses. Not many companies [8] _____ (buy) new equipment, so it means that our Training Division [9] _____ (not/do) very well. Still, our Financial Services Division [10] _____ (manage) to get new customers, because in the current climate there are a lot of people who [11] _____ (look) for good financial advice.

Read the following passages about changes that are taking place in the software industry. Fill in the blanks with the verbs from the box, using the present continuous.

spend	come	sell	shrink

After two years in which the price of PCs has fallen by half, the price of software [1] *is coming* down too. The big software houses [2] _____ software at lower and lower prices, and a price war looks inevitable. The profit margins of major companies like Borland, Lotus, and Microsoft [3] _____ . In the last quarter Borland were down to a mere 2.6%. In addition, they [4] _____ less and less on R&D, which may affect their long-term product plans.

become	begin	take over	turn

Now the major software companies [5] _____ their attention to the less profitable home computer market, and software packages for children, such as Microsoft's 'Creative Writer' [6] _____ from business software. Specialist computer shops are [7] _____ less popular, as families are unwilling to spend their weekends there, and computers [8] _____ to appear in supermarkets such as Wal-Mart and Costco.

....
Task 1

Continue these sentences using a verb in the present continuous.

1   I'm afraid the MD is busy. *He's having a meeting with the auditors.*
2   Could you call the maintenance people? _____
3   The meeting room isn't free. _____
4   I've just seen Jane in the cafeteria. _____
5   Shh! Listen! _____

....
Task 2

Answer these questions about yourself and your company's current projects.

1   What new product or service is your company currently working on?

_____

2   What are you doing at work these days?

_____

3   What training courses are you doing?

_____

4   What examinations or professional qualifications are you studying for?

_____

5   What other aims and objectives are you trying to achieve outside work?

_____

....
Task 3

Complete the following paragraph about a temporary situation. Say how people are dealing with one or more of the following problems.

No transport (trains, buses, underground, etc.)
No emergency services (ambulances, fire brigade, etc.)
No local government services (rubbish collection, etc.)
No postal service

The General Strike is now in its second week, and is causing widespread chaos and disruption in the capital ...

....
Task 4

Write about changes currently taking place in the car market, using the prompts.

1   size   *On the whole, cars are getting smaller.*
2   safety   Nowadays ... _____
3   the Japanese   These days ... _____
4   reliability   _____
5   electric cars   _____
6   pollution   _____

3 Present simple vs present continuous

Read through the following examples comparing the present simple and present continuous.

A Routine vs moment of speaking

1 *James **works** for an investment magazine. Every month he **writes** articles about new investment opportunities.*
2 *Take these figures to James. He needs them for an article **he's writing**.*

In 1, we are talking about something that James does as a routine.
In 2, we are talking about something he is doing at the moment of speaking.

B General activities vs current projects

1 *I work for 'Teletraining'. We **make** training videos.*
2 *At the moment **we're making** a training video for British Telecom.*

In 1, we are talking about a general activity.
In 2, we are talking about a specific current project.

C Permanent vs temporary situations

1 *Peter **deals with** enquiries about our car fleet sales.*
2 *I **am dealing with** enquiries about fleet sales while Peter is away on holiday.*

In 1, this is seen as permanently true.
In 2, this is seen as a temporary situation.

D Facts vs slow changes

1 *As a rule, cheap imports **lead to** greater competition.*
2 *Cheap imports **are leading to** the closure of a number of inefficient factories.*

In 1, we are making a statement about a general fact that is always true.
In 2, we are talking about a change that is taking place at the moment.

E Stative verbs

There are a number of verbs which describe states rather than actions. They are not normally used in the continuous form. Common examples are:

Verbs of thinking:	**believe, doubt, guess, imagine, know, realize, suppose, understand**
Verbs of the senses:	**hear, smell, sound, taste**
Verbs of possession:	**belong to, have** (meaning **possess**), **own, possess**
Verbs of emotion:	**dislike, hate, like, love, prefer, regret, want, wish**
Verbs of appearance:	**appear, seem**
Others:	**contain, depend on, include, involve, mean, measure, weigh, require**

These are usually found in the simple form because they do not refer to actions:

*I'm sorry, I don't **understand** what you mean.*

Exercise 1
Routine vs moment
of speaking

Decide if the speaker is talking about routine activities or activities going on at the moment of speaking. Put the verbs into the present simple or the present continuous.

A: How (1) *do you usually organize* (you/usually organize) the delivery of milk to the factory? (2) _____ (the farmers/bring) it here themselves?

B: No, (3) _____ (we/always collect) the milk ourselves, and the tankers (4) _____ (deliver) it to the pasteurization plant twice a day.

A: What sort of safety procedures (5) _____ (you/have)?

B: As a rule we (6) _____ (test) samples of every consignment, and then the milk (7) _____ (pass) down insulated pipes to the bottling plant, which (8) _____ (operate) 24 hours a day. I'll show you round a bit later, but the production line (9) _____ (not work) at the moment because the employees (10) _____ (change) shifts.

Exercise 2
General activities vs
current projects

Decide whether the verbs refer to general activities or current projects. Put the verbs into the present simple or present continuous.

Our company was founded fifteen years ago, and we (1) *manufacture* (manufacture) and (2) _____ (supply) clothing to large organizations such as the police, hospitals, and so on. We always (3) _____ (spend) a long time talking to the customers to find out their needs. At the moment we (4) _____ (produce) an order for 18,000 shirts for the police. The next order is for a local electronics factory, and our head designer (5) _____ (have) discussions with them to find out what sort of clothes they (6) _____ (require).

Exercise 3
Permanent vs temporary
situations

In the following exercise, decide whether these situations are permanent or temporary. Put the verbs into the present simple or present continuous.

1 He joined the company 25 years ago and he still *works* (work) for us.

2 We _____ (not/send) out any orders this week because we're waiting for the new lists.

3 I _____ (deal) with Mr Jarman's clients this week because he's away.

4 Go down this road, turn right, and the road _____ (lead) straight to the industrial estate.

5 Because of the high cost of sterling, exports _____ (not/do) very well.

6 The stock market can be risky because the price of shares _____ (vary) according to economic conditions.

7 She would be excellent as a European sales rep because she _____ (speak) French fluently.

8 I'm Heinrich Brandt, I'm German, and I _____ (come) from a small town near Munich.

9 We _____ (spend) a great deal on phone calls due to a postal strike.

A   In the following passage, decide whether the verbs refer to general statements about change, or changes that are currently taking place. Put the verbs into the present simple or present continuous.

Political parties cannot last for ever. Normally they [1] _enjoy_ (enjoy) a period of great popularity in their early years; then they [2] _____ (go) through a period of stability and [3] _____ (put) their ideas into practice. After that, they [4] _____ (run) out of ideas, and the opposition [5] _____ (take) power. Now the present government [6] _____ (become) old and tired. It [7] _____ (make) mistakes and it [8] _____ (lose) popularity, and the opposition party [9] _____ (start) to look like a possible alternative.

B   Fill in the blanks with the verbs in the box, using the present simple or present continuous.

fall   grow   begin   go   demand   make

In many ways, the economic outlook is good. Unemployment [1] _is falling_ and is now down to 8% from 14%. The economy [2] _____ at a rate of 2.5%. However, the real danger is that inflation [3] _____ to rise. This is dangerous because every time that inflation [4] _____ up, people always [5] _____ higher wages, and this in turn [6] _____ the problem worse.

In each of the following sentences, put one of the verbs into the present simple and the other into the present continuous.

1   We _are interviewing_ (interview) people from outside the company for the new post in the export department, but I _think_ (think) we ought to give the job to Mr Jackson.
2   At the moment we _____ (carry) out a survey to find out what sort of after-sales service our customers _____ (want).
3   We've got a competition on at work to do with our new range of cosmetics. The marketing people _____ (try) to find a brand name that _____ (sound) natural and sophisticated.
4   _____ (you/know) what Mrs Ericson _____ (do)? She's not in her office and nobody has seen her since lunch.
5   Could you help me? I _____ (try) to translate this letter from a Spanish client and I don't know what this word _____ (mean).
6   I _____ (apply) for a transfer to our London office, but I don't know if I'll be successful. It all _____ (depend) on whether or not they have any vacancies.
7   Their new 'Own brand' instant coffee _____ (taste) very good, so it's not surprising that it _____ (become) more and more popular.

| Task 1 | Make up sentences using the following prompts. The first verb should be in the present simple, and the second verb in the present continuous. |

1 come from/but/live
   I come from Austria, but at the moment I'm living in Switzerland.

2 speak/and/learn

   _____

3 normally/like my work/but/not enjoy

   _____

4 go on a lot of training courses/and/do a course in CAD

   _____

5 work from 9 to 5/but/stay late

   _____

6 travel a lot/and/visit Australia

   _____

7 have several subsidiaries in Europe/and/set up another one in Brussels

   _____

8 normally/export a lot to Greece/but/not get many orders

   _____

| Task 2 | Make questions to go with the answers. Use either the present simple or present continuous. |

1 *Where do you come from?*
   I come from a little town called Zug, near Zurich.

2 _____
   I'm writing to Markson's to ask for an up-to-date catalogue.

3 _____
   I think he's a consultant.

4 _____
   I usually cycle in, but sometimes I bring the car.

5 _____
   Our Sales Director goes abroad about three or four times a year.

6 _____
   No, not at all well. In fact, the factory is doing a three-day week.

7 _____
   Yes, very well. We met in 1980.

8 _____
   No, not at the moment. But we'll start taking on new staff again in May.

4 Simple past

A Form

The simple past (positive) is formed by using the past tense form. Regular verbs add **-d** or **-ed** to the bare infinitive to form the past tense. For negatives and questions we use the auxiliary **did** and the infinitive:

I/you/he/she/it/we/they **worked/did not** (**didn't**) **work**.
Did I/you/he/she/it/we/they **work**? (**Yes**, I/you/etc. **did./No**, I/you/etc. **didn't**.)

COMMON MISTAKES: A common mistake is to use the past tense form in negatives and in questions. We use the auxiliary **did** and bare infinitive:

WRONG: ~~Did you checked~~ the figures? No, I ~~didn't checked~~ them.
RIGHT: **Did you check** the figures? No, I **didn't check** them.

The verb **to be** follows a different pattern:

I/he/she/it **was/was not** (**wasn't**) ...
We/you/they **were/were not** (**weren't**) ...
Was I/he/she/it ... ? (**Yes**, I/he/she/it **was./ No**, I/he/she/it **wasn't**.)
Were we/you/they ...? (**Yes**, we/you/they **were./No**, we/you/they **weren't**.)

B Irregular verbs

Many common verbs do not add **-ed** to the bare infinitive to form the simple past, but change in other ways. Look at these common examples:

*I **went** to a very interesting presentation last week.* (BARE INFINITIVE: **go**)
*I **rang** her yesterday, but she **wasn't** in the office.* (BARE INFINITIVE: **ring**, **be**)

(A full list of common irregular verbs is in Appendix 2.)

C Completed actions

The simple past is used to talk about completed actions in the past:

*James Sainsbury **set up** a dairy in 1869. The business **expanded** and **diversified**, and eventually **became** the largest chain of supermarkets in Britain.*

D Time expressions with prepositions

As in the example above, the simple past is often used with expressions that refer to points of time in the past. Look at the following common examples and at the prepositions that are used with them:

at	6 o'clock/1.15/the end of the year/Christmas
on	Tuesday/15th May/the 21st/New Year's Day
in	January/1987/the 1980s/summer
no preposition	yesterday/yesterday morning/last Monday/next April/a few days ago/the day before yesterday/when I was young

Use the verbs in the box to complete the sentences. Some of the sentences are positive statements, some are negative, and some are questions.

accept	complain	hire	place	realize	study	visit

1 Oh, I'm sorry to disturb you. I _didn't realize_ you had a visitor.
2 _____ you _____ economics when you were at university?
3 She _____ _____ the job because the salary was too low.
4 Last week a number of customers _____ about slow service.
5 _____ you _____ the Acropolis when you were in Greece?
6 I am writing with reference to the order I _____ with you last week.
7 At last year's launch party, who _____ you _____ to do the catering?

A Write in the missing form of each of the irregular verbs below. Each verb can be used with the expressions on the right.

BARE INFINITIVE	PAST TENSE	EXPRESSIONS
run	ran	... a business, ... out of something, ... up a bill
do	_____	... a job well, ... your best, ... business (with)
make	_____	... a profit, ... a mistake, ... a complaint
_____	went	... abroad, ... out for a meal, ... bankrupt
write	_____	... a letter, ... a report, ... out a cheque
_____	had	... lunch, ... a meeting, ... problems
pay	_____	... by credit card, ... cash, ... in advance
_____	sold	... something at a profit, ... at a loss, ... out

B Choose a past tense form and one of the expressions above to complete the following sentences.

1 He made some calls from his hotel room and _ran up_ a large phone _bill_.
2 We _____ with that company a few years ago, but then we stopped dealing with them.
3 The company lost money in its first year, but last year it _____ of £2.5m.
4 He couldn't find a suitable job in his own country, so he _____ to look for work.
5 When the consultants had finished their study they _____ for the directors, giving a list of recommendations.
6 The engineers _____ with the gearbox, so they made some modifications to it.
7 They didn't want cash or a cheque, so I _____ .
8 The product was very popular. We _____ on the first day and ordered more stock.

4 Practice

Complete the following passage by putting the verbs into the past tense.

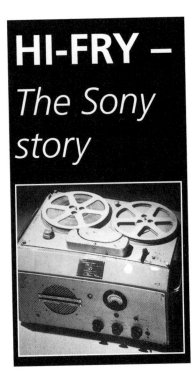

After the Second World War, Akio Morita, the co-founder of Sony,[1] *joined* (join) forces with a friend, Masaru Ibuka. Both men [2] _____ (know) a great deal about telecommunications, so they [3] _____ (use) all their money, about £100, and [4] _____ (set) up a small engineering company, Tokyo Tsushin Kogyo. They [5] _____ (find) a small broken-down building to use as a laboratory in Tokyo. There [6] _____ (be) so many holes in the roof that when it [7] _____ (rain), they [8] _____ (have) to continue working under umbrellas.

  Their first task [9] _____ (be) to decide what to make. They [10] _____ (not want) to make radios because of the competition from much larger companies. Instead, they [11] _____ (decide) to create an entirely new product, a tape recorder. They [12] _____ (succeed) in making a machine, but unfortunately they [13] _____ (not have) any tape, and they [14] _____ (not know) how to produce it.

  So they [15] _____ (start) to experiment, and [16] _____ (try) using a number of different materials. Finally, they [17] _____ (make) a breakthrough. They [18] _____ (cut) up strips of paper to make a reel, and [19] _____ (paint) them with a magnetic material that they [20] _____ (heat) on a frying pan in their small room. It [21] _____ (work), and they gradually [22] _____ (improve) the process. In 1950, they [23] _____ (begin) trying to sell their revolutionary machine.

And the rest is history!

Make questions from the prompts and complete each answer by using **in**, **on**, **at**, or no preposition.

1 When/she/complete/the report   *When did she complete her report?*
   She completed her report <u>on</u> Friday.

2 When/they/set up/the company   _____
   They set up the company _____ the 1950s.

3 When/you/go abroad   _____
   I went abroad _____ June.

4 When/the meeting/finish   _____
   The meeting finished _____ 3.15.

5 When/you/order the parts   _____
   We ordered the parts _____ 11 August.

6 When/you/pay for them   _____
   I paid for them _____ the day before yesterday.

In 1990, a small shoe company lost a great deal of money. Then a new group of managers arrived and made it profitable. Say what they did, using the past tense.

1   There were fourteen very old directors on the board.
    They made all the directors redundant.

2   Their offices were too small.

    _____

3   The factory where they made shoes used very old machinery.

    _____

4   The workers in the factory disliked their working conditions.

    _____

5   The company had two loss-making subsidiaries.

    _____

6   The company only had two salesmen.

    _____

7   All the company's customers came from the local area.

    _____

8   The company's products were very old-fashioned.

    _____

9   The company's suppliers always complained about late payment.

    _____

10 The Accounts Department did all the book-keeping by hand.

    _____

Write a short paragraph about your career history, giving the dates where possible. Here is an example:

Roderick Salmon went to university in 1973, where he studied economics. He graduated in 1976 and joined Arthur Andersen. He qualified as a Chartered Accountant in 1980, and worked for the company for three years. In 1983, he did an MBA at INSEAD in France, and then got a job with Yamaichi, a Japanese investment bank. In 1987 he left the bank and became the Financial Director of a television company.

_____

_____

_____

_____

_____

5 Present perfect (1)

A Form

The present perfect tense is formed by using the present tense of the auxiliary **have** and the past participle:

> I/you/we/they **have taken/have not (haven't) taken.**
> He/she/it **has taken/has not (hasn't) taken.**
> **Have** I/you/we/they **taken?** (Yes, I/you/we/they **have.**/No, I/you/we/they **haven't.**)
> **Has** he/she/it **taken?** (**Yes**, he/she/it **has.**/No, he/she/it **hasn't.**)

(The past participles of regular verbs end in **-d** or **-ed**, and have the same form as the past tense. For a list of irregular verbs, see Appendix 2, page 188.)

B Present result of the past

We use the present perfect to talk about a present situation which is a result of something that happened at an unspecified time in the past. Therefore we do not use specific time expressions such as **yesterday**, **last week**, etc.:

*I **have given** your report to the MD.*
(I gave him your report and he has it now.)
*I **have sent** them the samples they wanted.*
(I sent them. They are in the post now.)

C Specific and non-specific time

If we need to mention the specific time when something happened, we use the simple past, not the present perfect:

WRONG: *I ~~have spoken~~ to her yesterday.*
RIGHT: *I spoke to her yesterday.*

Similarly, with expressions such as **on Monday, in 1987, at 3.30**, etc. (see Unit 4), or with questions beginning **When ...?** and **How long ago ...?**, we use the simple past and not the present perfect.

D Just

The present perfect is often used with the word **just** to talk about actions that have taken place very recently. The exact time is not mentioned:

*I'm sorry, Mrs Smith is not here. **She has just left.***

E Been and gone

Notice the difference between **has been** and **has gone**:

*I'm afraid Mr Smith is not here at the moment. He **has gone** to a meeting in London.*
(He is still at the meeting.)

*Amanda **has been** to the travel agent. She has your tickets for Hong Kong.*
(She went to the travel agent and has returned.)

Exercise 1
Form

Complete the following sentences by putting the irregular verbs into the present perfect.

1 I'm going to send them a reminder. They *haven't paid* (not pay) us for their last order.
2 Their shares _____ (fall) by over 23% and now look like a good buy.
3 _____ (you/write) to them about that shipment, or do you want me to phone them?
4 We _____ (spend) a lot on modernizing the factory, and it is now very well equipped.
5 Unemployment is very high here because a lot of factories _____ (shut) down.
6 The lawyers _____ (draw) up the contracts, so we are now ready to go ahead with the deal.
7 I _____ (not speak) to the MD about your proposal, but I will soon.
8 _____ (you/find) a suitable replacement for Mr Chambers, or is the post still vacant?
9 Anne _____ (just/get) back from lunch. Why don't you call her now?
10 Peter, _____ (you/meet) David Long? He's our new Finance Director.

Exercise 2
Present result of the past

Match each sentence in column A with the two sentences in column B that give more information about: (i) the action in the past, and (ii) the result in the present.

A	B
1 *I have missed my flight to Rome.*	A We moved offices two months ago.
	B We bought some new machinery.
2 I have lost that file on Inchcape.	C It dropped in value yesterday.
	D The factory is now very efficient.
3 We have relocated to Corby.	E It is trading at $1.90 to the pound.
	F A lot of firms are in trouble.
4 The dollar has fallen sharply.	G *I arrived at the airport late.*
	H The economy slowed down last year.
5 We have automated our production lines.	I I don't know where it is.
	J *I am waiting for another plane.*
6 The recession has been very severe.	K We have a new address.
	L I put it somewhere.

5 Practice

Exercise 3
Specific and non-specific time

Read the following newspaper extracts and say when these actions took place. If you do not have the information, write **don't know**.

(Financial Times, page 5, 31 January 1994)

China (1) **has extended** its freeze on new capital spending projects until the end of this year as part of an effort to combat inflation. The State Council, China's cabinet, (2) **announced** at the weekend that 'no new fixed-asset investment projects' would be approved.

(The Times, page 21, 29 January 1994)

The seemingly unstoppable success story of J Sainsbury, Britain's biggest supermarket group, (3) **came** to an abrupt halt yesterday when they (4) **warned** that profits in the current year would be substantially lower than market expectations. The news (5) **hit** Sainsbury's shares, which (6) **plummeted** from 481p to 393p.

(Financial Times, page 14, 31 January 1994)

Two years ago it (7) **seemed** as though Mr Trump might no longer have his desk, his office, his tower, or any of the rest of the property and casino empire he (8) **built up** during the 1980s. And yet, he (9) **has survived**. Helped by the cashflows from his casinos, he (10) **has paid** off a large part of his debt.

1	has extended	*don't know*	6	plummeted	_____
2	announced	*at the weekend*	7	seemed	_____
3	came	_____	8	built	_____
4	warned	_____	9	has survived	_____
5	hit	_____	10	has paid off	_____

Exercise 4
Just

Complete the sentences with one of the verbs in the box, using **just** and the present perfect.

announce arrive buy give leave read speak

1 I'm afraid Mr Jamieson isn't here. He *has just left*.
2 A: There's an article in the paper about BMW.
   B: Yes, I know. I _____ it.
3 He's feeling very pleased. They _____ him a pay rise.
4 I _____ a new car. Would you like to come and have a look at it?
5 A parcel for you _____ in reception. Shall I send it up to you?
6 I _____ to the MD about your proposals, and he wants to discuss them with you.
7 The company _____ that it is going to close the Glasgow factory next month.

Exercise 5
Been and **gone**

Fill in the blanks with **have/has been** or **have/has gone**.

1 I'm afraid Mr Davis has gone to Bali and won't be back for two weeks.
2 Ask Amanda where to stay in New York. She _____ there a few times.
3 I _____ to the printers to collect the brochures. They're in my car.
4 Mr Lund _____ to Oslo. I can give you the phone number of his hotel if you like.
5 I don't know where their new offices are. I _____ not _____ there.

Complete these sentences. Use a verb in the present perfect to explain why the present situation has occurred.

1   Our sales are improving because …
    we have introduced some new product lines.

2   Our agent wants the brochures delivered urgently because …
    _____ .

3   Maria is off work for three months because …
    _____ .

4   It is now much easier for us to export because …
    _____ .

5   At the moment the government is very unpopular because …
    _____ .

6   This year's coffee crop in Colombia will be very small because …
    _____ .

7   I think it would be a good time to buy shares now because …
    _____ .

Write short paragraphs about the changes that have taken place.

1   The new supermarket is attracting a lot of new customers.
    The new managers have refurbished the building completely and they have put in a new delicatessen section. They have improved their range of fresh foods and have added a cafeteria.

2   The office isn't the same as it was when you were here.
    _____
    _____

3   The company is now in a much better financial position.
    _____
    _____

Complete or continue these sentences using **just** and the present perfect.

1   *I have just seen Jane.* She wants to have a word with you.
2   He probably won't come in to work today because _____ .
3   Yes, the report is ready. _____ .
4   Boeing's financial future now looks very secure. _____ .
5   Why don't we have lunch in that new restaurant that _____ ?
6   I think she must be out. _____ .
7   No, I won't have a coffee, thank you. _____ .

6 Present perfect (2): **ever**, **never**, **already**, **yet**

A Ever and **never** +
present perfect or simple
past

The present perfect is often used with the words **ever** and **never** to talk about general life experience:

*Have you **ever worked** abroad?* (i.e., In all your life up to now?)
*I **have never been** to America.* (i.e., Not in all my life up to now.)

The present perfect with **ever** is often followed by the simple past. We use the simple past to give more information about a completed action, when referring to a specific time or context:

*Have you **ever been** to Hong Kong?*
*Yes, I **have**. I **worked** there when I was with Coopers and Lybrand.*

B Already and **yet**

The present perfect is often used with **already** and **yet**:

*They are getting on well with the new building. They **have already**
modernized the warehouse, but they **haven't decorated** the reception area **yet**.*

Already is used in positive sentences. It often indicates that something has taken place slightly earlier than expected. Notice its position in the sentence:

*She **has already shown** me the figures.* (NOT: *She has shown already …*)

Yet is used in questions and negatives. It shows that we expect an action will take place if it has not happened up to now. Notice the position of **yet**, and **not yet**:

*Have you **talked** to Peter **yet**?* (NOT: *Have you talked yet to Peter?*)
*I **have not talked** to him **yet**.* (NOT: *I have not talked yet to him.*)

C Finished and unfinished
periods of time

The present perfect is often used with prepositions or prepositional phrases indicating periods of time that have not finished yet. Common examples are: **today**, **this morning**, **this month**, **this year**, **so far**, **to date**, **over the last few weeks**, **up to now**, etc.:

*This month we **have received** a lot of complaints about late deliveries.*
(The month has not finished, and there may be more complaints.)

If we are speaking after one of these time periods, we use the simple past because we are referring to a period of time that has finished. Compare:

Have you seen John this morning?
(It is now 11.15 in the morning; the morning has not finished.)

Did you see John this morning?
(It is now 2.30 in the afternoon; the morning has finished.)

Exercise 1

Ever, **never** +
present perfect

Make up typical interview questions and answers, using the prompts.

1   work for yourself
    A: _Have you ever worked for yourself?_
    B: _Yes, I have._ or _No, I have never worked for myself._

2   work for a multinational company
    A: _____?
    B: _____

3   have experience of managing people
    A: _____?
    B: _____

4   hold a position of responsibility
    A: _____?
    B: _____

5   study economics or accountancy
    A: _____?
    B: _____

6   give a presentation in English
    A: _____?
    B: _____

Exercise 2

Ever + present perfect or
simple past

Read the following dialogues. Put the verbs into the present perfect or the simple past.

1   A: _Have you ever been_ (you/ever/be) to South Africa?
    B: Yes, I have. I _went_ (go) there last year.
    A: How long _did you stay_ (you/stay)?
    B: I _was_ (be) only there for a couple of days for a meeting.

2   A: _____ (you/ever/be) on a skiing holiday?
    B: Yes, I have. We _____ (have) a family holiday in the
        Alps last year.
    A: Which resort _____ (you/go) to?
    B: We _____ (stay) in Wengen.

3   A: _____ (you/ever/be) to one of Karl Mason's seminars?
    B: Yes, I have. I _____ (go) to one a couple of months ago.
    A: What _____ (it/be) like.
    B: I _____ (think) it _____ (be) very interesting.

4   A: _____ (you/ever/hear) of a place called Hindhead?
    B: Yes, it's in Surrey. I _____ (do) a training course there when I
        _____ (be) with the bank.
    A: Which bank _____ (you/work) for?
    B: Lloyds, but I _____ (not/stay) with them very long.

6 Practice

Exercise 3
Already and **yet**

Complete the dialogue by putting the verbs into the present perfect.

A: Good afternoon, Mr Jackson here. How you are getting on with the car I brought in this morning? [1] *Have you finished it yet* (you/finish it/yet)?

B: Nearly. We [2] _____ (already/do) most of the work on it. We [3] _____ (not/find any major problems/yet), but we [4] _____ (already/fix) the things you mentioned.

A: [5] _____ (you/check) the headlights? I think they need adjusting.

B: Yes, we [6] _____ (already/fix) them. The only other thing is that you need two new tyres, but I [7] _____ (not/order them/yet), because they're £50 each.

A: That's fine, go ahead with that. Do you know what the bill will be?

B: No, I [8] _____ (not/work it out/yet), but it'll be about £180. Are you coming to get the car now?

A: No, I [9] _____ (not/finish work/yet). I'll be there in about an hour.

Exercise 4
Unfinished periods of time

Read this passage about the performance of the computer manufacturer, Compaq. Fill in the blanks with the verbs in the box, using the present perfect.

be	go	grow	have	manage	already/reach	open

This [1] *has been* an excellent year so far, and we [2] _____ most of our sales targets. Worldwide unit shipments [3] _____ up to 2.5m over the last eight months, and every region [4] _____ to set new records. In North America, we [5] _____ sales of $3.1 billion, and sales in Europe and the Pacific Rim [6] _____ by 38% and 94%. Our international expansion plans are going well. We [7] _____ a new office in Beijing and are planning to open five more next year.

Exercise 5
Finished and unfinished periods of time

Match each of the sentences from column A with a suitable context from column B.

	A		**B**
1	*I hope you enjoyed the launch party.*	A	Mary has gone home. It is 5.15.
2	I hope you have enjoyed the launch party.	B	The launch party is about to finish.
3	Has the post come this morning?	C	Max rings on Monday or Tuesday. It's Thursday.
4	Did the post come this morning?	D	Mary is still at the office. It is 2.30.
5	Has Max rung this week?	E	It is 10.00 in the morning.
6	Did Max ring this week?	F	Max rings on Monday or Tuesday. It's Tuesday.
7	Has Mary finished that report?	G	It is 3.00 in the afternoon.
8	Did Mary finish that report?	H	*The launch party was last week.*

Task 1

Complete these sentences using **never** and the present perfect.

1 I'm feeling rather nervous.
I have never given a presentation to so many people.

2 I don't like taking unnecessary risks with money, so

_____ .

3 _____ ,

but I would like to go there for a holiday.

4 What are Nigel Seymour's books on management like?

_____ .

5 I can definitely recommend Hewlett Packard printers. I've had one for
years, and _____ .

6 Their record of industrial relations is excellent.

_____ .

Task 2

Write short paragraphs saying what you have already done and what you
haven't done yet.

1 The new model is almost ready for production. _We have done a lot of
research and we have finalized the design. We have solved the problems we
had with the prototype and we have already set up a production unit in
Cambridge. We haven't decided who will lead the project yet, but we are
interviewing three possible candidates._

2 I am nearly ready to start my own business.

_____
_____
_____

Task 3

Complete the sentences, using the present perfect to make it clear that the
periods of time have not finished yet.

1 I must get a new alarm clock. _I have been late three times this week._
2 GM's new saloon car has been a great success. To date,

_____
_____

3 British Coal is cutting its workforce dramatically. So far this year

_____
_____

4 I think they must have put the wrong phone number on the
advertisement because up to now we _____

_____

7 Present perfect (3): **for** and **since**

A Stative verbs + **for** and **since**

The present perfect simple is often used with **for** and **since** and stative verbs to talk about things that began in the past and have continued up to now:

*I **have known** about the takeover bid **for** several weeks.* (And I know now.)
*She **has owned** shares in ICI **since** she started work there.* (She owns them now.)

B For or **since**?

We use **for** to talk about the duration of periods of time and **since** to talk about when a period started. Look at the time line and the examples:

for ten minutes/five days/three months/two years/a long time/ages/etc.
since 10.15/Monday/the 18th/last week/June/1989/I left school/etc.

*I **have been** with this company **for** six years.*
*I **have been** in computing **since** the beginning of 1989.*

C How long ...?,
for and **since**

To ask questions about periods of time, we can use **How long ...?** + the present perfect:

***How long have you been** in England? I **have been** here **since** August/**for** six months.*
COMMON MISTAKES: We do not use the present simple tense with **for** and **since** to talk about something that began in the past and has gone on up to the present:
WRONG: *I ~~am here~~ since December.*
RIGHT: *I **have been** here **since** December.*

D Negatives

We can use the present perfect negative to talk about the amount of time that has passed between now and the last time something happened:

*We **haven't had** any large orders from them **for** several months.*
*I'm not sure if his trip is going well. I **haven't heard** from him **since** Monday.*

E Completed actions over a period of time

If we talk about a completed action, (particularly if we give details about how much, how many, etc.), we can use the present perfect and **since** (but not **for**). We can also use other phrases of duration such as **to date**, **recently**, **over the past five years**, etc. The action itself is finished, but the period of time extends up to the present:
*We **have opened** six new branches **since July**.* (From July until now.)

Exercise 1
For and **since** with stative verbs

Some of the following sentences are right and some are wrong. Put a tick [✔] next to the ones that are right, and correct the ones that are wrong.

1   I am here since last week.   *I have been*

2   He has had a company car for two years.   _____

3   I know Mr Smith since we did an MBA together.   _____

4   How long are you with ICI?   _____

5   We have had an office in Japan for several years. _____

6   She has an account with FN Bank since 1980.   _____

7   CPT is in financial difficulties for several months. _____

8   How long has the office been vacant?   _____

Exercise 2
For or **since**?

Fill in the blanks with **for** or **since**.

1   They have operated as joint directors *since* the company started.
2   Orders have increased _____ the advertising campaign in June.
3   Our sales executives have used the same hotel _____ over 20 years.
4   Sorry, Mr Smith is not available. He has been in a meeting _____ 8.30.
5   _____ I joined the company, I have been to over twenty countries.
6   Car sales have gone up by 10% _____ the tax cuts in December.
7   Portugal has been a member of the European Union _____ 1986.
8   It isn't a new Mercedes. He has had it _____ years.

Exercise 3
How long...?, **for** and **since**

Make questions and answers, using the prompts.

1   How long/you/be/in charge of the Finance Department?
   A   *How long have you been in charge of the Finance Department?*
   B   (I/six months) *I have been in charge of it for six months.*

2   How long/you/have a phone line for investors?
   A   _____
   B   (We/three months) _____

3   How long/the property/be on the market?
   A   _____
   B   (It/six months) _____

4   How long/you/have an office in Spain?
   A   _____
   B   (We/1992) _____

5   How long/Jason/be in the States?
   A   _____
   B   (He/the 18th) _____

7 Practice

Exercise 4
Negatives

Rewrite the sentences using the negative form of the present perfect, with **for** or **since**.

1 The last time I saw Mr Ng was in September.
I haven't seen Mr Ng since September.

2 The last time the company made a profit was three years ago.
_____

3 The last time I had a pay rise was two years ago.
_____

4 The last time we looked at their proposal was in July.
_____

5 The last time we raised our prices in real terms was in 1992.
_____

6 The last time we played golf together was three months ago.
_____

7 The last time there was a fall in unemployment here was in 1990.
_____

8 The last time I went on a sales trip abroad was in January.
_____

Exercise 5
Completed actions

Look at the chart and read through this extract from an advertisement about the Emerging Markets Fund. Put the verbs into the present perfect tense.

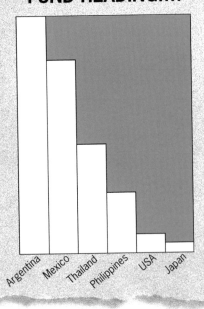

EMERGING MARKETS FUND HEADING...?

Over the past five years, the capital returns from many emerging Asian and Latin American stock markets [1] _have been_ (be) substantially higher than those of the developed world, as the chart shows.

For example, the market in Argentina [2] _____ (rise) by 793% and Mexico [3] _____ (increase) by 645%. In Asia, the booming market in Thailand [4] _____ (go up) by 364%, and investors in the Philippines [5] _____ (see) a return of 204%.

The major developed nations [6] _____ (not/manage) to make anything like such significant returns. The market in the USA [7] _____ (grow) by 69.8%, and in Japan, the market [8] _____ (fall) by 32.2% over the same period. The growth rates that these emerging markets [9] _____ (enjoy) in recent years is little short of phenomenal. And we are firmly convinced, much more is yet to come. Our new Emerging Markets Fund, therefore, offers you an easy and attractive way of investing now in the world of tomorrow and its many exceptional growth opportunities.

....

Task 1

Read the following notes. In each pair, decide which sentence should be in the simple past and which should be in the present perfect.

1   I/meet/Mr Christiansen/1988
    I met Mr Christiansen in 1988.

2   I/know/Mr Christiansen/1988
    _____

3   Nissan/build a car plant in the UK/1986
    _____

4   Nissan/have/a car plant in the UK/1986
    _____

5   Greece/be/a member of the European Community/1986
    _____

6   Greece/join/the European Community/1986
    _____

....

Task 2

Continue these sentences. Use a verb in the present perfect negative.

1   I'm not sure what my bank balance is.
    I haven't had a statement for several weeks.

2   I don't know how my investments are doing.
    _____

3   I am not sure how the negotiations are going.
    _____

4   They used to be one of our major clients, but
    _____

5   I used to be quite good at Japanese, but
    _____

....

Task 3

Using the notes, write about what has happened in the recent past.

1   Turnover – up 25%   Profits – double   New contracts – 3
    New employees – 50
    Since the new management team took over at Berisford ...

2   Productivity – up 20%   Absenteeism – down 50%
    Days lost to strikes – 1   Staff turnover – down 50%
    Since we adopted Japanese-style working practices ...

8 Present perfect (4): continuous and simple

A Form

The present perfect continuous is formed by the present perfect of **be** (**have been**) and the **-ing** form of the verb.

> I/you/we/they **have been working/have not (haven't) been working**.
> He/she/it **has been working/has not (hasn't) been working**.
> **Have** I/you/we/they **been working?** (Yes, I/you/we/they **have./No,** I/you/we/they **haven't**.)
> **Has** he/she/it **been working?** (Yes, he/she/it **has./No** he/she/it/**hasn't**.)

B Unfinished activities

The present perfect continuous is used with **for**, **since**, and **How long ...?** and other expressions of duration (e.g., **all day**), to talk about activities that started happening in the past and are still happening now. The activity may have been going on continuously or repeated several times:

*They **have been producing** cars here for 10 years.*
(They started producing cars 10 years ago. They are still producing cars.)

*I **have been trying** to ring them all day.*
(I started trying to ring them this morning. I am still trying to ring them.)

However, we normally use the present perfect simple with stative verbs, or about situations we consider permanent (see Unit 3):

*Ken **has been** in London since 9 o'clock this morning.* (NOT: *has been being ...*)
*I **have lived** in London all my life.* (NOT: *have been living ...*)

C Finished and unfinished activities

We use the present perfect simple if we are talking about a completed action, particularly if we give details of how much or how many. We use the present perfect continuous when something is still going on:

*I've **written** a report for Janet.* (It is finished.)
*I've **been writing** a report for Janet.* (I am still writing it.)

D Negatives

In the negative, the focus on the present perfect simple is on the amount of time that has passed since something happened. The focus of the present perfect continuous is on the verb itself. Compare:

*I **haven't had** a holiday for two years.* (The last time was two years ago.)
*I **haven't been feeling** well recently.* (This has been continuing for days.)

E Recently finished activities

We use the present perfect continuous to talk about an activity that was in progress, but has just finished. Normally there is some evidence. Compare:

*There's glass everywhere! Someone **has broken** the window.*
*The ground is very wet. It **has been raining**.*

Complete the sentences by putting the verbs into the present perfect continuous.

1 I didn't realize you had moved to Ciba Geigy. How long *have you been working* (you/work) for them?

2 We _____ (export) a lot of high technology equipment to Russia since the government relaxed export regulations.

3 The price of cigarettes fell sharply when Philip Morris started a price war, and it _____ (fall) ever since.

4 Because of the recession, many businesses _____ (not/invest) in capital equipment over the last couple of years.

5 We _____ (not/use) DFT's Express delivery service very much recently because we are trying to keep our costs down.

6 They _____ (try) to sell their food distribution division, but so far there has been very little interest in it.

7 I _____ (make) contributions to my pension for the last five years.

8 How long _____ (you/send) your trainees on management courses?

Ironstand is a company that manufactures exhibition equipment, and organizes exhibitions of books and magazines. Using the notes, continue the interview with the chairman of the company.

1986	Alan Franks joins the company as chairman
1986	Ironstand starts manufacturing equipment for exhibitions
1990	Ironstand starts exporting to Europe
1992	Ironstand starts organizing exhibitions
1993	Ironstand starts representing UK publishers in Europe
1994	Ironstand starts selling books in the USA

How long have you been running the company?
I have been running the company since 1986.

_____
_____
_____
_____
_____
_____
_____
_____

Put the verbs in brackets into the present perfect simple or the present perfect continuous.

1   We are thinking about opening an office in Tokyo, so I *have been learning* (learn) Japanese at evening classes for the last two months.
2   By the way, I *have worked* (work) out those figures. They are on your desk now.
3   Do you know where that order form is? Peter _____ (look) for it.
4   I'm sorry, I didn't know that you were here. _____ (you/wait) long?
5   Since January, our turnover _____ (increase) by 18%.
6   The film company is a reasonable investment. They _____ (make) four very successful films.
7   The lawyers _____ (look) through the contract, but they say they need another day to read it all.
8   We _____ (visit) potential sites for the new workshops, but we haven't found anything suitable yet.

Rewrite these sentences, using the present perfect simple or the present perfect continuous.

1   I didn't feel well on Monday, Wednesday, Thursday, and Saturday.
(not feel/recently)   *I haven't been feeling well recently.*

2   The last time I had a meeting with them was two weeks ago.
(not have/two weeks) _____

3   My fax machine didn't work properly on three different days this week.
(not work/properly/recently) _____

4   The last time they gave their workers a pay rise was three years ago.
(not give/three years) _____

Match the questions in column A with the replies or explanations in column B.

A	B
1 *Why is your office in such a mess?*	A They've been travelling so much that they never have time to do any.
2 Why has the wages bill been so high recently?	B We've been losing a lot of stock because of shoplifting.
3 Why have you got three new store detectives?	C I've been having a lot of problems with it recently.
4 Why are they so behind with their work?	D *I've been looking for that letter from Graylings, but I can't find it.*
5 What's you car doing at the garage?	E Yes, but I've been interviewing people all day.
6 You look tired, Anne. Are you OK?	F Because everyone's been doing a lot of overtime.

Task 1

Write short paragraphs answering the questions, giving details about the activities that have been going on.

1   Why do you think Peter should be dismissed?
He has been coming in late and he hasn't been doing any work. He's been spending hours every day talking to his friends on the phone and he's been upsetting the customers.

2   Why do you think you deserve a pay rise?
_____
_____

3   What have you been doing to improve your English?
_____
_____

4   What have you been doing at work recently?
_____
_____

Task 2

Reply to the following questions using a verb in the present perfect continuous.

1   Is it wet outside? *Yes, it's been raining.*

2   You look terrible. What have you been doing?
_____

3   Have you seen your face? You're covered in black ink.
_____

4   How come your golf has improved so much?
_____

5   Why do you think she's been having so many days off?
_____

6   Why are you under so much stress at the moment?
_____

7   Why is your expenses claim so high this month?
_____

How come your golf has improved so much?

9 Review: simple past, present perfect, and present perfect continuous

A The simple past

We normally use the simple past to talk about actions that took place at a time that is separated from the present. It is used with expressions like **yesterday**, **on Monday**, **last week**, **in 1989**, **at 6.30**, **How long ago ...?**, etc.:

*Yesterday GKN **launched** a takeover bid for Westland.*
*He **did** his MBA at Cranfield in 1991.*

We can use the simple past and **for** to talk about something that happened during a period that has now finished:

*I **lived** in Singapore **for** three years; then I **came** back to England.*

B The present perfect

The present perfect is used to talk about the present result of past actions and recent events, and is often used with words like **ever**, **never**, **just**, **already**, **yet**, and phrases of unfinished time such as **so far**:

*British Telecom **has cut** the price of peak rate phone calls by 20%.*
***Have** you **ever tried** Swiss wine?*
*We have spoken to each other on the phone, but we **have never met**.*
*Don't worry about the order from Siemens. I **have already dealt** with it.*
*I'm afraid I **haven't done** that sales forecast **yet**. I'll do it tomorrow.*
*The film was released two weeks ago and **so far** it **has taken** $45m.*

C Present perfect simple + **for** and **since**

The present perfect can be used with **for** and **since** and stative verbs, or to refer to actions that are seen as long term or permanent. We use **for** to talk about the duration of a period of time and **since** to talk about the starting point of an action or state:

*I **have been** with the company **since** 1986.*
*I **have lived** here **for** 20 years.*

It is also used in the negative with **for** and **since** to talk about the last time something took place:

*I **haven't seen** her **since** Monday.*
*I **haven't seen** her **for** three days.*

It is used with **since** to talk about completed actions:

*Our market share has increased by 11% **since** we started advertising on TV.*

D Present perfect continuous

The present perfect continuous can be used with **for** and **since** to talk about actions or activities that have gone on repeatedly or continuously for a period of time, and are still going on:

*We've **been producing** over 1,000 units a week **since** the new factory opened.*

Look at the graph and read the sentences. Put a tick [✔] next to the ones that are right, and correct the ones that are wrong.

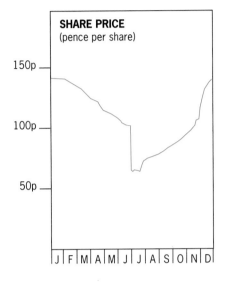

SHARE PRICE
(pence per share)

150p —

100p —

50p —

J F M A M J J A S O N D

1 Over the last year or so, shareholders in the holiday group Owners Abroad have had a turbulent ride. ___✔___

2 The shares have risen sharply at the beginning of the year on the news of the Airtours bid. _rose_

3 Then the shares have fallen steadily for three or four months, ending up at 100p at the end of June. _____

4 In July the shares plummeted to 60p because of the company's difficulties. _____

5 The shares have stayed at around 60p for most of July. _____

6 At the beginning of August, the shares began to recover again. _____

7 Since August the shares have managed to recover. _____

8 The share price has now climbed back to where it has been before the Airtours bid. _____

In the dialogue, put the verbs into the simple past or the present perfect.

A: Can I have a word about your trip to Athens?

B: Yes, of course. Is everything OK?

A: Yes. Your tickets (1) _have arrived_ (arrive) and they're in my office now. And I (2) _____ (just/had) a fax from the hotel confirming your reservation.

B: Thank you. What about money?

A: I (3) _____ (already/order) some drachmas for you. I (4) _____ (ring) the bank yesterday, and they'll have them tomorrow. But there's a problem with your Eurocheque book. I (5) _____ (ask) them to send one a week ago, but it (6) _____ (not/arrive) yet.

B: That's all right. I (7) _____ (never/need) a Eurocheque before. I normally use a credit card.

A: Really? Are you sure you can do that?

B: Yes, I think so. Certainly when I (8) _____ (go) to France last October I (9) _____ (take) my Visa card and my Mastercard, and I (10) _____ (not/have) any problems. But I'll check about Greece. (11) _____ (you/ever/be) there?

A: No, but have a word with Alison Morgan in Production. She (12) _____ (be) there a couple of times this year, so I expect she would know.

Underline the correct form of the verb.

1 I've *stayed*/*been staying* in a hotel for the last ten days, but I hope to find an apartment of my own soon.

2 I wonder how Jim is getting on. I haven't *heard*/*been hearing* from him for nearly a week.

3 Graham is a natural salesman. He has *sold*/*been selling* eight cars since the beginning of the week.

4 I didn't realize that you and David were friends. How long have you *known*/*been knowing* him?

5 This report is a nightmare. I have *written*/*been writing* it for two weeks, and it is still not finished.

Read the following letter. Put the verbs in brackets into the simple past, present perfect, or present perfect continuous.

Darwin, 24 October

Dear Ken,

I am writing to let you know how I am getting on with the marketing trip here. I am sorry I ⁽¹⁾ _haven't been_ (not/be) in touch for so long, but I ⁽²⁾ _____ (be) very busy since I ⁽³⁾ _____ (arrive) here on the 18th.

There is a great deal of interest in the new fertilizer. Last week I ⁽⁴⁾ _____ (be) in Sydney, where I ⁽⁵⁾ _____ (visit) a number of farmers and ⁽⁶⁾ _____ (see) a couple of potential agents. The feedback at all of those meetings ⁽⁷⁾ _____ (be) very positive, and I ⁽⁸⁾ _____ (already/receive) a number of orders. I ⁽⁹⁾ _____ (never/have) such an enthusiastic response about a new product, so I am confident it will be a great success. I ⁽¹⁰⁾ _____ (come) up to Darwin on Tuesday, and since then I ⁽¹¹⁾ _____ (be) to some more farms and I ⁽¹²⁾ _____ (make) two or three useful contacts. Yesterday I ⁽¹³⁾ _____ (have) a meeting with Barry Thomas, who you may remember. He ⁽¹⁴⁾ _____ (work) with Agrichem in London for a couple of years in the early 90s, then ⁽¹⁵⁾ _____ (set) up his own business over here, and he ⁽¹⁶⁾ _____ (act) as a distributor of some of our agricultural machinery for the last year or so. Towards the end of our meeting he ⁽¹⁷⁾ _____ (ask) about becoming the sole distributor for the fertilizer. The question is an interesting one, but I feel that we ⁽¹⁸⁾ _____ (not think) enough yet about the precise sales and distribution network that we will need. We must talk about this when I get back.

Anyway, I must fax this off to you now. I ⁽¹⁹⁾ _____ (just/have) another phone call from someone who wants to hear about the fertilizer, so I'll do that now. I'll be in touch again soon, and in the meantime send my congratulations to everyone in R&D.

Jim

Task 1

Write a short paragraph about one of your or your company's current projects. Talk about what is happening now, what you have already done, and what you haven't done yet. Here is an example:

1 *We're going to the Hamburg Book Fair next week. We've reserved a 20 metre stand, so the display will be quite impressive. We have sent most of the stock on ahead, but there are one or two books that haven't come out yet, and we're going to take them with us. We have already arranged a lot of meetings, but there are still a few people that we haven't contacted yet.*

2 _____
_____
_____
_____

Task 2

Write a paragraph from a covering letter applying for a job. You should give details of your general experience, and mention some specific dates when you did something. Here is an example:

1 *As you will see from the enclosed CV, I have worked in the financial services sector for several years. I spent two years with Allied Dunbar as a pensions salesman, and then moved to Sun Alliance, where I have been working in the Life Assurance division. I have had considerable managerial experience, and I recently became Area Manager.*

2 _____
_____
_____
_____

Task 3

Complete each of the following sentences in two ways. In one sentence, use the present perfect to say what these people have done, and in the other use the present perfect continuous to say what they have been doing.

1 I got into trouble for not working hard enough last week. Since then ...
I have stayed late three times. I have been working very hard.

2 I handed in my resignation a month ago. Since then ...
_____
_____

3 We got a new manager a few weeks ago. Since he arrived ...
_____
_____

4 The new product is going to be a big success. Since its launch ...
_____
_____

10 Past continuous

A Form

The past continuous is formed with **was/were** + the **-ing** form of the verb:

> I/he/she/it **was/was not** (**wasn't**) **working**.
> You/we/they **were/were not** (**weren't**) **working**.
> **Was** I/he/she/it **working**? (**Yes**, I/he/she/it **was working**./**No**,
> I/he/she/it **wasn't working**.)
> **Were** you/we/they **working**? (**Yes**, you/we/they **were working**./**No**,
> you/we/they **weren't working**.)

B Points of time in the past

We use the past continuous to talk about an action or activity that was in progress at a particular moment of time in the past:
*At 3.15 yesterday afternoon, Mr Jansen **was seeing** some clients in London.*

C Interrupted past action

We can use the past continuous to talk about an action or activity that was already in progress, and which was interrupted by another action:
*We **were discussing** our expansion plans **when** the chairman suddenly **announced** his resignation.*

We can rephrase this sentence using **while** + the past continuous:
***While** we **were discussing** our expansion plans, the chairman suddenly **announced** his resignation.*

The activity may or may not continue after the interruption:
*Paul **was doing** some filing **when** his boss **asked** him to fetch an invoice.*
(Paul fetched the invoice and then probably carried on with the filing.)

*Paul **was doing** some filing **when** the fire **broke out**.*
(Paul probably stopped doing the filing at this point.)

D Sequence of tenses

With a time clause like **when the phone rang**, we can use either the past continuous or the simple past.

The past continuous tells us what was happening up to the point when the phone rang:
*When the phone rang, I **was talking** to a client.*

The past simple tells us what happened afterwards:
*When the phone rang, I **answered** it.*

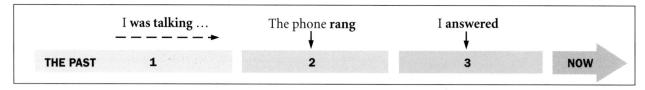

David's colleague Jack (who doesn't have enough work to do) has tried to phone him several times without success. Complete their conversation by putting the verbs in brackets into the correct form of the past continuous.

David's Activities – Wednesday

9.00 - 10.00	make some phone calls to clients
10.00 - 11.00	see Sue Tims (her office)
11.00 - 11.15	have coffee with JC (canteen)
11.15 - 1.00	meeting with designer
1.00 - 2.00	lunch with designer

JACK: I rang at 9.15 and again at 9.30 but the phone was engaged. Who (1) _were you talking_ (you/talk) to?

DAVID: Oh, I (2) _____ (call) some clients.

JACK: And I tried again at 10.15, but there was no reply.

DAVID: At 10.15? I think I (3) _____ (discuss) the new catalogue with Sue Tims.

JACK: And then I rang back again at 11.10.

DAVID: Yes, I was out. I (4) _____ (have) a coffee in the canteen.

JACK: I thought so, so I rang again at 11.30.

DAVID: I was out again. The new designer and I (5) _____ (organize) the artwork for some adverts.

JACK: What (6) _____ (you/do) at 1.30, then? I called again, and tried to leave a message but even the answering machine (7) _____ (not/work)!

DAVID: I'd better have a look at it, but the designer and I (8) _____ (have) lunch. Anyway, what did you want to talk about?

JACK: Oh, nothing special. I just wanted to try out my new mobile phone.

Choose the correct tense, simple past or past continuous.

I (1) _met/was meeting_ an old business colleague of mine while I (2) _travelled/was travelling_ to New York for a conference. She (3) _noticed/was noticing_ me while I (4) _stood/was standing_ in the queue at the airport check-in desk. We decided to travel together, and while we (5) _waited/were waiting_ for the flight to leave, we (6) _realized/were realizing_ that we were going to the same conference and staying at the same hotel. We talked about old times, and while we (7) _had/were having_ lunch on the plane, she (8) _said/was saying_ that she was going to look for a new job. I didn't think of it at the time, but later on when the plane (9) _came/was coming_ in to land, I suddenly (10) _remembered/was remembering_ that we had a vacancy for a lawyer. I told her about the terms and conditions, and later that evening, when we (11) _had/were having_ dinner, she (12) _accepted/was accepting_ the position.

Exercise 3
Sequence of tenses

Read each set of sentences. Decide the order in which things happened. Write two sentences about each set of information. Begin each pair of answers with the same words.

1 His car broke down. He went the rest of the way by taxi. He was driving to Bonn.
A *When his car broke down, he was driving to Bonn for a conference.*
B *When his car broke down, he went the rest of the way by taxi.*

2 We left the building. We were having a meeting. The fire alarm went off.
A _____
B _____

3 They took our company over. We were losing a lot of money. They made a number of people redundant.
A _____
B _____

4 My secretary brought it down. I was having lunch in the canteen. The fax arrived.
A _____
B _____

5 Mr Yamaichi arrived at the airport. He came straight to the office. The chauffeur was waiting.
A _____
B _____

Exercise 4
Review

In the following sentences, put one of the verbs in brackets into the past continuous, and the other verb into the simple past.

1 (walk, notice) The security guard *noticed* the broken window while he *was walking* round the warehouse.
2 (go, meet) I first _____ Mr Rodriguez when I _____ round Mexico on a marketing trip.
3 (interrupt, give) When she _____ her presentation, someone at the back of the room _____ to ask a question.
4 (finalize, ring up) While my PA _____ arrangements for my trip to Brazil, the clients _____ to cancel the visit.
5 (notice, look) The auditors _____ a large unauthorized withdrawal when they _____ through the account.
6 (happen, clean) The worker who died _____ the chemical tank when the accident _____ .
7 (drop, take) One of the removal men _____ my computer when he _____ it into my office.
8 (work, approach) A headhunter _____ her when she _____ for ICL.

Complete each sentence in two ways. In A, use the past continuous to say what was happening at the time. In B, use the simple past to say what happened next.

1   When I got to the airport, ...
A   *the company driver was waiting for me.*
B   *I went straight to the meeting.*

2   When I got to work this morning, ...
A   _____
B   _____

3   When the accident happened, ...
A   _____
B   _____

4   When they decided to close down the factory, ...
A   _____
B   _____

Explain what was happening up to the point when the following events took place. Use **because** + the past continuous.

1   He decided to see a doctor ... *because he wasn't feeling well.*

2   Peter handed in his resignation ...

    _____

3   They gave Jane a new company car ...

    _____

4   We offered our agents an extra 5% discount ...

    _____

5   Helen phoned the service engineer ...

    _____

Write a short paragraph about one of the following events. Say what you were doing when it happened, and what you did next.

Write about the time ...
when you had or saw a car crash   when you got your present job
when you had to go to hospital   when you were stopped by the police
when you lost some money   when you met your partner

_____
_____
_____
_____
_____

11 Past perfect

A Form

The past perfect is formed with **had** + the past participle of the verb:

I/you/he/she/it/we/they **had worked.**
I/you/he/she/it/we/they **had not (hadn't) worked.**
Had I/you/he/she/it/we/they **worked?** (**Yes,** I/you/etc. **had./No,** I/you/etc. **hadn't.**)

B Previous and subsequent events

The past perfect is used to refer back to completed actions that happened before other events in the past. Compare:

1   *When I **arrived** at the office, the meeting **started.***
    (I arrived at the office, and then the meeting started.)

2   *When I **arrived** at the office, the meeting **had started**.*
    (The meeting started before I got to the office. I was late.)

In 1, it is also possible to use **As soon as** and **After** in place of **When.**
In 2, it is also possible to use **By the time** in place of **When.**

C Present perfect and past perfect

The past perfect acts as the past form of the present perfect (see Units 5–9). It is often used with adverbs like **just, already, never.** Compare:

*I am nervous because I **have never given** a presentation.*
(I am about to give a presentation.)

*I was nervous because I **had never given** a presentation.*
(I gave a presentation yesterday.)

The past perfect is often used in reported speech structures (see Units 30–31) and in 3rd conditionals (see Unit 21).

D Past perfect continuous

The past perfect continuous is formed by using the auxiliary **had been** + the **-ing** form of the verb (I/he/you/etc. **had (not) been working**).

We use the present perfect continuous to talk about how long an activity has been going on up to the present (see Unit 6). We use the past perfect continuous to talk about the duration of an activity up to a point in the past. Compare:

*I **have been working** here for six months.*
(I am still working here now.)

*When I left my last job, I **had been working** there for four years.*
(I started in 1990 and I left in 1994.)

We do not use the past perfect continuous with stative verbs like **know, like,** etc. (see Unit 3). Instead, we use the past perfect:

*When they met again, they **had not seen** each other for 15 years.*

Complete the sentences by putting the verb into the past perfect.

1 Did you manage to see the Director, or _had he gone_ (he/go) by the time you got there?

2 I couldn't get into the office yesterday morning because I _____ (leave) my keys at home.

3 We could not call our new low-fat spread Mono, because one of our competitors _____ (already/choose) the name.

4 I found out about the vacancy too late. When my application form arrived, they _____ (appoint) someone.

5 By the time he sold off the shares, his original investment _____ (grow) by 83%.

6 He found his first few weeks at Ernst & Young very difficult because he _____ (not/study) accountancy before.

7 When I got back to the office, I was surprised to hear that the manager _____ (put) someone else in charge of my main project.

8 The bank returned the cheque to me because I _____ (not/sign) it.

Complete each of the following sentences in two ways, using **because** + past perfect and **so** + simple past.

1 When I left the office, the building was empty ...
(everyone/go home) _because everyone had gone home._
(I/lock the doors) _so I locked the doors._

2 When I arrived at the office the next morning, the place was in a terrible mess ...
(I/phone the police) _____
(someone/break in) _____

3 The chairman was in a very good mood ...
(we/win/a major contract) _____
(we/open/a bottle of champagne) _____

4 The negotiators realized another meeting would be necessary ...
(they/not reach an agreement) _____
(they/get out/their diaries) _____

5 I did not know their phone number ...
(I/call/Directory Enquiries) _____
(they/move/to new premises) _____

6 The Marketing Manager's flight from Japan arrived late ...
(she/go/straight home from the airport) _____
(there/be/a security alert in Tokyo) _____

11 Practice

Exercise 3

Present perfect and past perfect

Change the following sentences into the past perfect.

1 'I don't want lunch because I've already eaten.'
   I didn't want lunch because I had already eaten.

2 'We can't give him the job because he hasn't had enough experience.'
   We couldn't give him the job because _____

3 'I'm phoning Jane to say a fax has just arrived for her.'
   I phoned Jane to say that _____

4 'I can't give Peter a lift because I haven't finished work.'
   I couldn't give Peter a lift because _____

5 'I'm looking forward to my trip because I've never been to Russia.'
   I was looking forward to my trip because _____

6 'He is calling a press conference because we've just closed a major deal.'
   He called a press conference because _____

Exercise 4

Past perfect continuous

Look through the notes about the history of Biogen, a genetic engineering company that specializes in producing medical products. Write sentences about the company's activities until it went public in 1993.

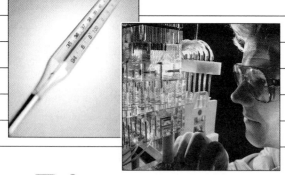

(1987)	company starts producing pregnancy test kits
(1988)	company starts marketing test kits in USA
(1989)	Dr Pierce starts running the company
(1990)	Dr Warner, new Medical Director joins
(1991)	company starts manufacturing thermometers
(1992)	company opens a new production unit in Spain

Biogen

1 When the company went public, (we/produce/pregnancy test kits/6 years)
  we had been producing pregnancy test kits for six years.

2 When the company went public, (we/market the kits/USA/5 years)
  _____

3 When the company went public, (Dr Pierce/run it/4 years)
  _____

4 When the company went public, (Dr Warner/be the Medical Director/3 years)
  _____

5 When the company went public, (We/manufacture thermometers/2 years)
  _____

6 When the company went public, (we/have/a production unit in Spain/one year)
  _____

....

Task 1   Complete the following sentences using the past perfect.

1   She found working from 9 to 5 very difficult because ...
     she had never had a full-time job before.

2   The company decided to take legal action because ...
     _____

3   The company was forced to pay a fine to the tax authorities because ...
     _____

4   My trip to the airport to collect Mr Olivera was a waste of time. When I got there I found that ...
     _____

5   She was not worried when the stock market fell because ...
     _____

....

Task 2   Continue each of the paragraphs. Use the simple past to describe the results of the change, and the past perfect to describe what had happened before.

1   When the new version of the car came out, it was a great success. *The price was the same but the manufacturers had fitted electric windows, air bags, and power steering as standard. They had modified the engine, and they had managed to increase the car's efficiency. There was more room in the back because they had changed the design of the seats, and the car was much safer because they had made the side doors stronger.*

2   When the management consultant went back to see the company, she found that it had followed her advice.
     _____
     _____
     _____

....

Task 3   Continue the sentences. Say what activities had been going on.

1   He felt very tired at 4.30 because *he had been working at the VDU all day.*

2   They realized that none of their confidential information was safe because _____

3   She felt that a change of job would be good for her because
     _____

4   The accountant finally discovered why the phone bill was so high. One of the night security guards _____

5   There was a very long delay at the airport. When we finally left, we _____

12 The future (1): **will**

A Spontaneous decisions

We can use **will** (or **'ll**) + bare infinitive to refer to the future when we make an instant or spontaneous decision to do something:

A   *'We've run out of paper for the printer.'*
B   *'**I'll** go and get some from the stockroom.'*

We often use the **will** future after **I think** and **I don't think**:
A   *'**I think I'll** go home now. It's getting late.'*
B   *'Yes, you're right. **I don't think** I'll stay either.'*

The negative of **will** is **won't** (**will not**):
*I **won't** stay long. I'm in a hurry.*

COMMON MISTAKES: We don't use **won't** after **I think**.
WRONG: *~~I think I won't~~ come to the conference.*
RIGHT: *I don't think I'll come to the conference.*

B Predictions

We can use **will** to make predictions and to state facts that will be true in the future:

*Over the next few years, interactive TV **will** make a great impact on consumer behaviour, and advertisers **will** have to approach customers in a completely new way.*

C Future time words + present simple

We use a present tense (not **will**) to refer to the future with time words like **if**, **when**, **before**, **as soon as**, **after**, etc.:

*I **will** contact you **as soon as** I get the information.* (NOT: *will get*)

(See also Unit 19, Conditionals)

D Offers, promises, requests, etc.

Will can also be used to ask if someone is willing to do something, to make requests, promises, and threats, and to offer help:

*Hello, caller. I am afraid the line is busy. **Will** you hold?*

A   *'**Will** you give me a hand with these boxes?'*
B   *'Yes, of course I **will**.'*

*Don't worry about the meeting. I **will** support you.*

The word **won't** can mean **is not willing to** or **is refusing to**:

*There's something wrong with the printer. It **won't** print copies in reverse order.*

Exercise 1
Spontaneous decisions

Match the comments in column A with the responses in column B.

A	B
1 *There's going to be a train strike tomorrow.*	A I didn't realize. I'll order some more.
2 I'm afraid the line is busy.	B I'm not sure. I'll give him a ring.
3 I insist on seeing the manager.	C Thanks, I'll have a look at them later.
4 We're running very low on floppy disks.	D Is it? Then I'll stay at the Hilton.
5 Is John in his office?	E No thanks, I'm driving. I'll have a coffee.
6 The Holiday Inn is full.	F Don't worry, I'll call back later.
7 Here are the plans for the new building.	G *Is there? Then I'll bring the car.*
8 Another whiskey?	H Very well, madam. I'll go and call her.

Exercise 2
Predictions

Match the notes to the graphs and forecast the changes in the economy in the last quarter of the year using **will**.

Industrial production/rise sharply
Unemployment/fall slowly
Inflation/rise slowly
Consumer prices/remain stable
Interest rates/fall sharply

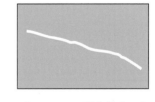

1 *Unemployment will fall slowly.*

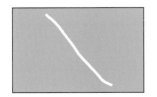

2 _____

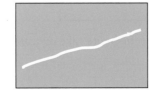

3 _____

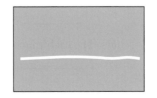

4 _____

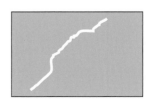

5 _____

12 Practice

Practice

Exercise 3
Future time words +
present simple

Put the verbs in brackets into the **will** future or the present simple.

1 Sally is working on the sales forecast at the moment. I _will give_ (give)
   you the figures as soon as I _get_ (get) them.
2 The shipment isn't in yet, but the agent _____ (phone) us as soon as
   it _____ (arrive).
3 If they _____ (not receive) payment next week, I think they _____
   (take) legal action against us.
4 Give me the report and I _____ (show) it to the lawyers before they
   _____ (leave).
5 Analysts believe the share price of ICI _____ (rise) after it _____
   (announce) its interim profit forecast next week.
6 When they _____ (close) the factory next year, a lot of small local
   businesses _____ (suffer).
7 When I _____ (come) to England next year, I _____ (give) you a
   ring and maybe we can arrange dinner.
8 When the strike (be) _____ over, everyone (feel) _____ happier.
9 I am sure that our sales (fall) _____ when we (put up) _____ prices.
10 Don't worry about the office. I (tidy) _____ it up before Mr Kosser
   (get) _____ back.

Exercise 4
Offers, promises, requests

Rewrite the following sentences using **will** or **won't**.

1 Has anyone offered to collect you from the airport?
   Will anyone collect you from the airport?

2 I promise not to be late again.

   _____

3 The finance group 3i has agreed to loan us £18m for the project.

   _____

4 The company has offered a 5% pay rise in return for a no-strike deal.

   _____

5 I promise not to discuss this information with anyone.

   _____

6 They have refused to increase our discount.

   _____

7 The company has offered to pay me relocation expenses.

   _____

8 The cash machine is refusing to take my card.

   _____

9 Let me give you a hand with those boxes.

   _____

Make spontaneous decisions based on the comments below.

1 You won't be able to get to Paris. The air traffic controllers are on strike.
Really? Then I'll take a train through the tunnel.

2 I'm sorry. The wine waiter says we have no more Château-Lafite '64.

_____

3 I am afraid that we don't accept cheques.

_____

4 We can't deliver the fax machines you ordered for three months.

_____

5 I'm afraid that the British Airways flight on Tuesday is fully booked.

_____

6 One of your clients – Mrs Mason – just rang. She sounded very upset about something.

_____

Write a short paragraph predicting what the world will be like in 2100 AD.

Medicine in 2100
The world of medicine will be very different in 2100. *There will be new ways of curing disease, and there will be drugs that will make people younger. People will live longer, and transplants will be very simple and effective. On the other hand, there will also be new problems. There will be new diseases, and some common bacteria will become resistant to drugs.*

The world of work in 2100
(You may like to comment on one or more of these aspects: technology, communication, methods of production, transport, working conditions, company size.)

In 2100, the office as we know it will be completely different.

_____
_____
_____

Complete the sentences using a verb in the present tense.

1 Don't worry, I'll go and see the lawyer *before I sign the contract.*
2 I think our Sales Director will leave as soon as _____
3 You needn't wait for Mr Takashi. I'll stay here until _____
4 My boss will be delighted if _____
5 Everyone is very stressed, but things will get better when _____
6 I am fairly sure that I will get promoted as soon as _____

13 The future (2): the present continuous and **going to**

A Present continuous – arrangements

The present continuous (see Unit 2) is often used to talk about appointments or things we have arranged to do in the future. We generally use it with a future time phrase:

*What **are you doing** on Friday afternoon?* (What have you arranged to do?)
*I **am seeing** the accountants.* (I have arranged to see them.)

We do not use the present continuous with stative verbs (see Unit 3).

B **Going to** – decisions and intentions

We use **going to** + bare infinitive to talk about something we intend to do, or have already decided to do:

*The D.V. Group is **going to open** a new Fiat dealership this summer.*

C **Going to** – predictions

We can also use **going to** for making firm predictions when there is some physical evidence that an event will take place:

*Based on these figures, we are **going to make** a loss of £1.5m this year.*

In many cases, however, it is possible to predict future events using either **going to** or **will**. There is little difference in meaning, but **going to** usually suggests that the event will happen soon. Compare:

*I don't think the present government **will win** the next election.*
*I don't think the present government is **going to win** the next election.*

D **Will**, present continuous, or **going to**?

The most important differences between the present continuous, **going to**, and **will** are as follows:

We use the present continuous for arrangements (except with stative verbs):
*I'**m having** a meeting with the Export Manager on Thursday at 2.15.*

We use **going to** for decisions and intentions:
*I've made up my mind. I'm **going to buy** a BMW 730i.*

We use **going to** for firm predictions:
*It's already 28°C. It's **going to be** very hot today.*

We use **will** for spontaneous decisions:
*I wonder if Peter is back from his marketing trip. I'**ll give** him a ring.*

We use **will** for promises, offers, and requests:
*I'**ll give** you a hand with those boxes if you like.*

We use **will** for general predictions:
*In the next century, computers **will play** a vital role in everyone's life.*

(For details of when the present simple is used to refer to the future, see Unit 1.)

Exercise 1
Arrangements

Two managers of an engineering company are trying to arrange a meeting. Put the verbs in brackets into the present continuous.

PETER: Jack, Peter here. Could we arrange a time tomorrow to talk about the new freight schedules? Say, er ... 9.15?

JACK: I'm a bit busy first thing because I [1] _am having_ (have) a meeting with a new driver. Would 10 o'clock suit you?

PETER: I'm afraid not. I [2] _____ (go) over to the factory, and after that I [3] _____ (see) Mr Henderson for lunch.

JACK: What time [4] _____ (you/come) back?

PETER: At about 2.30 I suppose, but I [5] _____ (not/do) anything special after that. Would you be free then?

JACK: No, I don't think so. I [6] _____ (see) a sales rep from Mercedes from 2.00 until about 3.30. So shall we say 3.45?

PETER: Fine. I'll ask Janet to come along as well. I [7] _____ (have) lunch with her today, and I'll tell her about it.

Exercise 2
Going to – decisions and intentions

Use the verb in brackets to say what the following people are going to do.

1   The Unions have been offered a 3.9% pay rise.
    (not accept) _They are not going to accept it._

2   We have ordered over £1.5m of new equipment for the factory.
    (modernize) _____

3   Mrs Mason has booked three weeks' leave in October.
    (have a holiday) _____

4   The engineers have finished the design for the new engine.
    (build/prototype) _____

5   Our trials have shown that the new vaccine is commercially viable.
    (produce) _____

Exercise 3
Going to – predictions

Use the words in brackets to make predictions with **going to**.

1   The stock market is very over-valued.
    (be/correction) _There is going to be a correction soon._

2   Demand for tin is rising, but supply is falling.
    (price/rise) _____

3   The company is in serious financial difficulty.
    (go bankrupt) _____

4   My boss is looking for another job.
    (leave the company) _____

5   We should have left much earlier.
    (be late) _____

13 Practice

Exercise 4

Will or present continuous?

The export manager of an agricultural machinery company is talking to his PA about a sales trip. Put the verbs in the following sentences into the **will** future or the present continuous.

JANET: I've booked your flight and hotels for your trip to Ethiopia. You (1) *are leaving* (leave) on the 18th at 6.30 a.m., and that means you (2) _____ (be) in Addis Ababa late afternoon.

DAVID: What about hotels?

JANET: You (3) _____ (stay) at the Addis Ababa Hilton, and you (4) _____ (have) to get a taxi there from the airport. Your first meeting is on Monday, and you (5) _____ (see) Mr Haile Mariam from the Ministry of Agriculture at 10.30.

DAVID: (6) ___ ___ (I/need) any vaccinations?

JANET: I'm not sure, but leave it with me. I (7) _____ (phone) the travel agent, and I (8) _____ (let) you know what she says.

Exercise 5

Will or **going to**?

Fill in the blanks with the correct form of the future, using **will** or **going to**.

1 A: I'm afraid the fax machine isn't working.
  B: Don't worry, it's not a very urgent letter. I *will post* (post) it.

2 A: We've chosen a brand name for the new biscuits.
  B: Really? What _____ (you/call) them?

3 A: Why are you taking the day off on Friday?
  B: I _____ (look) at a new house.

4 A: I'm afraid there's no sugar. Do you want a coffee without any?
  B: No, I _____ (not have) one, thanks.

5 A: Have you decided what to do about improving the circulation of the magazine?
  B: Yes, we _____ (cut) the cover price by 10% as from October.

6 A: I'm afraid I can't take you to the airport. Something important has just come up.
  B: Never mind. I _____ (take) a taxi.

7 A: Do you need any help?
  B: Oh, yes please. _____ (you/carry) the display stand for me?

8 A: Could you make sure Mr Wilson gets my message?
  B: Yes, I _____ (tell) him myself when he gets in.

I'm going to jump!

Really? Will you drop this in to Accounts on your way down?

Task 1 Write a short paragraph about the arrangements that have been made for the CEO of a major American bank to open the new European HQ in London.

18 JUNE	9.00	Arrive at Heathrow
	10.15	Meeting with Executive Vice-Presidents
	1.00	Lunch with officials from Department of Trade and Industry
	3.00	Official opening of new office in Threadneedle Street
	7.00	Speech: *'Financial Deregulation in the EU'*
	8.00	Dinner at the Guildhall
19 JUNE	11.30	Return flight to New York (Concorde)

The CEO is arriving at Heathrow at 9.00, and _____

_____

_____

_____

Task 2 Look at the following subjects. Write sentences about any definite plans you or your company have. Use **going to** and/or **not going to**.

1 training and courses   3 new equipment   5 holidays
2 new products and services   4 staffing changes

1 *I'm going to do a course in business Japanese in September, but*
   I'm not going to take any exams.

2 _____

3 _____

4 _____

5 _____

Task 3 Add comments to the sentences. Use the present continuous, **going to**, or **will**.

1 I'm afraid that I can't meet you for lunch on the 30th.
   I'm seeing Mr Karlssen in Oslo.

2 The management have announced how they intend to reduce costs.

   _____

3 I'm sorry, I didn't realize you were busy.

   _____

4 Our Sales Manager has finally chosen what he wants as a company car.

   _____

5 I need some time to think about this proposal.

   _____

6 Our Export Manager is in Peru at the moment looking at new offices.

   _____

14 The future (3): other future tenses

A Was going to

We can use **was going to/were going to** to talk about changed plans or intentions. Read this short dialogue:

A *'I've decided that I'm going to resign.'*
B *'Don't do that – I've just heard that the management want to promote you.'*
A *'OK, perhaps I'll stay then.'*

When we report this change of plan, we can say:

*'I **was going to** resign, but in the end I decided to stay.'*

B Was doing/were doing

When we talk about an arrangement that has been changed, we can use the past continuous (**was/were doing**):

*I **was meeting** her on Friday, but she had to go to the States, so I am seeing her next Wednesday instead.*

This is similar to **was going to**, but the past continuous is normally used to report changed arrangements rather than changed plans or intentions.

C Will be doing

The future continuous (**will be doing**) is used to talk about an activity that will be in progress at a particular moment in the future:

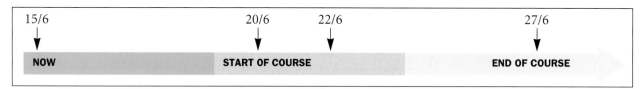

*I'm afraid I can't see you on the 22nd because I **will be attending** a training course in England.*

D Will have done

We use the future perfect (**will have done**), and a time phrase with **by**, to talk about something that will be completed before a particular time in the future:

*We **will have paid back** the loan by August.*

Compare this with the use of the future with **will**:

*We **will** make the last payment in July.*

Was going to – changed plans

Two colleagues are discussing the changes in the plans for a new office. Fill in the blanks with **was/were going to** and **is/are going to**.

A: Have you seen the revised plans?

B: Yes, they are much better. You remember that originally the office [1] _was going to_ be open-plan and that they [2] _____ put up screens?

A: Yes, it sounded terrible.

B: Well, now they [3] _____ divide it up into six separate offices, and there [4] _____ be one or two desks in each one.

A: That sounds a lot better. What about the IT set-up?

B: They've taken our advice on that one too. We [5] _____ have twelve stand-alone PCs, but now everyone [6] _____ be linked to a network, and there [7] _____ be one central computer, which is much better.

Exercise 2
Changed arrangements – problem solving

Look at the schedule (A) for a programmer's visit to a client. All these appointments must be rearranged for the following day. Look at the notes. Work out a new schedule (B) and write sentences about the changes.

(A) original schedule:

WEDNESDAY 18 MAY
10.00 –11.30
– visit the new warehouse
11.30 –1.00
– give presentation to IT Department
1.00 –2.00
Lunch at Nelson's restaurant
2.00 –3.30
– have meeting with Mr Barber
3.30 –5.00
– see the Finance Director

(B) new schedule:

THURSDAY 19 MAY
10.00 –11.30
....
11.30 –1.00
....
1.00 –2.00
Lunch at Gee's restaurant
2.00 –3.30
....
3.30 –5.00
....

NOTES: Nelson's is closed on Thursdays. Gee's restaurant is shut on Mondays. The IT Department is busy all morning. Mr Barber is not free at 2.00. The Finance Director is busy all afternoon. The warehouse shuts at 3.30. The programmer must see Mr Barber before the Finance Director.

1 _____

2 _____

3 _He was having lunch at Nelson's, but now he is having lunch at Gee's._

4 _____

5 _____
_____

Exercise 3

Will be doing and **will have done**

Look through the notes about the building of a new factory. Say what **will be happening** and what **will have happened** at each of the times below.

NOVEMBER – JANUARY:	demolition of the existing building
FEBRUARY – APRIL:	building the new factory
MAY – JULY:	installation of equipment
AUGUST – OCTOBER:	testing of new machinery
NOVEMBER:	start of production

1   In December, _we will be demolishing the old building_.
2   By the end of January, _we will have demolished the old building_.
3   In March _____
4   By the end of April, _____
5   In June, _____
6   By the end of July, _____
7   In September, _____
8   By the end of October,_____
9   By the beginning of December,_____

Exercise 4
Review

Look at the information. Then put the verbs into the right tense.

1   **BUSINESS SEMINAR 10.00–11.00**   *Speaker: Mr AG Wright*

A   The talk (start) _will start_ at 10.00.
B   Mr Wright (give) _will be giving_ his seminar at 10.23.
C   The talk (finish) _will have finished_ by 11.15.

2   **Itinerary for Miss T Wilson:**
    Depart London Heathrow 18.00
    Arrive Athens 22.00

A   The plane (take off) _____ at six in the evening.
B   At 19.35, Miss Wilson (travel) _____ to Athens.
C   Miss Wilson (arrive) _____ in Athens by 11.30.

3   **Law Finals:** *Paper I 10.00–1.00, Paper II 2.00–5.00*

A   The first exam (start) _____ at 10.00.
B   We (have) a break at 1.30.
C   We (finish) _____ by six.

Task 1

Complete these sentences using **was/were going to** or **was/were doing**.

1 *I was going to accept a job in Qatar*
   ... but in the end I decided that I probably wouldn't enjoy it.

2 _____
   ... but I couldn't get a flight until the 18th.

3 _____
   ... but in the end we felt it was too expensive.

4 _____
   ... but she was ill, so we had to cancel.

5 _____
   ... but in the end we decided that three was enough.

6 _____
   ... but it was fully booked.

Task 2

Answer the following questions about yourself in 20 years' time.

1 Who will you be working for 20 years from now?
   _____

2 What position will you have in the company?
   _____

3 What sort of things will you be doing as part of your job?
   _____

4 What will you have achieved by then?
   _____

5 What changes will have taken place in your family life?
   _____

Task 3

Complete these sentences.

1 I hope that, by the time I am your age, _____
   _____

2 This time next week _____

3 There's no point trying to get to the meeting now. By the time you do
   _____

4 By the way, they've changed the venue for the sales conference.
   _____

5 This time tomorrow _____

15 The future (4): possibility and probability

A Definitely, probably, etc.

We often use the words **definitely**, **probably**, and **perhaps/maybe** to show how probable we think a future event is:

DEGREE OF CHANCE:

100% *We **will definitely** increase our turnover next year.*
75%   *The journey **will probably** take about an hour.*
50%   ***Maybe/perhaps** we **will** get some bigger orders soon.*
25%   *The Financial Director **probably won't** be at the meeting.*
0%   *The shipment **definitely won't** get there on time.*

Notice that **won't** normally comes after **probably** and **definitely**.

B Likely to, certain to

We can also use the verb **be** + (**un**)**likely/certain** + infinitive to refer to the future. We use the present tense of the verb **be** and we do not say **will be certain to**. We use **certain to** to refer to things that we think are certain, **likely to/expected to** to refer to things that are probable, and **unlikely to** to refer to things that are improbable:

*You'll meet Jane at the Sales Conference next week. She is **certain to be** there.*
(She will definitely be there.)

*The final cost of the project **is likely to be** higher than the current estimates.*
(It probably will be higher.)

*The Bundesbank **is unlikely to lower** interest rates again this year.*
(It probably won't reduce them.)

C I think, I doubt

There are a number of verbs and other expressions that can show how probable we think a future event is. Here are some common examples:

HIGH PROBABILITY
I'm quite sure that ...
I'm confident that ...
I expect that ...
The chances are that ...   *they will give you a pay rise.*
I should think that ...
I shouldn't think that ...
I doubt if ...
I doubt very much whether ...

LOW PROBABILITY   *I'm quite sure that + (won't) ...*

D Modal verbs

We can use **may**, **might**, and **could** + bare infinitive to refer to the future:

*I believe that unemployment **may/might/could** fall over the coming months.*

(For further information on modal verbs, see Units 23–6.)

Exercise 1
Definitely, probably

Look at the results of an opinion poll asking voters which party they will support at the next election. Complete the sentences about the likely results using **definitely**, **probably**, or **maybe** + **will/won't**.

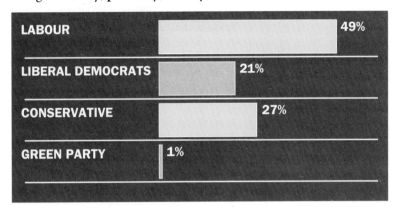

LABOUR	**49%**
LIBERAL DEMOCRATS	**21%**
CONSERVATIVE	**27%**
GREEN PARTY	**1%**

1   The Liberal Democrats *will definitely* do better than the Green Party.
2   The Labour Party _____ get the most votes.
3   _____ the Labour Party _____ get an overall majority.*
4   The Conservatives _____ come second.
5   The Liberal Democrats _____ beat the Conservatives.
6   The Green Party _____ form the next government.

   * *i.e. More seats in Parliament than all the other parties put together.*

Exercise 2
Likely to, certain to

Complete the sentences with **be** + **certain to**, **likely to**, or **unlikely to**.

1   They have very little experience of the entertainment industry, so they *are unlikely to* win the contract for a national television network.
2   She _____ get the job. She has the experience and the qualifications, and none of the other applicants were any good.
3   I will offer them a 10% discount, but they _____ ask for more because they are sometimes very tough negotiators.
4   Of course the stock market goes up and down, but you _____ lose all your money in such a safe investment.
5   I can give Harriet the message. She _____ be here at some stage tomorrow, because she usually comes in to the office on Thursdays.
6   The consortium _____ need some extra finance for the bridge; they have spent all of their money and the project is only half-finished.
7   We are relocating to a site that is quite close, so most of the staff _____ stay with the company.
8   I have booked a hotel room in London for the 18th, because the dinner _____ finish before 11 p.m., and then it will be too late to get a train back to Liverpool.
9   The new manager _____ make a number of changes in the department; the only question is exactly what those changes will be.

15 Practice

A Arrange the expressions in the box in the appropriate columns.

| I'm quite sure + (won't) ... I'm confident that ... I doubt if ... |
| I should think that ... The chances are that ... I'm quite sure that ... |
| I expect that ... I shouldn't think that ... I doubt very much whether ... |

DEFINITELY	PROBABLY	PROBABLY NOT	DEFINITELY NOT
I'm confident that ...			

B Match the sentences in column A with sentences in column B that have a similar meaning.

A	**B**
1 *I'm quite sure they will sign the deal.*	A They are unlikely to sign the deal.
2 The chances are that we'll win the contract.	B They definitely won't sign the deal.
3 I doubt very much if they will sign the deal.	C We probably won't win the contract.
4 We will definitely win the contract.	D We're very unlikely to win the contract.
5 I should think they will sign the deal.	E We'll probably win the contract.
6 I'm quite sure they won't sign the deal.	F We are certain to win the contract.
7 I doubt if we'll win the contract.	G They are likely to sign the deal.
8 I doubt very much whether we'll win the contract.	H *They are certain to sign the deal.*

Rewrite the sentences, using the word in brackets in your answer.

1   He says we are certain to get the contract.
    (confident) *He is confident that we will get the contract.*

2   I shouldn't think that their new store will attract many customers.
    (unlikely) _____

3   I don't imagine they will give us better terms.
    (probably) _____

4   I'm likely to be very busy early next week.
    (probably) _____

5   They are unlikely to deliver the equipment this month.
    (think) _____

Reply to the following questions about your future in two different ways.

In the next few years, what are your chances of ...

1   ... working abroad?
     A   *I should think I'll work abroad in the next few years.*
     B   *Perhaps I'll work abroad in the next few years.*

2   ... changing jobs?
     A   _____
     B   _____

3   ... getting rich ?
     A   _____
     B   _____

4   ... getting promoted?
     A   _____
     B   _____

5   ... marrying someone English?
     A   _____
     B   _____

6   ... taking over control of your company?
     A   _____
     B   _____

7   ... having to spend some time doing military service?
     A   _____
     B   _____

Make predictions about what changes will happen in the next few years.

1   the economy *I should think that the economy will continue to improve in the short term, but the recovery may slow down because of political uncertainty. There will definitely be an election, and taxation is likely to be increased.*

2   your company _____
     _____
     _____

3   new technologies _____
     _____
     _____

4   the countries of the Pacific Rim _____
     _____
     _____

16 The passive (1): actions, systems, and processes

A Form

The passive is formed by using the verb **be** and the past participle (e.g., **broken**, **driven**, **used**). For example, the present tense passive is formed with **am/is/are** + past participle:

I **am/am not driven.** **Am** I **driven?**
He/she/it **is/is not** (**isn't**) **driven.** **Is** he/she/it **driven?**
We/you/they **are/are not** (**aren't**) **driven.** **Are** we/you/they **driven?**

B Focus on actions

We often use the passive to focus on something that happens to someone, when we do not want to focus on the person who does the action:

*Over 36% of Guatemalan workers **are employed** in the agricultural sector.*

We use the passive here because we do not know, or need to say, who employs them.

C Systems and processes

The passive is often used to talk about systems and processes:

*Many of the world's diamonds **are mined** in South Africa. The stones **are sent** to Amsterdam, where they **are sold** to international dealers. The stones **are cut** in Antwerp, and they **are** then **sold** on to jewellers.*

D Active or passive?

If it is important to say who performs an action, we can use the active or we can use the passive and the word **by**:

ACTIVE: *Peter Franks **runs** the Marketing Department.*
PASSIVE: *The Marketing Department **is run by** Peter Franks.*

Both of these sentences are correct. If we were already talking about Peter Franks, we would probably use the active:

*Peter Franks is an old colleague of mine. He works for Butterfield International, and he **runs** the Marketing Department.*

If we were talking about the the Marketing Department, we would probably use the passive:

*The Marketing Department is a large and very successful division that employs over 100 people. It **is run by** Peter Franks.*

Exercise 1

Form

Put the verbs in brackets into the present simple passive.

A: What is the difference between this new Paycard and ordinary phonecards?

B: The Paycard [1] *is not designed* (not/design) for public telephones; you can use it with any phone, for example in a hotel. Each Paycard has an account number on the back, and that is a bit like a bank account. This account [2] _____ (credit) with money from your Visa card or Access card. When you want to make a call, you ring the Paycard operator, and then you [3] _____ (connect) with the number you want. The cost of the call [4] _____ (deduct) from your Paycard balance.

A: How do you know what the balance of your Paycard account is?

B: At the beginning of the call, you [5] _____ (tell) by the operator, for example, that you have £15 in the account, and you can talk as long as you like. And if the money runs out, you [6] _____ (warn) that you only have one minute left.

A: Who is the new card for? [7] _____ (it/aim) at tourists or the general public or business people?

B: Business people will find it very useful. Business people often complain that they [8] _____ (charge) too much for phone calls at hotels. With this system, you can use the hotel phone, but the cost of the call [9] _____ (not/put) on your hotel bill. It [10] _____ (take) from the balance in your Paycard account, so of course it is much cheaper and more convenient, and you can use almost any phone anywhere.

Exercise 2

Avoiding the subject

Many of the following sentences sound unnatural because they are in the active. Rewrite them in the present simple passive, but do not mention the agent (e.g., **by workers**, **by people**).

1 Workers in China make these telephones.
   These telephones ... *are made in China.*

2 Employers pay many manual workers weekly.
   Many manual workers ... _____

3 They keep a large amount of gold at Fort Knox.
   A large amount of gold ... _____

4 Workers build a lot of the world's supertankers in South Korea.
   A lot of the world's supertankers ... _____

5 Farmers grow a third of the world's cocoa in the Ivory Coast.
   A third of the world's cocoa ... _____

6 Countries store most nuclear waste underground.
   Most nuclear waste ... _____

7 Scientists test most new drugs extensively before they go on sale.
   Before they go on sale, most new drugs ... _____

8 Workers print a lot of our books in Hong Kong.
   A lot of our books ... _____

Exercise 3
Systems and processes

Read this information about DHL, a company that delivers parcels and documents worldwide. Put the verbs into the present simple passive.

DHL FROM START TO FINISH

One phone call is all it takes to get your shipment moving.

Quick off the mark

As soon as you book your shipment over the phone, your details (1) *are programmed* (program) into the DHL system. Within minutes, a courier receives a pick-up message.

Rapid collection

The data (2) _____ (transfer) to a printer in the van, so our driver will know where you are. Your consignment (3) _____ (collect), and a bar code scanner (4) _____ (use) to record all the details of the shipment. That shipment (5) _____ (drive) to a DHL centre, where the most suitable air route (6) _____ (choose).

Prepared for take off

Your shipment (7) _____ (check in) by DHL ground staff at the airport, and they make sure that it (8) _____ (load) onto the right flight.

Satellite technology

While the plane is in the air, all the details of the shipment (9) _____ (transmit) to the local DHL import agents. As soon as the plane lands, the information (10) _____ (give) to customs.

Personal delivery

As soon as your shipment (11) _____ (clear), it (12) _____ (deliver) to its final destination. All the information about delivery (13) _____ (held) on computer, allowing you to check delivery with one quick phone call.

Exercise 4
Active or passive?

Read each of the following statements. Then say if it should be followed by sentence A or sentence B. Underline the correct answer.

1 Roche is one of the world's leading pharmaceutical groups.
A *It manufactures vitamins, perfumes, and antibiotics.*
B Vitamins, perfumes, and antibiotics are manufactured by it.

2 Qantas is the second oldest international airline.
A The Australian government currently owns it.
B It is currently owned by the Australian government.

3 Bass PLC is the largest global hotel operator.
A It owns Holiday Inns and a number of other hotel chains.
B Holiday Inns and a number of other hotels chains are owned by it.

4 Australian born Rupert Murdoch is Chairman of News Corporation.
A He controls 39% of the company through Cruden Investments.
B 39% of the company is controlled by him through Cruden Investments.

A person who works in the Personnel Department is explaining how they select candidates in her company.

'If there's a vacancy, I usually advertise it in-house first of all, and if I don't find any suitable candidates, then we advertise the job in the papers. We ask applicants to send in their CVs, and we invite some of the candidates to an interview. After that, we draw up a shortlist and ask some of the applicants back for a second interview. We choose the best candidate, and then I check his or her references, and if everything's OK, we offer the applicant the job.'

Complete the sentences below to give a general description of the recruitment process. Use the passive in your answer.

1   The vacancy ... _is advertised in-house._

2   If there is a suitable in-house candidate ... _____

3   The vacancy ... _____

4   Applicants ... _____

5   Some candidates ... _____

6   A shortlist ... _____

7   Selected candidates ... _____

8   The best candidate ..._____

9   The references ... _____

10   The successful candidate ... _____

Write a short paragraph describing a system or process you know well. You may find the following linking words helpful.

| First of all, ... | Then, ... | Next, ... | After that, ... | Finally, ... |

_____
_____
_____
_____
_____

17 The passive (2): tenses

A Other tenses

The examples below show how to form the passive with other tenses.

Present continuous passive: **am being**, **is being**, or **are being** + past participle:

*I **am being asked** to do a lot of extra work at the moment.*
*I can assure you that your complaint **is being dealt with**.*

Simple past passive: **was** or **were** + the past participle:

*Our company **was founded** in 1848.*
*Most of the senior managers **were fired** after the takeover.*

Note the passive form **be born**:
A *When **were** you **born**?*   **B** *I **was born** in 1968.*

Past continuous passive: **was being** or **were being** + the past participle:

*I couldn't use the company car yesterday because it **was being serviced**.*
*We only noticed the mistakes when the brochures **were being printed**.*

Present perfect passive: **has been** or **have been** + the past participle:

*A design fault **has been found** on some of our washing machines.*
*All of the machines **have been recalled**.*

Past perfect passive: **had been** + the past participle:

*They faxed us to say that the shipment **had been delayed**.*

Future passive: **will be** or **going to be** + the past participle:

*The shipment **is going to be** delayed.*
*It **will be** delivered next Tuesday.*

B Personal or impersonal?

The passive is also often used in business correspondence, because it is less personal than the active. Compare:

*Peter Jason, who opens our post at this branch, **received** your letter yesterday. He **has forwarded** it to Head Office.* (ACTIVE)

*Thank you for your letter which **was received** at this branch yesterday. It **has been forwarded** to Head Office, as complaints **are dealt with** there.* (PASSIVE)

C Changes

The present perfect passive is often used when we are describing changes that have taken place, and we are more interested in the changes than who has made them:

*The factory is completely different. The whole place **has been modernized** and **computerized**, and a lot of people **have been made redundant**.*

Exercise 1
Tenses in the passive

A Put the verbs in brackets into the present continuous active or passive.

Less than a month after the fire at its plant in Ludwigshafen, Germany, the air bag manufacturer HTS is back in business. Sales Director Klaus Schiller explained: 'The factory in Ludwigshafen [1] *is working* (work) again, because one part was not destroyed by the fire. So, for the moment, some of the other components [2] _____ (import) from the States, and the bags [3] _____ (assemble) at our other plant in Poland.' The company [4] _____ (plan) to build a much larger production plant at Ludwigshafen. This will be a large investment, but the air bag market [5] _____ (grow) rapidly, and more and more air bags [6] _____ (fit) in cars as a standard safety device.'

B Put the verbs in brackets into the past continuous active or passive.

Three armed men escaped yesterday with over $1million in used European banknotes after an attack at Heathrow airport. The money [1] *was being transported* (transported) from a Middle Eastern country to a London bank and [2] _____ (carry) by an unarmed courier. The three robbers, who [3] _____ (wait) for the courier in the short-stay car park, attacked the man and stole the money. A passer-by told the police that a man [4] _____ (attack), but when they reached the scene, the robbers had driven off.

C Put the verbs in brackets into the past perfect active or passive.

SAMANTHA PHILLIPS SAID yesterday that she was 'delighted' with the decision of an Industrial Tribunal after she [1] *had been awarded* (award) £18,000 for unfair dismissal. Miss Phillips, a 28-year-old City worker, told the court that she [2] _____ (sack) because she [3] _____ (reject) the sexual advances of her boss. Her former employers said that Miss Phillips [4] _____ (dismiss) because she [5] _____ (not/do) her job properly. The judge agreed that Miss Phillips [6] _____ (make) some 'foolish' business decisions, but said that Miss Phillips [7] _____ (not/treat) fairly by the company.

Exercise 2
Future passive

Put the verbs in brackets into the **will** future active or passive.

JANET: I've booked you on the 8.30 flight, so you [1] *will arrive* (arrive) at 11.00 local time. You [2] _____ (meet) at the airport by one of their drivers, and you [3] _____ (take) straight to their Head Office.

HELEN: Fine. Have you organized a hotel?

JANET: Yes, you [4] _____ (be) at the Holiday Inn.

HELEN: OK. Do they know how long the meeting [5] _____ (last)?

JANET: They expect that you [6] _____ (be able) to finish at about 5.30. I have told the hotel that you [7] _____ (not arrive) before 6.30. But that's fine and they have said that the room [8] _____ (keep) for you, and that it [9] _____ (not/give) to anyone else.

....

Exercise 3
Present perfect: changes

Look at the staff changes that have taken place at a small UK engineering company. Complete the dialogue between a company employee and a friend who used to work there. Put the verbs in brackets into the present perfect active or passive (**has/have done** or **has/have been done**).

PREVIOUS ORGANIZATION

CURRENT ORGANIZATION

JOHN: Are things different now?

SARA: Yes. What has happened is that the Sales and Marketing Department [1] *has been turned* (turn) into three separate divisions – there is now an International Division, a UK Division, and there's a new office that [2] _____ (set up) in the US.

JOHN: Is Peter still in charge?

SARA: No, they [3] _____ (make) him a Senior Director, so he doesn't have much to do with the department now. Laura [4] _____ (promote) to Sales Director, so they all report directly to her. Benedict Warner and Katie Lang [5] _____ (put) in charge of the International Division and the UK Division.

JOHN: [6] _____ (they/send) Ken to the US?

SARA: No, not at all. He didn't get on with Laura, basically, so he [7] _____ (demote) to UK Sales Assistant, and he works for Katie. Obviously he's not very happy about it and he doesn't think that the company [8] _____ (treat) him fairly. I don't expect he'll stay long.

Task 1

Write sentences from the prompts using one of the verbs from the box.

| build | discover | elect | found | invent | open |

1 The Berlin Wall/1961

The Berlin Wall was built in 1961.

2 The Channel Tunnel/1994

_____

3 Radium/Marie and Pierre Curie

_____

4 The wireless/Marconi

_____

5 Fiat SPA/1899

_____

6 President Clinton/1992

_____

Task 2

Add a comment to each of the following questions.

Have you heard what ...

1 ... has happened to their Spanish subsidiary? *It has been sold.*
2 ... is happening to the department? _____
3 ... happened to the chairman at the meeting?_____
4 ... has happened to the strikers? _____
5 ... is happening to the price of petrol? _____
6 ... happened to our office in Singapore?_____
7 ... has happened to the lira? _____

Task 3

Read the information about AMS Trading. Then write a similar short paragraph about the history of your company.

AMS Trading was founded by Alan Sugar in 1968, and the company's name was changed to Amstrad in 1972. The company sold electronic consumer goods, and then moved into computers. Amstrad was floated on the Stock Exchange in 1980. It expanded rapidly until 1988, when it launched the PC 2000 series of personal computers.

_____

_____

_____

18 The passive (3): passive verbs and infinitives, **have** something **done**

A Passive + infinitive

The verbs **believe**, **expect**, **know**, **report**, **say**, **think**, **suppose**, and **understand** are often used in the passive and are followed by an infinitive (**to be**, **to do**). Compare:

*People **say** that Taikichiro Mori **is** the richest person outside the USA.*
*Taikichiro Mori **is said to be** the richest person outside the USA.*

To refer to the past we can use **to have done**:

*They **believe** that the company **lost** a great deal of money on the deal.*
*The company **is believed to have lost** a great deal of money on the deal.*

To refer to something happening at the moment we can use **to be doing**:

*People **believe** that George Soros **is planning** a major new investment.*
*George Soros **is believed to be planning** a major new investment.*

B **Have** something **done**

We can use the structure **have** something **done** to talk about things we pay or employ other people to do for us. We use the verb **have** + the object + past participle:

HAVE	+	OBJECT	+	PAST PARTICIPLE
We **have**		our books		**printed** in Singapore.

COMMON MISTAKES: We put the object before the past participle, not after:
WRONG: *We ~~have serviced our cars~~ by a local garage.*
RIGHT: *We **have** our cars **serviced** by a local garage.*

In most cases we can also use **get** instead of **have**. This is more informal:

*We **get** our brochures **printed** in Hong Kong.*

C **Have** something **done**
– tenses

We can use **have something done** in different tenses. To do this, we use the correct tense of the verb **have** (or the verb **get**). Look at the following examples:

PRESENT SIMPLE:	*We **have** the machines **cleaned** regularly.*
PRESENT CONTINUOUS:	*He **is having** the letter **typed** out.*
SIMPLE PAST:	*They **had** the order **sent** by courier.*
PRESENT PERFECT:	***Have you had** your accounts **checked**?*
GOING TO:	*I'm **going to have** a new fax **installed**.*
MODALS:	*You **must have** your office **repainted**.*

Read the following article about the richest man in Britain. Fill in the blanks with a verb in the passive and a suitable form of the infinitive.

THE RICHEST MAN IN BRITAIN

The publisher Paul Raymond (1) *is said to be* (say/be) the richest man in Britain, and he (2)_____ (believe/have) a personal fortune of over £1,650,000,000. His magazine publishing company (3)_____ (think/make) annual profits of around £14 million, and he (4)_____ (believe/own) a number of other companies. He (5)_____ (know/have) houses in London and the Caribbean, but at the age of 68 he (6)_____ (say/live) a very quiet life.

However, most of his wealth does not come from the magazines; it comes from the property he owns in central London. He (7) *is known to have started* (know/start) buying up properties over forty years ago, when prices were about £10,000. He (8)_____ (say/buy) another fifty properties in 1974, and he (9)_____ (believe/purchase) another hundred in 1977 just before the property market recovered. Each of these investments (10)_____ (believe/rise) in value many times over, so he is much richer than the Queen.

He is now nearing retirement, but he (11) *is thought to be making* (think/make) major new property investments at the moment. He (12)_____ (say/try) to buy a number of properties in Rupert Street, London, and (13)_____ (believe/buy) additional houses in Chelsea. However, he (14)_____ (not think/plan) to expand his publishing empire any further.

18 Practice

The manager of a British company is explaining how its computers are made. Look at the map and make sentences using **have** something **done**.

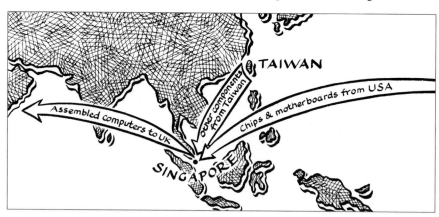

1 We/chips and motherboards/make/in the USA.
We have the chips and the motherboards made in the USA.

2 Then we/them/fly/Singapore.

_____

3 We/other components/manufacture/Taiwan.

_____

4 We/them/send/Singapore.

_____

5 We/computers/assemble/Singapore.

_____

6 We/the finished products/ship/the UK/every 3 months.

_____

Rewrite the following sentences using **have something done**.

1 Someone makes my suits in London.
I have my suits made in London.

2 Someone is going to print 5,000 new catalogues for us.
We _____

3 Someone is designing a new office for them.
They _____

4 Someone has checked these figures for me.
I _____

5 Someone should mend the photocopier for you.
You _____

6 Someone delivered the new furniture for us yesterday.
We _____

Task 1

Answer the questions using the verbs in brackets in the passive, and another verb in the infinitive.

What do you know about ...

1 the Sultan of Brunei? (suppose)
He is supposed to be the richest man in the world.

2 the Prime Minister or President in your country? (believe)

_____

3 the Chairman of your company? (think)

_____

4 your main competitors? (know)

_____

5 American companies? (say)

_____

6 Saudi Arabia? (suppose)

_____

Task 2

Write a short paragraph for the company log book using a suitable passive form. Say what happened to:

the storeroom   the carpets and curtains
the money in the safe   the work you had on the computer
a lot of the windows   one of the firemen

We had a fire at our office last night, and the storeroom was burned to the ground. There was quite a lot of damage to the rest of the building too ...

_____

_____

_____

_____

Task 3

You have just been on an all expenses paid trip to one of the best conference centres in the world, where they did everything for you. Say what you had done for you while you were there.

1 (clothes) *I had my clothes cleaned and returned within 12 hours.*
2 (breakfast) _____
3 (letters) _____
4 (room) _____
5 (presentation) _____
6 (business cards) _____
7 (travel arrangements) _____
8 (bills) _____

19 Conditionals: **if you go**...

A Zero conditional

We can talk about general facts or things that are always true using an **if** sentence. This kind of sentence has the present tense in both parts:

> **IF + PRESENT TENSE,**   **PRESENT TENSE**
> **If** interest rates **fall,**   company profits **rise.**

In statements like this, **if** means the same as **when** or **every time**. This is sometimes called the zero conditional.

B First conditional:
if + present + **will**

When we talk about future events that are reasonably likely and their results, we can use an **if**-sentence. The **if**-clause states the condition, and the other clause states the result:

> **IF + PRESENT TENSE**   **WILL + BARE INFINITIVE**
> **If** the government **raises** taxes,   consumer spending **will fall.**
> (CONDITION)   (RESULT)

The **if**-clause can come in the first part of the sentence or the second:

*If the government **raises** taxes, consumer spending **will fall**.*
*Consumer spending **will fall** if the government **raises** taxes.*

COMMON MISTAKES: We do not use **will** in the **if** part of the sentence:
WRONG: *If the shipment ~~will arrive~~ tomorrow, I will collect it.*
RIGHT: *If the shipment **arrives** tomorrow, I **will** collect it.*

C If or when?

When we talk about events that will take place in the future, we can use **if** or **when**:

*I'm flying to the States tonight. I'll give you a ring **if** I can find a phone.*
(The speaker is not sure if he will be able to find a phone or not.)

*I'm flying to the States tonight. I'll give you a ring **when** I get there.*
(The speaker has no doubt that the plane will arrive safely.)

D Variations

In a sentence with an **if**-clause we can use the imperative, or other modal verbs (see Units 23–6), instead of **will** + infinitive:

*If you hear from Susan today, **tell** her to ring me.*
*If the traffic is bad, I **may** get home late.*
*If we sign the contract today, we **can** start production at the end of next month.*
*If Mr Duval rings, you **must** ask him to leave his number.*

Exercise 1
Zero conditional

Match the first part of the sentences in column A with the right endings in column B.

A	B
1 *Governments expect something in return*	A something is wrong with the management.
2 Every time Peter chairs a meeting	B it gets there the following morning.
3 People are more productive	C I usually look after them.
4 If you send a letter by Datapost,	D *if they give aid.*
5 If inflation rises,	E if we launch a new model.
6 When you have a high staff turnover,	F it goes on for a long time.
7 If anyone from our Hamburg office visits,	G if they work in pleasant surroundings.
8 We spend a great deal on promotion	H the value of people's savings goes down.
9 I always fly Club Class	I when I go on a long haul flight.

Exercise 2
First conditional

Look at the notes about each situation. Then put the verbs in brackets into the correct tense. Use the present simple and **will** + infinitive in each sentence.

1   A   If the meeting *finishes* (finish) late, I *will spend* (spend) the night in London.

    B   If the meeting *doesn't finish* (not finish) late, I *will catch* (catch) the train home.

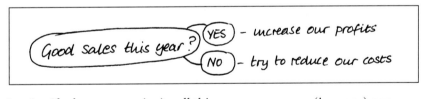

2   A   If sales _____ (go) well this year, we _____ (increase) our profits.

    B   If sales _____ (not/go) well this year, we _____ (try to) reduce our costs.

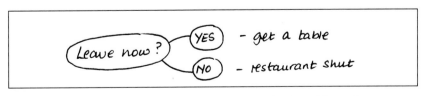

3   A   If we _____ (leave) now, we _____ (get) a table at the restaurant.

    B   If we _____ (stay) here for much longer, the restaurant _____ (shut).

Exercise 3
If or when?

Fill in the blanks with **if** or **when**.

1 I don't think you'll have any problems, but call me _____ you do.
2 Mrs Barton is coming this afternoon. Could you send her up _____ she arrives?
3 We won't be able to compete _____ we don't modernize our production plant.
4 Put that on my bill please, and I'll pay _____ I check out.
5 I will feel very disappointed _____ I don't get promotion this year.
6 Sales are low this spring, but they will improve _____ summer starts.

Exercise 4
Variations

Read the following dialogue, and choose the best option from the words in italics.

HANS: I'll be at a meeting this afternoon, so if Pierre (1) *will call/calls*, (2) *tell/you'll tell* him I'll give him a ring later.

CLAUDIA: OK, but there's one other thing. You've got a meeting with Mr Sachs at 5.00. Will you be back by then?

HANS: It depends, really, but I'll call you. If the meeting (3) *will go on/goes on* after 4.30, you (4) *will/can* cancel my appointment with Mr Sachs. But if it has already finished by then, I (5) *may/can* be able to get back in time.

CLAUDIA: Anything else?

HANS: Yes, if you (6) *will manage/manage* to get hold of Kevin, you (7) *must/will* get the October sales figures from him. I need them today. The Chairman (8) *may come/can come* to the sales meeting tomorrow, and if he does, he (9) *is going to want/must want* to see them.

Exercise 5
Right or wrong?

Some of the following sentences are right and some are wrong. Put a tick (✔) next to the ones that are right and correct the ones that are wrong.

1 If you finish everything that needs to be done before five, you are able to go home.   _____*you can go home*_____
2 Mr Lo probably won't want to go out for dinner if he has a meal on the plane.   _____
3 If it will be their first visit to England, I expect they might want to do some sightseeing.   _____
4 I may go and visit their headquarters if I will go to London next week.   _____
5 Please don't hesitate to contact me if you require any further information.   _____
6 What should I do if everyone will be still talking when I want to start my presentation?   _____
7 If you will go to Paris next week, I can give you the name of a good hotel I know.   _____

··
Task 1

Rewrite these sentences using a first conditional sentence with **if**.

1   For further information call us on 0800 726354.
    If you ring 0800 726354, they'll give you some more information.

2   We've got these products on a 'sale or return' basis.
    _____

3   Subscribe to Business Age before September 30 and save up to 33%.
    _____

4   The Ford Escort comes with a money-back guarantee.
    _____

··
Task 2

Complete these sentences.

1   If I have time this weekend, ... _____
2   If I go on holiday this year, ... _____
3   If I can afford it, ... _____
4   If I carry on learning English, ... _____
5   If I stay in my present job, ... _____
6   If I feel tired this evening, ... _____
7   If I finish work early, ... _____
8   If I move house at some stage in the future, ... _____

··
Task 3

You have been asked to speak on these topics at a meeting. Write short paragraphs about what you think will happen during the next two or three years, and what you or your company will do.

1   interest rates
    I think that interest rates will rise again during the next two or three years.
    If they do, we will have to try to reduce our costs and the amount we borrow
    as much as possible, and we will not be able to expand.

2   your market share
    _____
    _____
    _____

3   new competitors
    _____
    _____
    _____

4   the political situation
    _____
    _____
    _____

20 Conditionals: **if, unless**, etc.

A If and unless

Unless means the same as **if ... not**. It always refers to the conditional part of the sentence and not the result part of the sentence:

> **If** he doesn't **get** here soon, we will have to start the meeting without him.
>   (CONDITION)   (RESULT)

> **Unless** he **gets** here soon, we will have to start the meeting without him
>   (CONDITION)   (RESULT)

We often use **not + unless**, which means **only ... if**, when we want to emphasize a condition:

*They **will only sign** the contract **if** we give them an additional discount.*
*They **won't sign** the contract **unless** we give them an additional discount.*

B If and in case

We use **in case** to talk about precautions we will take before a problem happens. We use **if** to talk about what we will do after a problem happens:

*We are going to insure the shipment **in case** the goods get damaged in transit.*
(We will take out insurance first; the problem may or may not happen afterwards.)

If the goods get damaged in transit, we'll make a claim.
(The damage may happen, and we will make a claim afterwards.)

Note that in sentences with **in case**, we often use **going to** rather than **will** because we are often talking about something we have already decided to do (see Units 12–13).

C Provided that, as long as, etc.

We can use **provided that/providing**, **as long as**, and **so long as** when we want to emphasize a condition. **Provided that** and **as long as** mean **if** and **only if** (**providing** and **so long as** are a little less formal than **provided that** and **as long as**):

*I will agree to these conditions **provided that** you increase my salary by 8.5%.*
(I will only agree if you give me more money.)

*The strike will be successful **as long as** we all stay together.*
(It will only succeed if we all stay together.)

Note that we use the same sentence pattern as with other **if**-sentences.

D So that

We use **so that** to explain what the result or purpose of an action will be:

*I'll take a credit card **so that** we don't run out of money.*
(The credit card will stop us from running out of money.)

Exercise 1

If and **unless**

Match the first part of each sentence in column A with the right ending in column B.

A	**B**
1 *There's going to be a train strike tomorrow*	A unless we give her the salary she wants.
2 The union won't go on strike	B we will not make a loss this year.
3 She will accept the job	C we will make a loss this year.
4 She won't accept the job	D they will not take legal action.
5 Unless sales improve dramatically	E *unless we agree to their demands.*
6 If sales improve dramatically	F if we agree to their demands.
7 Unless we pay them immediately	G they will take legal action.
8 If we pay them immediately	H if we give her the salary she wants.

Exercise 2

If and **unless**

Rewrite the following sentences using **unless**.

1 If nothing goes wrong, we will sign the deal tomorrow.
We will sign the deal tomorrow *unless something goes wrong.*

2 We're not going to get that contract if we don't improve our offer.
We're not going to get that contract _____

3 Only phone me if it is an emergency.
Please don't phone me _____

4 If demand doesn't increase soon, we're going to have a bad year.
We're going to have a bad year _____

5 This project will only be viable if you can cut your overheads.
This project will not be viable _____

6 I'll accept an overseas posting if I can have my job back when I return.
I won't accept an overseas posting _____

Exercise 3

In case

A manager is going to Frankfurt to attend a trade fair. Complete the sentences about what he is going to do using **in case** + present tense.

The hotels may be busy.   It might be extremely cold.
He might want to hire a car.   The office might need to phone him.
He might have to see a doctor.   He may lose his passport.

1 He's going to book a room in advance ... ___ *in case the hotels are busy.*
2 He's going to photocopy his passport ... _____
3 He's going to take his driving licence ... _____
4 He's going to leave a contact number ... _____
5 He's going to take out medical insurance ... _____
6 He's going to take some warm clothes ... _____

Look through the list of possible problems you may have when giving a presentation. Look at the precautions you can take, and the possible solutions. Write sentences using **in case** and **if**.

	PRECAUTIONS	POSSIBLE PROBLEMS	SOLUTIONS
1	leave in plenty of time	the traffic may be heavy	
2		may have a lot of time to spare	read through my notes
3	inspect the room first	it may not be suitable	
4		the seating may not be right	see the organizers
5	take extra handouts	audience may be larger than expected	
6		audience may not be experienced	keep the talk simple

1   *I'm going to leave early in case the traffic is heavy.*
2   *If I have a lot of time to spare, I'll read through my notes.*
3   _____
4   _____
5   _____
6   _____

Underline the best option from the words in italics.

1   We'll sign the contract today *provided that/unless* there aren't any last minute problems.
2   The banks will support us *unless/as long* as the company is profitable.
3   I won't call you *unless/providing* I have a problem I can't deal with.
4   *So long as/Unless* we continue to order in bulk, they will go on giving us free delivery.
5   *Unless/Provided that* we solve the problem now, the situation is going to get worse.
6   We will be able to start this project in two months *as long as/unless* the board think it is a good idea.

In each of the following sentences, fill in the blanks with **in case** or **so that**.

1   The building has smoke alarms <u>so that</u> we can detect fires immediately.
2   Keep the insurance documents safe _____ we need to make a claim.
3   I'll send you a fax _____ you get all the information you need today.
4   I'm going to hold a meeting _____ everyone can say what they think.
5   I'll phone you later _____ you have any problems with the program.
6   I've left the answering machine on _____ anyone calls.

Task 1   Complete the following sentences.

1   I'll probably stay in my present job unless ...

_____

2   The economic situation will continue to improve as long as ...

_____

3   I won't be able to go to the interview on Thursday unless ...

_____

4   Provided that Boeing get the safety certificate for their new aeroplane, ...

_____

5   Unless I have to change the time of the meeting for some reason, ...

_____

6   We will allow you to become the sole distributor of our product providing ...

_____

Task 2   Finish each of the sentences in three ways, using **if**, **in case**, and **so that**.

1   I'm going to leave early ...
A   if   _my boss lets me._
B   in case   _I get caught up in the traffic._
C   so that   _I get to the airport on time._

2   I'll take some local currency with me ...
A   if   _____
B   in case   _____
C   so that   _____

3   I'll take my address book with me ...
A   if   _____
B   in case   _____
C   so that   _____

4   They haven't paid the invoice yet. I'll send them a reminder ...
A   if   _____
B   in case   _____
C   so that   _____

5   You will need to hire a car ...
A   if   _____
B   in case   _____
C   so that   _____

21 Conditionals: **if you went ...**

A Form

The second conditional is formed by using **if** + past tense and **would** + infinitive:

> IF + PAST TENSE   WOULD + INFINITIVE
> **If** I **knew** her number, I **would send** her a fax.

COMMON MISTAKES: We do not use **would** in the **if** part of the sentence:
WRONG: *If trains* ~~would~~ *be more reliable, more people would use them.*
RIGHT: *If trains **were** more reliable, more people **would** use them.*

The **if**-clause can come in the first part of the sentence, or the second:

*If I knew her number, I **would send** her a fax.*
*I **would send** her a fax if I knew her number.*

B Imaginary situations

We can use the second conditional to refer to an action or state we imagine:

1 *If these machines **were not** so expensive, we **would buy** them.*
   (But they are expensive, and we are not going to buy them.)
2 *If I **lost** my job tomorrow, I **would move** to London to find another one.*
   (I don't think I will lose my job, but I understand the possible consequences.)

In 1 we are talking about the present, and imagining a situation that is different from reality. In 2 we are talking about a possible event in the future; however, by using the second conditional we make it clear that we do not really think it will happen.

C Variations

It is also possible to use **might** and **could** instead of **would**:

*If we had the finance, we **could** expand much more rapidly.*
*If the terms of the contract were different, we **might** accept it.*

In the **if**-clause, we can use **were** instead of **was**. This is very common when we give advice using the expression **If I were you ...**

*If I **were** you, I would have another look through those figures.*

D First or second conditional?

If we think that a future event is reasonably likely, we use the first conditional:

If *the investment **grows** at 6% a year, it **will be** worth £20,000 in ten years.*
(This is likely.)
If we are talking about an event that we think is unlikely or impossible, we use the second conditional:

*If I **had** as much money as Bill Gates of Microsoft, I **would retire**.*
(But I haven't and I never will.)

Exercise 1
Form

Change the verbs in brackets using **would** + infinitive or the past tense.

A: My session with the career counsellor was a bit of a waste of time.

B: Really? Why?

A: Well, firstly, he recommended moving to London, but that's impossible. If I [1] _got_ (get) a job in London, I [2] _____ (have) to spend at least four hours a day on the train, and I'm not going to do that.

B: Couldn't you move?

A: No, because if I [3] _____ (move) to London, I [4] _____ (need) to sell the house, and I don't want to do that at the moment.

B: Did he have any other ideas?

A: He suggested retraining to become an accountant, but that's not a solution either. Even if I [5] _____ (start) next week, I [6] _____ (not/be) qualified for at least three years, and that is too long. So I don't really know what I'm going to do.

Exercise 2
Imaginary situations

Rewrite the following sentences with **if** and the second conditional.

1 The reason we don't use them is that they are so expensive.
But ... _if they weren't so expensive, we would use them._
But ... _we would use them if they weren't so expensive._

2 The reason I can't contact them is that I haven't got their address.
But ... _____

3 The reason I work so hard is that I enjoy my job.
But ... _____

4 The reason we are the market leaders is that we spend so much on R&D.
But ... _____

5 The reason I won't give you an answer is that I haven't got the authority.
But ... _____

Exercise 3
Variations

Complete the sentences with the correct form of verbs in the box.

change	be	think	speak	apply	earn	give	produce

1 I think they might _give_ me that job in Paris if I _applied_ for it, but I'm not interested in it.

2 If I _____ you, I would _____ very carefully before investing.

3 It's a pity you have refused to talk to him. He might _____ his mind if you _____ to him personally.

4 It's a pity the circulation of our magazine is so low. If it _____ higher, we could _____ a lot more from advertising.

5 If our labour costs _____ lower, we could _____ cheaper goods.

Exercise 4
First or second conditional?

Read through the following sentences. Decide whether the events in them are likely or imaginary, and put the verbs in brackets into the right tense.

1   If everyone _contributed_ (contribute) 10% of their salaries to charity, there would _be_ (be) no poverty.

2   I am sure we _____ (meet) our targets if we _____ (maintain) our current level of sales.

3   If I _____ (be) in your position, I _____ (insist) on having more staff in the department.

4   Please have a seat. If you _____ (wait) a couple of minutes, I _____ (give) you a lift.

5   I'm expecting a fax from Grayson's. If it _____ (come) today, please _____ (let) me know at once.

6   I _____ (apply) for the job if I _____ (have) a degree, but unfortunately I haven't.

7   What laws _____ (you/change) if you _____ (be) in Parliament?

8   I'm leaving now; I _____ (be) back at 8.30 if the traffic _____ (not/be) too bad.

Exercise 5
Culture Quiz

Read through the following situations. Say if you would do these things or not by putting a tick (✔) or a cross (✗) next to each of the sentences. When you have finished, look through the notes in the Answer Key.

CULTURE QUIZ

❶ If I were doing business in China and was asked about Taiwan, I would say 'It's a country I have never visited'.

❷ If I were having a meal with some Malay business colleagues in Kuala Lumpur, I would only pick up food with my right hand.

❸ If I asked a Japanese businessman to do something and he said 'Chotto muzukashi' (It's a little difficult), I would continue trying to persuade him to agree.

❹ If I were invited to a British person's home at 8 p.m. for dinner, I would try and arrive 15 minutes late.

❺ If I were doing business in Saudi Arabia, I would not speak Arabic unless I could speak it properly.

❻ If I were in Oman, I would not start talking about business until after the second cup of coffee.

....

Task 1

Answer the following questions using the second conditional.

What would you do if ...

1 ... you invented a new product?
   If I invented a new product, I would patent it immediately.

2 ... you lost your job?

   _____

3 ... you were offered a job in Saudi Arabia for five years?

   _____

4 ... your company's main competitors offered you a good job?

   _____

5 ... you lost all your money and credit cards?

   _____

....

Task 2

Write down the advice you would give in the following situations. Begin each answer with '**If I were you ...**'.

What would you say to ...

1 ... an 18 year old who wanted to join your company instead of taking up a place at a well-known university?
   If I were you I'd go to university, because you could join the company later.

2 ... a colleague who had not heard about the result of an interview?

   _____

3 ... a friend who asked you what kind of car he should buy?

   _____

4 ... someone who was looking for a job with your company?

   _____

5 ... a visitor to your town who asked which restaurants were good?

   _____

....

Task 3

Read the example and then write a short paragraph about the changes you would make in the following situation.

If I were the Prime Minister, I would raise taxes and spend more money on education. I would reduce bureaucracy and cut defence spending. I would abolish the monarchy, and move into the palace, which I would make my private home.

If I were Chairman of the company I work for ...

_____

_____

_____

22 Conditionals: **if you had gone …**

A Form

Read the following information about a past action and its result:

I went for a job interview. The interview was a success and they gave me the job.

This is what actually happened. But we can imagine a different past action and a different result:

IF + HAD (NOT) DONE   WOULD (NOT) + HAVE DONE
*If the interview **had not been** a success, they **would not have given** me the job.*

This is the 3rd conditional. In speech, these forms are often abbreviated:

A '*What **would've** happened if the interview **hadn't gone** well?*'
B *If the interview **hadn't gone** well, they **wouldn't have given** me the job.*'

The **if**-clause can come in the first part of the sentence or the second:

'*If the interview **hadn't gone** well, they **wouldn't have given** me the job.*'
'*They **wouldn't have given** me the job if the interview **hadn't gone** well.*'

B Positives and negatives

When we use the 3rd conditional we are imagining the opposite situation. If what actually happened was negative, we use a positive form. If what actually happened was positive, we use a negative form:

WHAT HAPPENED: *We didn't put up our prices (–), so we kept our market share. (+)*
3RD CONDITIONAL: *If we **had put up** our prices (+), we **would not have kept** our market share. (–)*

COMMON MISTAKES: We do not use **would** in the if clause.
WRONG: *If I ~~would have known~~ you were at the office I would have called in.*
RIGHT: *If I **had known** you were at the office I **would have called** in.*

C Variations

We can use **could** or **might** instead of **would**:

*If we had followed his advice, we **could** have lost a great deal of money.*
*If we had offered large quantity discounts, we **might** have won the order.*

D Mixed conditionals

The examples in **C** are about two actions in the past. However, if we talk about a past action and its result in the present we use **if** + past perfect and **would not** + infinitive:

PAST ACTION: *He did well on the training course.*
PRESENT RESULT: *He is head of department now.*
MIXED CONDITIONAL: *If he **hadn't done** well on the training course, he **wouldn't be** head of department now.* (NOT: *wouldn't have been*)

Exercise 1
Form

Put the verbs into the correct form. Choose either the past perfect (**had done**) or **would** + perfect infinitive (**would have done**).

1 If we *had known* (know) that the company was in financial difficulty, we would not have done business with them.
2 We would have won that contract if we _____ (make) a better offer.
3 They _____ (go) out of business years ago if they hadn't invested in new technology.
4 Would sales have been higher if the price _____ (be) lower?
5 If we _____ (wait) a few more months, we would have saved a great deal of money on the new computers.
6 The company _____ (move) earlier if it had found suitable premises.
7 _____ you _____ (accept) the new job if they had offered it to you?
8 If the flight had been delayed, I _____ (stay) at the airport hotel.

Exercise 2
Positives and negatives

Complete the sentences using the graph and the extract from a sales report.

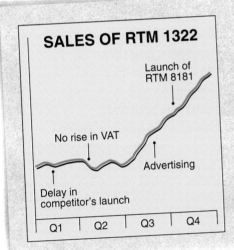

SALES OF RTM 1322

Launch of RTM 8181

No rise in VAT

Advertising

Delay in competitor's launch

Q1 | Q2 | Q3 | Q4

Sales of RTM fax machines

We were fortunate that sales of the old RTM 1322 fax held up well in the first half of the year. This was because the launch of our main competitor's new model was delayed due to technical problems. In the second quarter, we expected a rise in VAT and a drop in demand, but this did not happen and sales remained stable. We wanted to stimulate demand either by cutting prices or by launching an advertising campaign. We decided to advertise, and this led to an increase in sales, so we did not need to cut our prices. In the last quarter, sales went up again because of the launch of the improved model, the RTM 8181. This received very some favourable reviews. However, we did not win the 'Best Fax' award from Office News, and we narrowly failed to reach our target of 30% market share.

1 If our competitor *had brought out* (bring out) their new model in the first quarter, our sales *would not have held up* (not/hold up).
2 If they _____ (not/have) technical problems, their new model _____ (come out) sooner.
3 If there _____ (be) an increase in VAT, demand _____ (drop).
4 If we _____ (not/launch) an advertising campaign, our sales _____ (not/rise).
5 If the campaign _____ (not/be) successful, we _____ (cut) prices.
6 If we _____ (not/bring out) the new RTM 8181, our market share _____ (not/go up).
7 If we _____ (win) the Best Fax award, we _____ (reach) our target of 30% of the market.

22 Practice

Exercise 3
Common mistakes

Read through the sentences. Put a tick (✔) next to the ones that are right, and correct the ones that are wrong.

1 If I would have had the chance to study another foreign language, I would have learned Russian. _If I had had ..._

2 We would have moved to a bigger hall if there had been any more people for the presentation. _____

3 The company had made bigger profits if they had been able to cut down on salaries. _____

4 If they had dealt with the complaint more quickly, they didn't receive so much bad publicity. _____

5 If there wouldn't have been so many mistakes in the advertisement, we wouldn't have had to redo it. _____

Exercise 4
Might have, could have

Match the first part of the sentences in column A with the right ending in column B.

A		B	
1	_If we had had the right figures,_	A	he might have gone into insurance.
2	Could you have worked in Paris	B	they could have prevented the strike.
3	We might have lost a great deal of money	C	_we could have avoided a costly error._
4	If they hadn't won that order,	D	if you had wanted to?
5	If he hadn't gone into banking,	E	if she had been more prepared.
6	If you had left earlier,	F	they might have had to close the factory.
7	Her presentation could have been better	G	if we hadn't taken our lawyer's advice.
8	If they had offered a 15% pay rise,	H	you might have got there on time.

Exercise 5
Mixed conditionals

Rewrite the sentences using mixed conditionals.

1 We didn't order the parts at the end of June. They aren't here now.
If we had ordered the parts at the end of June, they would be here now.

2 We felt we could trust each other. Now we are partners.

_____

3 He lost his driving licence. Now he has to take taxis everywhere.

_____

4 You didn't go on the course. You don't know how to operate the new equipment.

_____

5 I went to school in France. Now I am bilingual.

_____

Task 1

Think back to the last time you went abroad on business. Write down what you would have done if the following things had happened.

What would you have done if ...

1   ... you had lost your passport while you were abroad?
If I had lost my passport the last time I was abroad, I would have gone to the embassy to get a replacement.

2   ... someone had stolen your credit cards and money?

_____

3   ... you had needed to contact the office urgently?

_____

4   ... you had fallen seriously ill?

_____

5   ... you had missed your return flight?

_____

Task 2

Read the passage about the Sinclair C5. Say what the company **should** or **shouldn't have done**, and explain why.

In 1985, the inventor Sir Clive Sinclair launched the C5. It was a three-wheeled electric car, but although it was a revolutionary vehicle, it was a commercial disaster. The company did very little research, but believed the product would be successful. The C5 did not have a very powerful engine, so it was not very fast. As a result, it did not appeal to adults. However, the C5 was not suitable for children either as it was so expensive, and it did not appear to be safe to use on the roads because it was so small. The result was that the C5 quickly became a national joke, and the company had to stop production almost immediately, after losing millions of pounds.

1   (market research) *First of all, the company should have done some more market research. If it had looked into potential demand, it would have realized that there was no demand for the product.*

2   (engine size)

_____

_____

3   (expense)

_____

_____

4   (size)

_____

_____

23 Modal verbs (1): suggestions, advice, and criticism – **shall, should, ought to**

A Making suggestions

We can use **shall** + infinitive to offer help and to make suggestions:

OFFERING HELP

A   I don't think I'm going to be able to get through all these letters.
B   **Shall** I give you a hand?

MAKING SUGGESTIONS

A   I need to have a word with you about the new project.
B   OK. **Shall** we meet this afternoon at 1.30?

Note that we can only use **Shall I ... ?** and **Shall we ... ?** in this way. We cannot say **Shall he ... ?**, **Shall you ... ?**, etc.

B Other ways of making suggestions

There are a number of other phrases we use in informal English for making suggestions:

A   *Where **shall we** go for lunch?*

B

Why don't we	go	
Let's		to that new Thai restaurant(?)
How about	going	
What about		

In more formal English we can use the verbs **suggest** and **advise**:
*I **suggest** that you read the contract through carefully.*
*I **advise** you to read the contract through carefully.*

C Advice and obligation

We can use **should** and **ought to** + infinitive (e.g., **do**), to give advice or to express obligation relating to the present or the future (see also **must** and **have to**, Unit 25):

*You **should** keep an account of all your expenses.* (This refers to the present.)
*When you go the conference next week, you **ought to** give Mr Franks a ring.* (This refers to the future.)

The passive is formed with **be** + past participle:
*Form BD222 **should be returned** to this office within 30 days.*

D Criticizing

We can make criticisms about past actions by using **should** and **ought to** with **have** + past participle (perfect infinitive):

*It was a mistake to get rid of those shares. You **shouldn't have sold** them.*
*It's too late to apply for shares now. You **ought to have applied** last week.*

The passive is formed with **have been** + past participle:
*This information **should have been given** to the tax authorities two years ago.*

Exercise 1
Making suggestions

Match the comments in column A with the comments in column B.

	A		B
1	*I'm afraid I'm tied up all this week.*	A	OK, I've got them here. Shall I fax them to you?
2	Can you turn the heating down?	B	That's OK. Shall I pick you up from the airport?
3	Is the next interviewee here yet?	C	That's OK. Shall I ring back this afternoon?
4	Is that the new screen I ordered?	D	Yes. Where shall I put it?
5	I'm sorry, but I'm in a meeting at the moment.	E	I'm not sure yet. Shall we send you a quote in a few days?
6	How much is this going to cost?	F	No, but shall I open the window for you?
7	I don't know London very well.	G	*That's OK. Shall we arrange a meeting for next week?*
8	I need to see the plans. Today, if possible.	H	Yes, she is. Shall I send her in?

Exercise 2
Other ways of making suggestions

Rewrite these suggestions. Use the word in capitals.

1   Shall we have lunch at Le Manoir? (WHY)
    Why don't we have lunch at Le Manoir?

2   I advise you to prepare for the interview carefully. (SUGGEST)
    _____

3   Why don't we wait until the next financial year? (HOW)
    _____

4   Let's organize a leaving party for Mr Simpson. (WHAT)
    _____

5   I suggest that you think about it and let me know your decision. (WHY)
    _____

6   How about sharing a taxi to the station? (LET'S)
    _____

7   I think you should check her references before offering her the job. (ADVISE)
    _____

8   Let's see if we can subcontract this work. (WHY)
    _____

Fill in the blanks with the verbs from the box in the active or passive.

ought/accompany	ought/not/bring	should/deposit
should/not/leave	should/meet	should/report

TO ALL STAFF: SECURITY

Following a number of recent thefts from the office, please remember the following points:

VISITORS

Visitors (1)_should be met_ at Reception by a member of staff. They (2)_____ at all times. You (3)_____ anyone who is acting suspiciously to a member of the security staff at reception.

VALUABLES

If possible, you (4)_____ large amounts of personal cash, or valuable items such as jewellery to the office. Handbags and wallets (5)_____ unattended. Any large amounts of cash or traveller's cheques (6)_____ in the safe.

Read the passage. Then use the prompts to make sentences about the Hoover campaign using **should(n't)** + **have done** (active or passive).

In 1991, Hoover launched a promotional campaign. It offered customers two free air tickets to the United States (worth about £400) if they bought any Hoover appliance worth over £100. There were not enough special conditions, and the total number of tickets was not limited. The company did very little research and it relied on outdated figures that showed that very few people ever took up 'special offers'. Potential customers were not targeted clearly enough, and the company made the offer much too attractive. The campaign was a sensational success. Thousands of people took up the offer and paid £100 to get their free air tickets. The company sold enormous numbers of appliances, but after paying for many thousands of air tickets, it ended up with a loss of about £48 million.

1   shouldn't/offer/valuable/air tickets
    It shouldn't have offered such valuable air tickets.

2   ought to/be/more special conditions

    _____

3   total number/tickets/should/limit

    _____

4   more research/ought to/do

    _____

5   should not/rely on/outdated figures

    _____

....

Task 1
Make suggestions referring to your own company. Use the expressions in the box.

I think we should ...	I don't think we should ...
We ought to ...	Why don't we ...
How about ...	Let's ...

1 Suggest a way of improving morale among the workforce.
   I think we should increase overtime rates.

2 Suggest a way of making working hours better for secretarial staff.
   _____

3 Suggest a way of reducing staff turnover.
   _____

4 Suggest a way of cutting costs.
   _____

5 Suggest a way of improving productivity in your company.
   _____

6 Suggest a way of increasing demand for your product or service.
   _____

7 Suggest a way of increasing incentives for managers.
   _____

....

Task 2
Read through the sentences about things that have gone wrong. Then explain why they happened using **should/shouldn't have done**.

1 The architect was nearly killed at the building site last week.
   The builder shouldn't have thrown his bag of tools down from the roof.

2 Helena lost all her savings when the company she had invested all her money in went bankrupt.
   _____

3 Our main competitor's last product was a total failure.
   _____

4 Peter has just lost an entire morning's work on his computer.
   _____

5 The government lost the election.
   _____

6 Their profits were down sharply last year.
   _____

24 Modal verbs (2): ability, possibility, and permission – **can**, **could**, **may**

We use **can** to talk about both ability and possibility, and it refers to the present or the future. It is followed by the bare infinitive (active or passive):

*I **can speak** fluent German.* (ABILITY)
*Your order **can be delivered** next Thursday.* (POSSIBILITY)

Can has no infinitive or present perfect form – we use **be able to**:

*I'd like to **be able to** help you, but I do not have the authority.* (NOT: *to can ...*)
*I **haven't been able to** finish the work.* (NOT: *haven't could ...*)

To refer to the future, we use **will be able to**:

*Soon people **will be able to** see videos by using ordinary telephone lines.*

B Past ability

The past tense of **can** is **could**. When we are talking about a general ability in the past or a verb of the senses (**see**, **hear**, **feel**, etc.) we use **could** + bare infinitive. However, when we are talking about one specific action, we normally use **was able to** or **managed to**:

*After a few months on the training course, I **could** speak Japanese quite well.*
*From my hotel room I **could** see the sea.*
*Janet phoned the airline and **managed to** get me on the flight.*

However, if the sentence is negative, it is possible to use **couldn't** to talk about either a general ability or a specific action:

*Even after two months, I **couldn't** speak Japanese at all.*
*Unfortunately I **couldn't** see the sea from the room.*
*Janet phoned the airline, but she **couldn't** get me on the flight.*

C Past possibility

We use **could** + **have done**/**could** + **have been done** to talk about something in the past which was possible, but which did not happen:

*It was foolish to leave so much money in your office. Someone **could have stolen** it.*
*There was a fire at the warehouse last night. We **could have lost** all our stock.*

D Requesting action and asking for permission

We use **can**, **could**, and **will**/**would** to ask people to do things. We use **can**, **could**, and **may** to ask for permission. **Can** and **will** are a little more direct than **could** or **would**:

***Can**/**Could** you give me hand with this machine?*
***Will**/**Would** you take this file to Peter?*
***Can**/**Could**/**May** I use your phone?*

Exercise 1
Abilities

Using your dictionary if necessary, match the adjectives from job advertisements (1–8) with the definitions (a–h).

	1	*flexible*	a	you can find practical solutions.
	2	bilingual	b	you can make firm decisions.
	3	logical	c	you can make others see your viewpoint.
If you are	4	computer literate	d	*you can adapt to changing circumstances.*
	5	pragmatic	e	you can deal with figures.
	6	persuasive	f	you can speak two languages.
	7	numerate	g	you can deal with IT problems.
	8	decisive	h	you can think clearly.

Exercise 2
Can and **be able to**

Two colleagues are rearranging a meeting. Complete the conversation with **can**, **can't**, **be able to**, or **been able to**.

HELEN: Jane, I'm afraid that I won't [1] <u>be able to</u> see you on Friday. I've got to see some clients and they [2] _____ make it any other time.

JANE: Don't worry, we [3] _____ easily meet next week. How would Tuesday morning suit you?

HELEN: That's fine. I [4] _____ come and pick you up at the station.

JANE: That's very kind of you, but my car will be back from the garage, so I will [5] _____ drive up.

HELEN: I'm sorry about the delay.

JANE: That's fine, really. I haven't [6] _____ do much work on the proposal, and now I've got an extra weekend, I'll [7] _____ look at it in more detail.

Exercise 3
Past ability

Complete the sentences using either **could** or **managed to**. (It is possible to use **was/were able to** in all these sentences.)

1 We had a very successful meeting, and we <u>managed to</u> make the publishers agree to giving us a 56% discount.

2 The walls in the hotel were very thin, and I _____ hear people talking in the next room.

3 Although the meeting finished early, we _____ cover the main points.

4 The machine was no longer in production, but at last we _____ find a spare part from a supplier in Scotland.

5 She was brought up in Paris, so by the time she was five she _____ speak French perfectly.

6 He was a brilliant salesman and _____ sell anything to anyone.

7 Although I was at the back of the hall, I _____ hear very clearly.

8 It was very difficult to find a suitable office, but in the end we _____ rent one near the Central Station.

Match the first part of the sentences in column A with the right endings in column B.

A

1 *Peter could have got a job in the overseas division,*

2 He was lucky that he was only slightly injured in the accident, because

3 We could have met our sales targets

4 I didn't think the presentation was very good, and that

5 The unions could have gone on strike

6 He could have stayed at the Hilton

7 The results last year were very bad

8 He could have been sent to prison for drinking and driving, so

9 He was lucky he sold his shares when he did, because

10 We could have done a great deal of business in Iraq

B

A he could have explained things more clearly.

B he was lucky they only fined him £500.

C he could have lost a great deal of money.

D but they decided to accept the 2.5% pay offer.

E but unfortunately one of our main customers cancelled a major order.

F but the political situation stopped us from opening an office there.

G *but he didn't want to live abroad.*

H but he decided to get a room at the Holiday Inn instead.

I he could have been killed.

J but they could have been worse.

In each of the following pairs of sentences, put a tick (✔) next to the one that is more polite.

1 A Give me a beer.
   B Could I have a beer? ✔

2 A Caller, I'm afraid the line's busy. Will you hold?
   B Caller, I'm afraid the line's busy. Hold, please.

3 A What do you want?
   B What can I do for you?

4 A What's your name?
   B May I ask who is calling?

5 A Could I borrow your pen?
   B Let me have your pen.

6 A I'm sorry, Mr Browning's busy. Can you come back later?
   B I'm sorry, Mr Browning's rather busy. Could you come back later?

7 A What did you say?
   B Could you repeat that?

8 A May I see some identification?
   B Who are you?

Complete the sentences using **can**, **can't**, or a form of (**not**) **be able to**.

1 If we send the parcel by second class post, it'll take a week. But if you like, ... _we can send it first class._

2 I've been trying to find a solution to the problem all week, but so far ...

_____

3 She could easily get a job as an interpreter because ...

_____

4 If business goes well this year, we will ...

_____

5 If you have a credit card, ...

_____

Complete the following sentences using **could** + perfect infinitive (**could have done**).

1 In the end I decided to turn down their offer of a job, but ...

_____

2 The machine had an electrical fault and was dangerous. You're lucky you didn't touch it, because ...

_____

3 She left the company a month before the top job became vacant. That was unfortunate for her, because ...

_____

4 It's a pity we placed such a large order just before they cut their prices. We ...

_____

You are on a long distance flight to New York. Write down what you would say in the following situations.

1 You are thirsty.

_____

2 The passenger next to you has a copy of 'Newsweek'. You would like to read it.

_____

3 You want to go to the toilet, but the passenger next to you is in the way.

_____

4 It's lunch-time. You are a vegetarian.

_____

25 Modal verbs (3): obligation and necessity – **must**, **have to**, **needn't**, **can't**, etc.

A Form

A number of different modal verbs can be used to express obligation. Look at the list below. All of the these are followed by the bare infinitive:

OBLIGATION	NO OBLIGATION	PROHIBITION
must	needn't	mustn't
have to	don't have to	can't
have got to	haven't got to	(be) not allowed to

B Expressing obligation, etc.

We use **must**, **have to**, and **have got to** to say that something is obligatory:

*Applicants **must** include the names of two referees.*
*I won't come to lunch today – I **have to/have got to** finish this report by 4.00.*

We use **needn't**, **don't have to**, and **haven't got to** if something isn't necessary:

*You **needn't** stay late – we have cancelled the meeting.*
*We **don't have to/haven't got to** pay our bill until the 30th.*

We use **mustn't**, **can't**, and **not allowed to** to say that something is forbidden:

*Passengers in the airport **mustn't** leave their luggage unattended at any time.*
*I'm sorry, but we **can't/aren't allowed to** give you your bank balance by phone.*

C Talking about obligations and telling people what to do

Have (got) to, **don't have to**, **can't**, and **(be) not allowed to** are more common when the speaker is talking about obligations and prohibitions. **Must**, **needn't**, and **mustn't** are more common when the speaker is giving an order or telling someone what to do:

A   *'I've got to be in London by 3.30.'*
B   *Then you **must** leave immediately, because the traffic is terrible.'*

Must, **need not**, and **must not** are also more common in written language.

D Past obligation

When talking about the past, we use **had to**, **didn't have to**, and **couldn't/wasn't allowed to**:

*In my last job, I **had to** be at the office by 8.00 a.m. We **didn't have to** work very hard, but we **couldn't** leave the office without asking for permission.*

E Didn't need to vs needn't have

There is a difference in meaning between **didn't need to** do something (it wasn't necessary, so you didn't do it), and **needn't have done** something (you did it, but it wasn't necessary).

*Because he was Spanish, he **didn't need to** get a visa to visit Britain.*
*We **needn't have** hurried to Heathrow as the plane was late.*

Exercise 1
Obligation, no obligation, and permission

Choose the correct word or phrase in italics to complete each sentence.

1 You *must*/*needn't* save a file before you turn the computer off, or you will lose it.
2 I'm afraid this is a non-smoking office, so you *haven't got to*/*can't* smoke in here.
3 Employees are reminded that they *mustn't*/*needn't* use the office phone to make personal calls.
4 You *needn't*/*mustn't* send that reminder to Eastwood's – they paid the invoice this morning.
5 In countries like Iran, you *don't have to*/*can't* buy or sell alcohol.
6 This income tax form *must*/*needn't* be completed and returned to the Inland Revenue within 30 days.
7 You *mustn't*/*don't have to* come to the meeting if you have more important things to do.
8 This information is highly confidential, so you *mustn't*/*needn't* discuss it with anyone.
9 As you are from the European Union, you *mustn't*/*don't have to* have a visa to go to France.
10 Drivers wishing to hire a car *must*/*aren't allowed to* be over 21 and have a full driving licence.

Exercise 2
Talking about obligations

Look at the chart and make sentences about the groups of people using **have to**, **don't have to**, or **are not allowed to/can't**.

	OBLIGATION	NO OBLIGATION	PROHIBITION
airline pilots union members university teachers army officers police officers	have good eyesight pay a subscription be graduates go to training college be over 1.75m tall	work office hours be qualified teachers carry guns (UK)	drink before flying work during a strike go on strike

1 A *Airline pilots have to have excellent eyesight.*
   B *They don't have to work office hours.*

2 A Union members _____
   B _____

3 A University teachers _____
   B _____

4 A Army officers _____
   B _____

5 A Police officers _____
   B _____

25 Practice

Telling people what to do

Write sentences using the prompts with **must**, **needn't**, or **mustn't**.

1 James needs these documents urgently. (fax them to him immediately)
   You must fax them to him immediately.

2 Good, we all seem to agree. (discuss the matter any further)
   _____

3 We've still got plenty of stock. (order any more yet)
   _____

4 Our health care products are selling really well. (make sure we keep our market share)
   _____

5 I hear you're coming over to England next month. (give me a ring)
   _____

6 I've got a very important meeting this afternoon. (be late).
   _____

Exercise 4
Past obligation

Read through this story of one businessman's travel experiences. Fill in the blanks with **had to**, **didn't have to**, or **couldn't**.

This happened several years ago when the former Soviet Union was still a communist state. I was working in Malaysia, and I (1) _had to_ get back to London for an urgent meeting. I (2) _____ take an Aeroflot flight because all the others were full, and we flew to Moscow. Unfortunately we missed the connecting flight, so we (3) _____ stay in the airport hotel and wait. I wanted to make a phone call but they said that it was 'not possible in Moscow'. I suggested sending a fax, but that was 'not possible in Moscow'. I wanted to transfer to a British Airways flight, but I (4) _____ do that either, because it was 'not possible in Moscow'. There were armed guards at the hotel doors, and we (5) _____ go outside or visit the city because we didn't have visas. On the other hand they were quite generous – we (6) _____ pay for the rooms and we (7) _____ pay anything for food either. So we just (8) _____ wait, and every morning there was a fight for tickets at the reception desk. In the end, after about five days, I managed to get a ticket and got back to London, but of course I had missed the meeting and I (9) _____ fly straight back to Malaysia – but not with Aeroflot!

Exercise 5
Didn't need to vs **needn't have**

Fill in the blanks with **didn't need to** or **needn't have**.

1 We were worried we might have to cut the workforce, but we got some large orders, so we _____ make anyone redundant.

2 We sent the manager of our Istanbul branch some important documents by air courier, but we _____ spent so much money because he was away on holiday at the time.

3 An interpreter came with us to a meeting with some Japanese clients, but we _____ hired her because they all spoke excellent English.

4 The negotiation in Hamburg went very well, so we _____ spend the whole week there and we came back a day early.

Task 1

Write down what the following people might say in these situations using **must**, **needn't**, or **mustn't**.

1   A supervisor in a supermarket hears a check-out operator being rude to a customer.
    'You mustn't talk to customers like that.'

2   A clerk in a store is explaining to a customer that refunds cannot be given without a receipt.

    _____

3   A pension salesman is explaining that there is no obligation to pay contributions every month.

    _____

4   You have just heard a colleague give a terrible presentation. Give him some advice.

    _____

5   You notice that a colleague uses the 'save' facility on his computer every ten minutes. You know that the computer has an 'auto-save' facility.

    _____

6   You overhear a temporary secretary discussing travel insurance with a travel agent. Your company has a policy that covers all the employees.

    _____

Task 2

Make notes in the columns about your current job. Then write a short paragraph about yourself using **have to**, **don't have to**, and **can't**. Here is an example:

OBLIGATION	NO OBLIGATION	PROHIBITION
discuss loans with clients	*financial analysis*	*no loans over $500,000*

I work as a lending officer for a London bank, and I have to discuss loans with clients and decide whether or not to authorize them. I don't have to do the financial analysis of the companies in question because we have a specialized team of analysts for that job. I can authorize loans of up to $500,000, but I can't authorize anything greater than that myself.

OBLIGATION	NO OBLIGATION	PROHIBITION
_____	_____	_____

_____
_____
_____
_____
_____

26 Modal verbs (4): speculation – **may**, **might**, **could**, **must**, **can't**

A Speculating about the future

We can use **may**, **might**, and **could**, followed by the bare infinitive (active or passive) to speculate about the future:

*In the next few months, the price of oil **may** rise.* (Perhaps it will rise.)
*I **might** be promoted at the end of the year.* (Perhaps I will be promoted.)
*The lawyers think it **could** take quite a long time to draw up the contract.*
(Perhaps it will take a long time; the lawyers are not sure.)

There is no significant difference in meaning between **may**, **might**, and **could** in this context.

(See Unit 15 for other ways of speculating about the future.)

B Speculating about the present

We use **must**, **may**, **might**, and **can't** to speculate about the present:

*There's no answer from David's extension. He **must** be out.* (I am sure he's out.)
*There's a lot of noise from room 420. They **must** be having a party.* (I am sure they're having a party.)
*Jane **may/might** know the address of the company because she did some work for them a few years ago.* (Perhaps she knows.)
*I can't get through to our office in Milan. They **may/might** be having problems with their fax machine.* (Perhaps they are having probems.)
*There's a charge of £85,000.00 for envelopes on this invoice! It **can't** be right!* (I am sure it isn't right.)
*Jane **can't** be looking for a new job already. She only started work a week ago.* (I am sure she isn't looking.)

C Speculating about the past

We use **may/might**, **must**, **can't/couldn't** followed by **have done**, **have been done**, or **have been doing** to speculate about the past:

*He bought the shares when they were cheap and sold them at their peak, so he **must have made** a lot of money.* (I am sure he did.)
*I am not sure why Mr Janssen wasn't at the meeting. He **might have been delayed** at the airport.* (Perhaps he was delayed.)
*You **can't/couldn't have seen** Mr Knowles at the sales conference, because he was in Mexico at the time.* (I am sure you didn't see him.)
*He arrived here this morning. He **must have been waiting** for hours.* (I am sure he has been waiting for hours.)

Exercise 1

Speculating about the future

Match the first part of the sentences (1–10) with an appropriate ending (A–J).

A	B
1 *I'll send you the letter now, so*	A they could go wrong at any time.
2 There are no vacancies at the moment, but	B there could be a strike soon.
3 The machines are getting very old, and	C *you might get it tomorrow morning.*
4 The Director is under a lot of pressure from the board, so	D she may want to discuss it with you.
5 The new range of sun creams looks very exciting, and we think	E there could be some in a few months.
6 I've shown your advert to the Marketing Manager, and	F I could be sent to the Argentina office next year.
7 The power generators are stockpiling supplies of coal because	G he may sell the company.
8 He's thinking of retiring from the family business, and	H they may sign it this afternoon.
9 We're expanding in Latin America, so	I it may capture about 15% of the market.
10 They're reading the contract now, and	J he might have to resign.

Exercise 2

Speculating about the present (problem solving)

In the Despatch Department of a mail order firm selling office supplies there are three packages, but the address labels are not complete. The packages are for three different customers, Mr Green, Mr Brown, and Mr Grey. The packages contain paper, a personal photocopier, and a computer. The packages weigh 18kg, 20kg, and 22kg.

PACKAGE:	A	B	C
NAME:	Mr Green		
CONTENTS:		computer	paper
WEIGHT:			18kg

A Complete the sentences using **must**, **might**, or **can't**.

1 Package B _____ be for Mr Brown or it _____ be for Mr Grey.
   Package C _____ be for Mr Green, because we know A is for him.

2 Package A _____ contain the photocopier, because the computer is in B and the paper is in C.

3 Package B _____ be heavier than C, but it _____ not be as heavy as A.

B Fill in the missing details on the labels using the following piece of information.

Mr Green's package is not as heavy as Mr Brown's.

Exercise 3
Speculating about the past

Write sentences using **might**, **can't**, **must**, and a suitable infinitive (e.g., **have done, have been done, have been doing**).

1   They say they definitely sent the shipment, but it never arrived.
    (They/must/send it/wrong address)
    They must have sent it to the wrong address.

2   You receive a memo saying that a company's phone number has changed. (They/must/move/new premises)
    _____.

3   You have come for a 10 o'clock meeting. It is now 10.15 and no-one else is there. (The meeting/must/be cancelled)
    _____.

4   It is 12.20. You ring a colleague but there is no reply. (He/might/go to lunch)
    _____.

5   She was engaged when I rang her but I don't know who she was talking to. (She/might/be phoning/Sales Department)
    _____.

6   The equipment was repaired last week, but it has gone wrong again. (It/can't/repair/properly)
    _____.

Exercise 4
Review

Rewrite each of the following sentences using **might**, **can't**, **must**, and a suitable infinitive.

1   It's possible that they will give us the discount that we want.
    They ... *might give us the discount we want.*

2   Judging by the phone bill, I am sure she has been making long international calls.
    Judging by the phone bill, she ... _____

3   The factory is on a 3-day week. I'm sure they aren't selling many cars.
    The factory is on a 3-day week. They ... _____

4   It was a very bad deal. I am sure they lost a lot of money.
    It was a very bad deal. They ... _____

5   There's a chance she will be promoted at the end of the year.
    She ... _____

6   She seemed surprised to see me, so I am sure she wasn't expecting me.
    She seemed surprised to see me. She ... _____

7   He went home at 4.30, so I am sure he hasn't heard the announcement.
    He went home at 4.30, so he ... _____

....

Task 1

Speculate about possible future events based on the following information.
Use **may**, **might**, or **could**.

1 The political situation in the Middle East is very unstable.
The price of oil might rise.

2 The Christian Democrats are doing very well in the opinion polls.

_____

3 The new Hoover 237 dishwasher has had excellent reviews.

_____

4 The government is spending much more than it is earning in taxes.

_____

5 There have been a number of delays in the project.

_____

....

Task 2

Speculate about these situations. Use **might**, **must**, **can't**, and a bare
infinitive or **be doing**.

1 I've phoned Jane three times this morning but there is no reply.
She must be out seeing a client.

2 Everyone in R&D is working very long hours at the moment.

_____

3 I've got a new Rolex watch. I bought it in Thailand for £5.

_____

4 Peter wasn't feeling well yesterday and he's not in the office today.

_____

5 I haven't got Henry's phone number, but I know that Ann has it.

_____

....

Task 3

Look at the graph. Use your own ideas to make comments on curves A and
B using **might**, **must**, or **can't** + **have done/have been doing**.

FIZZO SOFT DRINKS
Performance for
3rd and 4th quarters

Sales

A
B   Profits

J   A   S   O   N   D

Curve A

1 *They can't have sold much Fizzo in July.*

2 _____

3 _____

Curve B

1 *They must have made a loss in October.*

2 _____

3 _____

27 -ing and infinitive (1): verbs + -ing form or infinitive

Some verbs are followed by **to** + infinitive (e.g., I **want to finish** this report). Others are followed by the **-ing** form (I **enjoy going** abroad).

A Verbs followed by the **-ing** form

The following verbs are usually followed by the **-ing** form:

avoid	consider	delay	deny
dislike	enjoy	finish	can't help
involve	justify	like (=enjoy)	look forward to*
mind	miss	postpone	practise
risk	suggest	can't stand	carry on
put off			

*We **delayed launching** the product because of technical problems.*
*I **look forward to meeting** you again next week.*

* In the expression **look forward to**, the word **to** is a preposition. Prepositions (e.g., **in**, **on**, **at**, **with**, **from**, etc.) are always followed by the **-ing** form rather than the infinitive. (For more details see Unit 29.)

B Expressions + **-ing**

The expressions below are followed by the **-ing** form:

It's a waste of time/money ...	**It's no use ...**
There's no point (in) ...	**It's (not) worth ...**

*It's **not worth repairing** the machine. It would be cheaper to buy a new one.*

C Verbs followed by **to** + infinitive

The following verbs are usually followed by **to** + infinitive (e.g., **to do**):

afford	agree	arrange	attempt	claim
decide	demand	deserve	expect	fail
guarantee	hesitate	hope	learn	manage
neglect	offer	plan	prepare	pretend
promise	refuse	seem	tend	threaten
train	want	would like		

*I have **arranged to meet** the visitors at the factory.*

D Passive forms

There are passive forms of the **-ing** form and the infinitive. The passive of the **-ing** form is made with **being** + past participle (e.g., **being done**):

*Everyone **likes being congratulated** when they have worked hard.*

The passive infinitive is formed by **to be** + past participle (e.g., **to be done**):

*She **expects to be promoted** soon.*

Exercise 1
Verbs + **-ing** form

Complete the sentences using the verbs from the box in the **-ing** form.

apply	buy	film	lose	meet	negotiate	speak	wait

1 We won't know the final cost of the TV programme until the production company finishes _filming_.
2 Rupert Murdoch of News International risked _____ millions of pounds when he launched his satellite company Sky TV.
3 If you do a business course in England you will be able to practise _____ every day.
4 I have had to put off _____ the designers because I am too busy this week.
5 As a buyer for a large chain store, part of my job involves _____ competitive prices with suppliers.
6 I'm afraid the manager is busy at the moment. Would you mind _____ a few minutes?
7 There's no point _____ for the shares now – the offer closed last week.
8 It's a waste of money _____ a Pentium PC if you only want a computer for word processing.

Exercise 2
Verbs + infinitive

Complete the newspaper articles, using the verbs in the boxes in the infinitive form.

A

do	discover	give	prefer

Infotech – One man and his data log

Scientists in a field in Devon are hoping (1) _to discover_ a little more about the eating habits of sheep when a new research project gets under way next week. They are planning (2) _____ the sheep miniature computers which will monitor their eating habits. Farmers have known for a long time that sheep seem (3) _____ some types of grass to others, but so far no-one has tried (4) _____ any experiments.

B

earn	hire	last	pay

When a C++ can mean good money

Things are looking good for software engineers, according to Tony Coombes of the recruitment consultancy Systems Resources. 'There are a lot of big companies who want (1) _to hire_ engineers for short-term contracts, and most of them will agree (2) _____ good money. Someone with two years' experience, and who has been trained in C++ and Visual Basic, could expect (3) _____ about £1000 a week.' Most of the contract work tends (4) _____ for about six months, but some permanent jobs are becoming available.

Exercise 3
Review: **-ing** form or infinitives?

Complete the following letter. Put the verbs in brackets into either the **-ing** form or the infinitive with **to**.

Dear Mr Williams

Thank you for your letter of 12 June in which you stated that, following the visit of your chief buyer Mr Lindfield, you are considering ⁽¹⁾ <u>placing</u> (place) an order for our Riesling 92 table wine.

We can arrange ⁽²⁾ _____ (supply) you with an initial order of 1,000 cases, and I enclose our current price list, which I believe you will find very competitive. If you decide ⁽³⁾ _____ (go) ahead with the order, we will agree ⁽⁴⁾ _____ (give) you the 14% quantity discount you mentioned, and details are enclosed. Please note that we guarantee ⁽⁵⁾ _____ (deliver) firm orders within four weeks.

You mentioned also that you wanted ⁽⁶⁾ _____ (market) the wine under your own brand name, which will involve ⁽⁷⁾ _____ (change) the labels. I would suggest ⁽⁸⁾ _____ (get) the labels printed here, because it is probably not worth ⁽⁹⁾ _____ (print) them in the UK and ⁽¹⁰⁾ _____ (send) them here. I have contacted our personal printer for a quotation and I hope ⁽¹¹⁾ _____ (be) able to send you a price soon.

Please do not hesitate ⁽¹²⁾ _____ (contact) me if you have any further queries. I look forward to ⁽¹³⁾ _____ (hear) from you soon.

Yours sincerely,

P. Moewe

Piet Moewe
Managing Director

Exercise 4
Passives

Fill in the blanks with the verb in brackets, using the passive **-ing** form or the passive infinitive.

1 Our profits are up this year, so I expect *to be given* (give) a pay rise.
2 You'd better come back later. Mr Schmidt dislikes *being interrupted* (interrupt) when he's in a meeting.
3 You deserve _____ (pay) more because you do a lot of overtime.
4 When I am giving a presentation, I don't mind _____ (ask) questions.
5 Most of our sales team in Spain tend _____ (recruit) locally.
6 The company avoided _____ (take over) by splitting up into several different groups.
7 She hopes _____ (send) to our Paris office when it opens next year.
8 He took the telephone off the hook because he didn't want _____ (disturb).

Task 1

As part of their work, people often have to do the following things:

travel to work in the rush hour	take work home	attend meetings
deal with difficult customers	stay late	travel abroad
speak English on the phone	ask for more money	take clients out

A Choose four of these things and say how much you like them using the verbs in the box.

really enjoy   like   don't mind   dislike   can't stand

1 *I don't mind staying late.*
2 _____
3 _____
4 _____

B Now say what other things you like and dislike doing at work.
1 _____
2 _____
3 _____
4 _____

Task 2

Continue the sentences using the words in brackets with a verb in the infinitive.

1 We were very unhappy with the service they had provided. (refuse)
  We refused to pay them.

2 The company is taking on a lot of new staff. (plan)
  _____

3 He was angry about the way the company had treated him. (threaten)
  _____

4 Maria was getting tired of her job. (decide)
  _____

Task 3

Complete these sentences about yourself, using an **-ing** form or infinitive.

1 I enjoy my work, but I wouldn't mind ... *having a bit more responsibility.*
2 When I was 16, I decided ... _____
3 If I moved to another town, I would miss ... _____
4 At the moment I can't afford ... _____
5 I am really looking forward to ... _____
6 In a few years time, I hope ... _____
7 At the moment I am considering ... _____

113

28 **-ing** and infinitive (2): verbs and objects

A Verb + object + infinitive

There are a number of verbs that can take a direct object and **to** + infinitive. Common examples are :

advise	allow	ask	enable	encourage	force
invite	order	persuade	remind	tell	warn

*The lawyer **advised me to read** the contract carefully.*
*The negotiators **persuaded the union to accept** the pay deal.*

B Reporting what people say

Many of these verbs can be used to report what other people say (see also Units 30–31):

'Could you come back later?' he asked me.
*He **asked me to come** back later.*

The verb **warn** is usually used with **not to do**:

He said, 'Don't put all your money in one company'.
*He **warned me not to put** all my money in one company.*

C Make and **let**

The verbs **make** and **let** are followed by an object and the bare infinitive (e.g., **go**, **work**, **see**):

We use **make** to talk about something we have to do (but don't want to do):

*She wanted to go home, but her boss **made her stay** until the work was finished.*

We use **let** when we talk about being given permission for something:

*My boss **let me have** the afternoon off to go to my sister's wedding.*

The verb **help** can be followed by an infinitive with or without **to**:

*'Could you **help me** (**to**) **put** these boxes in the van?'*

D Verbs of perception

The verbs **see**, **watch**, **notice**, **hear**, **listen to,** and **feel** (called verbs of perception) are followed by a bare infinitive or by an **-ing** form (present participle). If we want to say that we heard or saw the whole action from beginning to end, we usually use the bare infinitive:

*I **saw** him **sign** the cheque.*
(He signed the cheque. I saw him do it.)

If we want to say that we only saw or heard part of the action, we use the **-ing** form (present participle):

*I **saw** the consultant **waiting** in reception.*
(I saw the consultant. He was waiting in reception.)

....

Exercise 1
Verb + object + infinitive

The words in the following sentences are in the wrong order. Rewrite them in the correct order.

1 new The law will allow on to open supermarkets Sundays.
The new law will allow supermarkets to open on Sundays.

2 finance bank persuaded project the the They to.
_____

3 court company compensation ordered pay The the to.
_____

4 The cut demand fall forced in us production to.
_____

5 at conference have invited me speak the They to.
_____

....

Exercise 2
Reporting what people say

Rewrite the sentences using the verbs in brackets + object + **to** + infinitive.

1 'Don't forget to post that letter!'
2 'Go on, apply for the job.'
3 'If I were you, I'd make a formal complaint.'
4 'Can you finish the report as soon as possible?'
5 'You can leave early if you like.'
6 'Don't rush into a decision.'

1 (remind) *He reminded me to post the letter.*
2 (encourage) _____
3 (advise) _____
4 (ask)_____
5 (allow) _____
6 (warn) _____

....

Exercise 3
Make and **let**

Rewrite the sentences beginning with **They made us ...** or **They let us ...**

1 We had to work extremely hard on the training course.
They made us work extremely hard on the training course.

2 We were allowed to go out at the weekends.
_____

3 We gave a presentation every morning.
_____

4 We spoke English all the time.
_____

5 There was a TV we could watch.
_____

28 Practice

Exercise 4
Review: verb + object +
infinitive

In each sentence, choose a verb from box A and a verb from box B.

A | allow   force   persuade   <u>want</u>   warn |

B | to advertise   not to smoke   to give up   <u>to start</u>   to buy |

'In the tobacco industry, we do not ⁽¹⁾ <u>want</u> young people ⁽²⁾ <u>to start</u> smoking. Anyway, the government does not ⁽³⁾ _____ us ⁽⁴⁾ _____ on TV or in magazines for young people. Our company spends a lot on advertising, because we believe these advertisements can ⁽⁵⁾ _____ those who already smoke ⁽⁶⁾ _____ our brand of cigarettes. We are a very responsible industry. On every packet, we ⁽⁷⁾ _____ people ⁽⁸⁾ _____ , and we give information about levels of nicotine and tar. But this is a free country, and nobody should ⁽⁹⁾ _____ smokers ⁽¹⁰⁾ _____ if they don't want to.'

Peter Wilson, spokesperson for a major tobacco company

Exercise 5
Review: **make, let, help**

Underline the correct word from each pair in italics.

'As a government, we ⁽¹⁾ *make/let* cigarette manufacturers ⁽²⁾ *to print/print* warning notices on every packet because we want to ⁽³⁾ *make/let* people ⁽⁴⁾ *realize/realizing* that it is a very dangerous habit. We do not ⁽⁵⁾ *make/let* them ⁽⁶⁾ *to advertise/advertise* on TV but we ⁽⁷⁾ *make/let* them ⁽⁸⁾ *sponsoring/sponsor* sporting events. In addition, recent studies show that things like nicotine chewing gum can ⁽⁹⁾ *make/help* people ⁽¹⁰⁾ *give up /giving up* more effectively, and we now ⁽¹¹⁾ *make/let* people ⁽¹²⁾ *buying/buy* these directly from pharmacies.'

Jane Godward, spokesperson for the Department of Health

Exercise 6
Verbs of perception

Rewrite these sentences using the verb in brackets.

1   He was talking to someone on the phone. I heard him. (hear)
    I heard him talking to someone on the phone.

2   Something was burning. I smelled it. (smell)
    _____

3   She left. I didn't see her. (see)
    _____

4   He gave a talk on 'Quality Control'. I heard it. (hear)
    _____

5   Some robots were assembling cars. The visitors watched them. (watch)
    _____

Task 1 Complete these sentences.

1 We made record profits last year, and this will enable us ...

_____

2 My parents encouraged me ...

_____

3 The government should train more young people ...

_____

4 The conference organizers have invited me ...

_____

5 Before I went to New York, a colleague warned me ...

_____

Task 2 Write a short paragraph using **make** and **let**.

1 Someone is being sent to Japan for an intensive training course. A friend has already been on this course, and is telling him what it will be like.

'They will probably make you work fairly hard, but I expect they'll let you have the weekends free. They'll make you learn a little Japanese, of course, but it's not very difficult. And you'd better learn some songs too because they'll definitely take you out to a Karaoke bar and make you sing.'

2 A colleague of yours is going to a health spa for a week. You went there last year. Tell him what life there will be like.

_____

_____

_____

_____

_____

Task 3 Say what advice you would give in these situations. Use the verbs in brackets in your answers.

1 Your accountants have made a number of mistakes, and you have to pay the tax authorities a large fine. (**ask, tell**)

_____

_____

2 The 16-year-old daughter of a friend comes to you to ask for advice about what career she should take up. (**encourage, advise**)

_____

_____

29 -ing and infinitive (3): changes in meaning

A Verb + -ing or infinitive?

Some verbs can be followed by either the **-ing** form or the infinitive and the meaning of the verb changes. Here are some common examples:

I remember sending them the cheque.	(I sent it and I can remember now that I did it.)
I remembered to send them the cheque.	(I remembered, and then I sent it.)
I will never forget meeting the President.	(I met him, and he impressed me.)
I won't forget to give her your message.	(I have made a note of it, and I will give it to her when I see her.)
We have stopped dealing with that firm.	(We used to deal with them, but we don't deal with them any more.)
At 12.00 we stopped to have a break.	(We stopped for a break.)
I regret saying that I was not interested in the work.	(I said I was not interested in the work, and I now think that was a bad mistake.)
I regret to say that we will not be able to give you the contract.	(I am sorry that I have to say this.)
If the printer doesn't work, try turning everything off and starting again.	(Do this and see what happens.)
I will try to negotiate a better deal.	(I will make an effort to do this.)
This advertisement needs redesigning.	(This advertisement needs to be redesigned.)
We need to increase productivity.	(It is necessary to do this.)

B Like and would like

When the verb **like** means **enjoy**, it is followed by the **-ing** form. However, if we use the expression **would like** (**want to**), it is followed by the infinitive:

*I **like going** abroad on marketing trips.* (I enjoy this.)
*I **would like to** go more often.* (I want to go more often.)

We can also use **prefer** and **would prefer** in the same way:

*I **prefer** working at home to working at the office.* (I enjoy this more.)
A *'Shall we go out for lunch?'* **B** *'I'd prefer to stay here.'* (I want to stay here.)

C to + -ing or infinitive?

The word **to** can be part of the infinitive (I want **to see** you). However, in the following examples, **to** is a preposition, so it is followed by the **-ing** form:

look forward to	**object to, an objection to**	**be used to, get used to**
react to, a reaction to	**in addition to**	**respond to, a response to**

Exercise 1
Verb + **-ing** or infinitive?

Match the beginning of the sentences in coloumn A with the right endings in column B.

A

1 *I am sure we have paid the bill. I remember*
2 Did you remember
3 On the way to the airport, he stopped
4 It's hard to find parts for this machine. The manufacturers stopped
5 I've given my PA a list of jobs that need
6 There are plently of hotel rooms available, so you don't need
7 He lost several hours' work. He switched off the computer but he had forgotten
8 I don't mind giving talks now, but I'll never forget
9 He wasn't at the office when I phoned, so I think I'll try
10 For a long time, the company tried

B

A to save the file.
B ringing him on his home number. He might be there.
C to give Peter my message?
D to book one in advance.
E *signing the cheque and sending it to them.*
F giving my first presentation. It was a disaster.
G to enter the Japanese market, but it was extremely difficult.
H to collect some traveller's cheques from the bank.
I producing this model over 15 years ago.
J doing before the sales conference starts.

Exercise 2
Verb + **-ing** or infinitive?

Fill in the blanks with the verbs in brackets, using the **-ing** form or **to** + infinitive.

1 There's nothing wrong with the photocopier. It just needs *servicing*. (service)
2 We need _____ (look) at this proposal very carefully before we make a decision.
3 I'll make a note in my diary so that I will remember _____ (send) you the information you need.
4 I'm not sure if I have met Mr Martino, but I remember _____ (hear) his name.
5 I will never forget _____ (walk) into the office on my first day at work.
6 Could you take this file to Mrs Armstrong? I meant to let her have it this morning, but I forgot _____ (give) it to her.
7 He found it very diffcult to get work because he was unemployed, and soon regretted _____ (resign) from his previous job.
8 We have appointed another candidate to the post, so I regret _____ _____ (say) that we will not be able to offer you the job.
9 If their Accounts Department is slow at paying bills, try _____ (send) a fax to the chairman. That usually works well.
10 As a company, we always try _____ (provide) our customers with the best service possible.

29 Practice

Exercise 3
Like and **would like**

Put the verbs in brackets into the **-ing** form or the infinitive.

1 Our Sales Director is very sociable. She likes _going_ (go) out and _meeting_ (meet) new people.
2 I'm afraid I'm fairly busy tomorrow, so I'd prefer _____ (arrange) the meeting for Monday.
3 He's afraid of flying, so he when he has to go to Frankfurt he prefers _____ (travel) by boat rather than _____ (take) a plane.
4 I'd like _____ (have) a word with you about next week's meeting.
5 I like _____ (work) with my new boss because she gives me a lot of encouragement.
6 Could you let me know when you would like me _____ (come) and see you?

....

Exercise 4
to + **-ing** or infinitive?

Read the following article about the use of the metric system (kilometres, metres, litres, etc.) in the United States. Put the verbs in brackets into the **-ing** form or the infinitive.

Drive down Spencer Road in St Peters, Missouri, and you will get a shock. Suddenly the speed limit changes from 35mph to 60. But take it easy! If you look closer, you will see a k in place of an m. These are kilometres you are dealing with.

Without warning, the St Peters City Street Department decided in May to (1) _change_ (change) its road signs to metric units. Officials said that the Federal Highway Administration had announced that all road signs must become metric by September 1996.

There was a public outcry, so the FHA decided to ask the public how they would react to (2) _____ (use) the metric system. Of those asked, 88% objected to (3) _____ (change) road signs to metric by 1996 – or whenever. They were supported by over 170 members of Congress, who said they would prefer to (4) _____ (spend) the estimated $200 million on urgent repairs to roads and bridges.

Under this pressure, the FHA postponed introducing the changes indefinitely, giving a victory to the opponents of metrification. The vast majority of Americans would not like to (5) _____ (convert) to the metric system. They are used to (6) _____ (drink) Coke from 2-litre bottles, but they would not look forward to (7) _____ (have) kilograms, kilometres, or degrees Celsius. As one person put it, 'We Americans have put 12 men on the moon. This metric system is a French idea, and we have nothing to learn from a country that reads the number 99 as "four twenties and nineteen"'.

[*The Economist, July 30 1994*]

120

Task 1   Complete these sentences with a verb in the **-ing** form or the infinitive.

1   I know for sure that we placed an order with them. I remember ...
sending them the form myself.

2   The meeting had gone on for two hours already, so we stopped ...

_____

3   I'll never forget ...

_____

4   I'm a very organized person. I like ...

_____

5   I have quite a lot of responsibilities at work. In addition to ...

_____

6   I am really looking forward to ...

_____

7   A lot of business people in this country object to ...

_____

Task 2   **A** Say which of the following you **like** or **prefer doing**, and why.

1   having holidays abroad/in your own country
I prefer having holidays abroad because the weather is much better.

2   starting work early/staying late

_____

3   working alone/working with other people

_____

4   eating out/eating at home

_____

B Say which of the following you **would prefer** or **would like**, and why.

1   be rich or be famous
I would prefer to be rich because if I was famous, I wouldn't be free.

2   have a larger house or a bigger car

_____

3   work for a man or a woman

_____

4   have a more demanding job or more time for yourself

_____

30 -ing and infinitive (4): other uses

A Infinitive of purpose

The infinitive (e.g., **to work**, **to stay**) can be used to explain why we do something:

*I have written to IBM **to get** their latest price list.*

COMMON MISTAKES: We do not use **for** + infinitive to explain why we do something.
WRONG: *I went to the warehouse ~~for to get~~ some more stock.*
RIGHT: *I went to the warehouse **to get** some more stock.*

B Infinitives after question words

We use the infinitive after question words (except **why**). We often use the infinitive in this way after verbs of thinking and knowing to talk about things we can do or should do:

*I don't know **how to operate** this machine.* (I can't operate this machine.)
*I'm not sure **what to do**.* (I'm not sure what I should do.)

C **-ing** form as the subject of a sentence

We can use the **-ing** form of the verb (the gerund) as the subject of a sentence:

***Developing** a high technology product like a compact disc requires a great deal of investment.*

D **-ing** form after prepositions

We use the **-ing** form (the gerund) after a preposition (**in**, **on**, **at**, **to**, **by**, **from**, **over**, etc.). We do not use the infinitive. Here are some examples of how we can use the following prepositions:

We can use **before** and **after** to talk about when something happened:

***Before opening** the Body Shop, Anita Roddick ran a hotel.*
*She borrowed the money from a friend **after being** refused a bank loan.*

We can use **without** to talk about something that didn't happen:

*She developed a range of cosmetics **without testing** them on animals.*

We can use **by** to explain how something happened:

*She became successful **by providing** the right product at the right price.*

We can use **instead of** to talk about something we did in the place of another action:

***Instead of opening** up new shops herself, she set up a franchise.*

(For adjective + preposition combinations, noun + preposition combinations, and verb + preposition combinations, see Units 42, 43, and 44.)

Exercise 1
Expressing purpose

Complete the sentences, using the words in the box.

attract	demand	go	increase	inform	miss
prevent	reduce				

1 I need a day off next week _to go_ to an interview.
2 He decided to take a later train _____ the morning rush hour.
3 I am writing _____ you of our change of address.
4 It is likely that the union will go on strike _____ a pay rise.
5 The company had to move to cheaper offices _____ its overheads.
6 We will have to employ more factory workers _____ production.
7 We have cut the price of our products by 10% _____ more customers.
8 The government may soon raise interest rates _____ inflation growing.

Exercise 2
Culture Quiz – visiting Britain

Complete the questions using a suitable question word and the infinitive.
Then choose a suitable answer. Check your answers on page 209.

Culture Quiz

1 I am going to visit Britain shortly on a training course, and I may go out to the pub with my British counterparts. I am not sure (what/do) _what to do_ about buying drinks. Which option is correct?

   A I should only pay for the drinks I have.
   B I should let other people buy me drinks.
   C each member of the group should take turns in buying everyone a drink.

2 I have been invited to an informal dinner at the house of a British business colleague in London. The invitation is for 8 p.m., but I am not sure (when/arrive) _____ at the house. Which of the following is more polite?

   A I should arrive a few minutes early, and certainly no later than 8 p.m.
   B I should arrive ten to fifteen minutes late.
   C I should arrive about 45 minutes late.

3 In Japan we often give business contacts small gifts to show we appreciate their hospitality. If I go to a British colleague's house for a meal, I don't know (whether/take) _____ a gift or not. Should I:

   A not take anything?
   B take a bottle of wine or some flowers?
   C offer to pay for the cost of the meal?

4 I am about to attend a conference in London. I have read about 'body language', and I am not sure (how close/stand) _____ when I am talking to British people. Should I stand:

   A about 30 cm away?
   B about 90 cm away?
   C about 2 metres away?

5 I find taxi drivers in London rather aggressive. If the fare is £5, I am not sure (how much/give) _____ the driver. Should I pay:

   A £5.00?
   B £5.50?
   C £6.00?

6 When leaving a group of colleagues after an informal evening out, we normally shake hands with everyone. I am not sure (how/behave) _____ in England. Should I:

   A shake everyone by the hand?
   B shake the men by the hand and kiss the women on the cheek?
   C do nothing?

30 Practice

Exercise 3
-ing form as subject

Match the beginnings of the sentences in column A with the right endings in column B.

A		**B**	
1	*Giving employees shares*	A	is difficult without local contacts.
2	Flying Business Class	B	can make overseas trips less stressful.
3	Taking over other businesses	C	*can help to increase motivation.*
4	Becoming a fully-qualified doctor	D	is one of the government's priorities.
5	Breaking into the Japanese market	E	takes about seven years.
6	Getting unemployment down	F	is one way of increasing market share.

Exercise 4
Prepositions + **-ing** form

Rewrite the following sentences, using the **-ing** form of the verb in italics and the preposition in brackets.

1 He left the office. He did not *speak* to his boss. (without)
   He left the office without speaking to his boss.

2 She *left* university. Then she got a job with Conoco. (after)
   _____

3 We will not *offer* them a discount. We will give them better credit terms.
   (instead of) _____

4 We managed to expand. We didn't *increase* our debts. (without)
   _____

5 He worked in industry for many years. Then he *joined* the government.
   (before)_____

6 The company *made* 700 workers redundant. That is how it became more
   profitable. (by) _____

Exercise 5
Review

Read the passage about the career history of one of the richest people in England. Choose the correct option from each set of words in italics.

After (1) *to leave/leaving* school at the age of 17, Peter Rigby went into the computer business. He trained as a program analyst, but moved into sales (2) *to make/making* more money. At 21, he moved to Honeywell (3) *to join/joining* the mainframe sales force, and became their top salesman. After (4) *to work/ working* there for seven years, he left (5) *to set up/setting up* his own business, Specialist Computer Holdings. After (6) *to see/seeing* Microsoft's Windows system, Rigby realized that computers would change into a mass-market industry. He set up a chain of large out-of-town superstores where people could see the products instead of (7) *to buy/buying* them from magazines. He has plans (8) *to expand/expanding* into Europe.

Task 1

Continue the following sentences. Say why people did these things.

1 I have written to the bank ...
to ask them for some more information about their charges.

2 The managers changed the layout of the department store ...
_____

3 Our Sales Director has gone to New York ...
_____

4 Next month I need a few days off ...
_____

5 I'll phone up the travel agent this afternoon ...
_____

Task 2

Brian Pelcinski is the agent for a number of people in the entertainment industry. Read his answers to the mini-interview.

1 Which part of your job do you find the most difficult?
Dealing with financial forecasts. It's a nightmare because I hate figures.

2 Which part of your job would most other people find the most difficult?
Dealing with the emotional problems of my clients. They can be very unreasonable.

3 Which part of your job gives you the most satisfaction?
Finding a new talent and seeing him or her become a star.

4 Which part of your job is the most glamorous and exciting?
Being invited to film premières and concerts, and knowing so many people.

5 Which part of your job are you not very good at?
Remembering appointments. But that's why I have a PA to do it for me.

Answer the same questions about the activities you do at work. Begin each answer with the **-ing** form of a verb as in the example above.

1 _____
2 _____
3 _____
4 _____
5 _____

Task 3

Write sentences about your career history. Begin each sentence with **after** + **-ing** form or **before** + **-ing** form.

_____

_____

31 Reported speech (1): statements, thoughts, commands, requests

A Introduction

When we report what someone else said, we can do it in three ways:

1 We can repeat the exact words using inverted commas (' '):
   The agent said: 'Sales are going well'.
2 We can use a reporting verb in the present tense:
   *The agent **says** that sales are going well.*
3 We can use a reporting verb in the past and change the tense:
   *The agent **said** that sales **were** going well.*

B Tense changes

The table shows how tenses change in reported speech when we use a reporting verb in the past tense (i.e., **said** in example 3 above):

ACTUAL WORDS	REPORTED SPEECH
*'I **work** for ICL.'*	*He said that he **worked** for ICL.*
*'I **am working** for ICL.'*	*He said that he **was working** for ICL.*
*'I **worked** for ICL.'*	*He said that he **had worked** for ICL.*
*'I **was working** for ICL.'*	*He said that he **had been working** for ICL.*
*'I **have worked** for ICL.'*	*He said that he **had worked** for ICL.*
*'I **will work** for ICL.'*	*He said he **would work** for ICL.*
*'I **may/can work** for ICL.'*	*He said he **might/could work** for ICL.*

We do not change the past perfect, or **might/could/should/would**.

C Reporting thought

We use the same tense changes when we are reporting what people think or know (e.g., after **I didn't realize, I knew, I thought, I had no idea**, etc.):

A *'I'm from Belgium.'*
B *'Are you? **I didn't realize** you **were** Belgian. **I thought** you **were** French.'*

D Reporting commands and requests

We report commands and requests using **tell** or **ask** and the infinitive:

'Sit down.'	*He **told** me **to sit** down.*
'Don't pay the invoice.'	*He **told** me **not to pay** the invoice.*
'Please wait.'	*He **asked** me **to wait**.*
'Please don't smoke.'	*He **asked** me **not to smoke**.*

E Other changes

It is sometimes necessary to change other words:

*'I saw him **yesterday**.'*	*She said she had seen him **the day before**.*
*'I met him **here**.'*	*She told me that she had met him **there**.*
*'I'll send them **this** report.'*	*She said she would send him **the** report.*
*'I'll do it **tomorrow**.'*	*She said she would do it **the next day**.*
*'I did it **a few days ago**.'*	*She said she had done it a few days **earlier**.*

Exercise 1
Tense changes

A customer came to a Mercedes showroom in a very old Fiat. There was an old lady in the back of the car. Look at some of the things the customer and the salesman said. Then rewrite the sentences in reported speech. (This is based on a true story.)

1 The customer said, 'I'm thinking about buying a new car'.
2 The salesman said, 'The new S500 is very good value'.
3 The customer said, 'I bought a Mercedes in 1985 and I liked it a lot'.
4 The salesman said, 'You can take it for a test drive'.
5 The customer said, 'I don't have any identification ...
     ... but the woman in the car is my grandmother'.
6 The salesman said, 'That will be fine'.
7 Two hours later, the salesman said, 'Your grandson is taking a long time'.
8 The woman said, 'He isn't my grandson ...
     ... He offered to drive me to the shops. I have never seen him before'.

1 The customer said that _he was thinking about buying a new car._
2 The salesman said that _____
3 The customer said that _____
4 The salesman said that _____
5 The customer said that _____
   but that _____
6 The salesman said that _____
7 Later on, the salesman said to the woman that _____
8 The woman said that _____
   and that _____

Exercise 2
Tense changes

Read the report about what a candidate said at an interview. Change the words in italics into direct speech.

Miss Briggs said that [(1)] _she was very interested in working for us_, and she explained that [(2)] _she had been working in the City for three years._ When I asked her about her reasons for leaving, she said that [(3)] _she liked what she did, but she wanted more responsibility._ She seems well-qualified for the post, as she said that [(4)] _she had a degree in Economics and an MBA._ As far as her terms of notice are concerned, she made it clear that [(5)] _she couldn't leave her job for another month._ I decided to offer her the job, and she said [(6)] _she would consider our offer, and would let us have her decision soon._

1 She said, _'I am very interested in working for you'._
2 She said, '_____'.
3 She said, '_____'.
4 She said, '_____'.
5 She said, '_____'.
6 She said, '_____'.

31 Practice

Exercise 3
Reporting thought

Match the comments in column A with those column B.

	A		**B**
1	*I'm just off to play golf.*	A	I thought you spoke Japanese.
2	Anna is working in London today.	B	I thought he'd already been on holiday.
3	These PCs are made in Taiwan.	C	I thought they were free.
4	John is moving to his new job next week.	D	I thought I saw her here this morning.
5	I will need an interpreter.	E	*I didn't realize you played.*
6	Peter is away on leave.	F	I had no idea he was leaving.
7	My boss needs more time to do the report.	G	I thought they were American.
8	We had to pay extra for phone calls.	H	I thought she had finished it.

Exercise 4
Reporting requests and commands

Report the requests or commands using **He asked me** ... or **He told me** ...

1 'Please come to dinner at 8.00.'
He asked me to come to dinner at 8.00.

2 'Send the letter immediately.'

_____

3 'Please don't mention the plans to anyone.'

_____

4 'Please return the form as soon as possible.'

_____

5 'Don't put any calls through to my office.'

_____

Exercise 5
Other changes

Read the situations, and underline the correct words.

1 At 10.00 this morning, Julia says to you, 'Dr Bangermann is arriving this afternoon'. At 10.30 the same morning you say to your boss, 'Julia said that Dr Bangermann was arriving *this afternoon*/that afternoon'.

2 The sales manager says to you, 'I'll show the visitors round the factory tomorrow'. Three weeks later, you say to your boss, 'He said he would show the visitors round the factory the following day/tomorrow.'

3 A client calls from his office and says, 'I'd like to hold the meeting here'. Later you speak to your boss in your own office and say, 'He said he'd like to hold the meeting here/there'.

4 A customer rings to say, 'We sent the cheque yesterday'. The same day you say to your boss, 'When I spoke to him, he said that he had sent the cheque yesterday/the previous day'.

5 A client rings you at your office and says, 'I'll meet you there tomorrow'. The same day at your office you say to your boss, 'He said he would meet me here/there tomorrow'.

....

Task 1

A headhunter took you out to dinner last night. Now a colleague is asking you about what you said. Answer his questions using reported speech.

1   'What personal details did you give him about yourself?'
    I told him I was married and that I lived in London.

2   'What did you tell him about the company?'
    _____

3   'What did you say your responsibilities were?'
    _____

4   'What did you tell him about the salary you would need?'
    _____

5   'What did he tell you about the new company?'
    _____

6   'What did he tell you about the new job?'
    _____

7   'So in the end what did you say to him?'
    _____

....

Task 2

Respond with surprise to the following comments.

1   A They are discontinuing this model at the end of the year.
    B Really? I thought *it was selling well.*

2   A It's my fortieth birthday next week.
    B Really? I had no idea _____

3   A You will have to wait about three months for delivery.
    B Really? I didn't realize _____

4   A I've just seen Mr Takashi in Reception.
    B Really? I thought _____

5   A The bill for dinner came to £145 each.
    B Really? I had no idea _____

....

Task 3

Complete the sentences using **ask** or **tell** + infinitive.

1   They were late paying the bill, so I phoned and *told them to pay at once.*
2   I was too busy to see Jane, so I _____ .
3   I could see that he had had too much to drink, so I _____ .
4   Peter said he was going to the bank, so I _____ .
5   The machine they sold us was faulty, so I _____ .
6   I wanted the mechanic to tell me how much the repairs would cost, so I
    _____ .

32 Reported speech (2): questions and reporting verbs

A Wh- questions

Some questions begin with a question word (i.e., **Who**, **Where**, **Which**, **Why**, **When**, **What**, **How**, **How much**, etc.). Look at the way we report these questions:

*'When **will you** let us know your decision?' they asked me.*
*They asked me when **I would** let them know my decision.*

COMMON MISTAKES: When we report a question, the word order changes from verb – subject (**will**, **you**) to subject – verb (**I**, **would**).
'Where is he?' she asked me.
WRONG: *She asked me where ~~was he~~.*
RIGHT: *She asked me where **he was**.*

B Yes/no questions

When we report **yes/no** questions, we use **if** or **whether** and the tense changes given in Unit 30:

DIRECT QUESTION: *'**Are you feeling** all right?'*
REPORTED QUESTION: *She asked me if I **was feeling** all right.*

DIRECT QUESTION: *'**Do you know** Lars Hansen?'*
REPORTED QUESTION: *He asked me if I **knew** Lars Hansen.*

C Embedded questions

When we begin a sentence with one of the following phrases, we need to use the same word order as for reporting questions. We do not need to change the tense if the introductory phrase is in the present tense:

'I wonder where that file is.'	(NOT: *...where is that file.*)
'I'm not sure if it is a good idea.'	(NOT: *...is it a good idea.*)
'Could you tell me what the time is?'	(NOT: *...what is the time?*)
'Do you know when the train leaves?'	(NOT: *...when does the train leave?*)

D Reporting verbs

We often use other verbs instead of **say**, **tell**, etc. to report what someone says.

The verbs **warn**, **order**, **advise**, **encourage**, **remind**, **persuade** are followed by an object + infinitive:

'I think you ought to see a lawyer.'   *He **advised** me **to see** a lawyer.*

The verbs **offer**, **refuse**, **promise** are followed by an infinitive:

'We will not pay any more.'   *They **refused to pay** any more.*

The verbs **admit**, **deny**, **apologize for** are followed by the **-ing** form:

'I am sorry I have kept you waiting.'   *He **apologized for keeping** me waiting.*

A speaker was asked these questions after a presentation. Report the questions.

1 'When will the new product be ready?'
2 'How much are you planning to spend on advertising?'
3 'Where do you intend to advertise?'
4 'What discount will you give to your distributors?'
5 'Why has it taken so long to develop?'
6 'How much market interest has there been in the new product?'
7 'Who is the product aimed at?'
8 'What sort of problems have you had in developing the product?'

1 They asked me *when the new product would be ready*.
2 They asked me *how much we were planning to spend on advertising*.
3 They asked me _____
4 They asked me _____
5 They asked me _____
6 They asked me _____
7 They asked me _____
8 They asked me _____

A colleague of yours came back from a business trip, and you asked her the following questions. Rewrite the questions using reported speech.

1 'Did you have a good trip?'
   I asked her if she had had a good trip.

2 'Have they signed the contract?'
   _____

3 'Will you need to go back again?'
   _____

4 'Was the hotel OK?'
   _____

5 'Did you have any time off?'
   _____

6 'Are you feeling tired?'
   _____

7 'Did you have any problems?'
   _____

8 'Do you feel confident about the project?'
   _____

9 'Did they like the idea of a joint venture?'
   _____

32 Practice

Exercise 3
Embedded questions

Rewrite the following sentences. Use the introductory phrases and either a question word or **if**.

1 Does the bank have a branch in Geneva, I wonder?
I wonder if the bank has a branch in Geneva.

2 When will the plane get in? Do you know?
Do you know when the plane will get in?

3 How are the negotiations going, I wonder?
I wonder _____

4 Is Peter coming to the meeting? Do you know?
Do you know_____

5 When is the talk going to start? Could you tell me?
Could you tell me _____

6 Should I take the job? I'm not sure.
I'm not sure_____

7 Where is their head office? I don't know.
I don't know _____

8 Will they accept our offer, I wonder?
I wonder _____

9 Have they sent us an order form? Could you tell me?
Could you tell me _____

10 How did they get this information, I wonder?
I wonder _____

Exercise 4
Reporting verbs

Match the sentences in column A with the reported statements in column B.

A	B
1 *'Don't forget to sign the contract.'*	A He apologized for signing the contract.
2 'I didn't sign the contract.'	B He warned me not to sign the contract.
3 'Go on, sign the contract. It's a really good idea.'	C He encouraged me to sign the contract.
4 'If I were you, I would sign the contract.'	D He ordered me to sign the contract.
5 'No, I will not sign this contract under any circumstances.'	E He refused to sign the contract.
6 'I am so sorry I signed the contract.'	F He admitted signing the contract.
7 'Yes, I am afraid to say that it was me who signed the contact.'	G *He reminded me to sign the contract.*
8 'I'll sign the contract if you like.'	H He offered to sign the contract.
9 'Sign the contract NOW!'	I He advised me to sign the contract.
10 'I really wouldn't sign the contract. You haven't read it. It could be a disaster.'	J He denied signing the contract.

A colleague has overheard you say the following things on the phone. Explain who you were talking to and what they asked you.

1   'Yes, the 15th would be fine.'
That was Mr Jackson. He asked me if he could change the date of our next meeting to the 15th, and I said it would be fine.

2   'No, I am afraid that 15% is the maximum.' _____
_____

3   'It will be there first thing on Wednesday.' _____
_____

4   'Yes, I am sure we have paid it. I remember writing the cheque myself.'
_____

5   '£16,000. _____
_____

Complete the sentence with a suitable embedded question.

1   The office is very different without Janet. I wonder ...
how she is getting on in her new job.

2   No, I'm afraid I don't know _____ .
I am a stranger here myself.

3   I'll just have a look at the new price list. I'm not sure ...
_____

4   I need to go to New York next Wednesday. Could you tell me ...
_____?

5   I can't understand this letter. Do you know ...
_____?

Complete the sentences using the verbs in brackets.

1   She was offered a very good job, so ...
(advise) *I advised her to accept it.*

2   He said that the guarantee was out of date, and ...
(refuse) _____

3   They said that they couldn't bring the price down any more, but ...
(offer) _____

4   The bank realized that they were in the wrong, and they ...
(apologize) _____

33 Relative clauses (1): **who**, **that**, **which**, **whose**, **whom**

A People and things

We can use a relative clause beginning with **who**, **that**, or **which** to describe and define a person or thing. To refer to people, we use **who** or **that**. To refer to things, we use **which** or **that**:

PEOPLE: *The accountants **who/that advised me** were very good.*
(The clause **who advised me** helps to identify the accountants.)
THINGS: *The computers **which/that they bought** were expensive.*
(The clause **which they bought** identifies the computers.)

B Subject and object relative clauses

Sometimes it is necessary to keep the relative pronoun in the sentence, and sometimes it is possible to leave it out.

If the relative **who**, **which**, or **that** is followed by a verb, we must keep it:

*We've got a machine **that prints in colour**.* (NOT: *a machine prints in colour*)
(In this sentence, **that prints in colour** is a subject relative clause.)

If the relative **who**, **which**, or **that** is followed by a noun or pronoun + verb, we can leave it out. So we can say:

*The computers **that you ordered** have arrived.* OR *The computers **you ordered** have arrived.*
(In this sentence, **that you ordered** is an object relative clause.)

In object relative clauses, it is possible to use **whom** to refer to people. However, this is only found in formal langauge, and rarely used in speech:

*The candidate **whom they selected** had extensive experience of industry.*
(In conversation, we would say : *The candidate [that] they selected ...*)

C Whose

The relative pronoun **whose** is used to show possession:

Yesterday I met someone. His brother works in your department.
*Yesterday I met someone **whose** brother works in your department.*

D To whom, from which, etc.

It is possible, particularly in formal or written language, to put words like **to**, **from**, **about**, **on**, etc. in front of **whom**, **which**, and **whose** (but not **who** or **that**):

*The woman **to whom** I spoke was extremely helpful.*

However, it is much more common to put words like **to**, **from**, **about**, **on**, etc. at the end of the relative clause:

*The woman (**that**) **I spoke to** was extremely helpful.*

Exercise 1

People and things

Complete the sentences in this job advertisement with **who** or **which**.

SALES MANAGER
£29,500 plus car

Our client manufactures leisure clothing (1) _which_ is distributed to major high-street retailers. We have a vacancy for a Sales Manager (2)_____ will be responsible for the overall control of a Sales Department (3)_____ consists of 15 representatives.

We are looking for someone (4)_____ has a proven track record of success in sales and (5)_____ will be able to motivate the existing sales team. This is a job (6)_____ will involve a great deal of dedication, flair, and enthusiasm, and priority will be given to applicants (7)_____ have experience in the retail clothing sector. We are offering a salary (8)_____ is highly competitive, and benefits (9)_____ include a company car, free health insurance, and generous pension contributions.

If you would like to work for an organization (10)_____ is expanding fast, and (11)_____ can offer you the chance to fulfil your potential, send your CV to:

Peter Hodgson & Co, 28 Barton Road,
Kingston-upon-Thames, Surrey KT2 5EE

PETER HODGSON & COMPANY   HUMAN RESOURCE CONSULTANTS

Exercise 2

Subject and object relative clauses

Look at the sales brief describing a desktop business accessory, the CTRX 501. Write sentences about the CTRX 501, describing what each feature does and its benefits for the customer.

Features	Selling points
phone	has a 60 number memory
	you can use it without picking up the handset
answering machine	can store up to 100 messages
	you can call it from another phone
photocopier	prints at different resolutions
	you can use it to copy A4 documents
fax	has an automatic sheet feeder
	you can program it

1   It's got a phone _that has a 60 number memory._
2   It's got a phone _that you can use without picking up the handset._
3   It's got an answering machine_____
4   It's got an answering machine_____
5   It's got a photocopier _____
6   It's got a photocopier _____
7   It's got a fax _____
8   It's got a fax _____

In which of the above sentences can you leave out the word **that**?

33 Practice

Exercise 3

Whose

Finish each sentence using one of the pieces of information in the box. Join the two parts with **whose**.

> Her department was doing well.   Their car had broken down.
> Its key competitors are Sony and Sanyo.   Their CVs were very good.
> Her mother tongue must be English.   Its headquarters are in Helsinki.

1   We drew up a shortlist of candidates _whose CVs were very good._
2   We are looking for a secretary _____
3   Nokia is a large Finnish company _____
4   I gave a lift to a couple of colleagues _____
5   Casio is a Japanese electronics company _____
6   They promoted one of the managers _____

Exercise 4

To whom, from which, etc.

Complete the sentences with **who**, **whom**, or **which**.

1   The salesperson to _whom_ you spoke was correct in saying that goods must be returned to the store from _which_ they were purchased.
2   I was ordering some supplies on the phone, and then the person _____ I was talking to suddenly hung up.
3   The profit we make from the sales depends on the country in _____ we are operating.
4   I can give you the name of an accountant _____ I deal with.
5   The client from _____ we have received this complaint wishes us to take action immediately.
6   The hotel has a large conference hall in _____ presentations and exhibitions can be held.

Exercise 5

Prepositions in relative clauses

Rewrite the sentences without relative pronouns, putting the prepositions at the end of the relative clause.

1   I was talking to a man. He is the head of AT&T.
    The man I was talking to is the head of AT&T.
2   You were looking for an invoice. Peter has found it.
    Peter has found the _____
3   I deal with customers. Most of them are very pleasant.
    Most of the _____
4   We wanted to stay in a hotel. It was fully booked.
    The hotel _____
5   She works for a company. It has a very good reputation.
    The company _____
6   We went to a restaurant. It wasn't very good.
    The restaurant _____

Task 1

The word in the box is the name of a large industrial corporation. Find this name by answering the clues below. Some of the answers are provided.

1 `I N V O I C E`
2 ☐☐☐☐☐☐☐☐
3 `S A L A R Y`
4 ☐☐☐☐
5 `S U B S I D I A R Y`
6 ☐☐☐☐☐☐
7 `C A T A L O G U E`
8 ☐☐☐☐☐
9 `C O L L E A G U E`
10 ☐☐☐☐☐☐☐☐

Clues

2 A legal document that gives details of an agreement between two or more people.
4 A building or company in which people keep their money.
6 A person whose job it is to give legal advice.
8 A list of things that are discussed at a meeting.
10 A machine that allows you to talk to people who are in a different place.

Now write clues for the words that you were given, using relative clauses.

1 An invoice is _____

3 A salary is _____

5 A subsidiary is _____

7 A catalogue is _____

9 A colleague is _____

Task 2

Complete the following sentences about yourself and your work, using relative clauses.

1 I work for a company *that manufactures components for aircraft.*
2 I have a boss _____
3 I am in a department _____
4 In my work, I deal with people _____
5 I sometimes have to do things _____
6 I prefer to work with people _____
7 I dislike working with people_____
8 In my spare time, I like to do things _____

34 Relative clauses (2): **where**, **with**, **what**, and non-defining clauses

A Where

The relative pronoun **where** is used to refer to places.

*The hotel **where** we stayed was very expensive.*

Where is not used if there is a preposition at the end of the clause:

WRONG: *The hotel where ~~we stayed in~~ was very expensive.*
RIGHT: *The hotel **we stayed in** was very expensive.*

B Use of with

When we want to describe what someone or something has, we can use a relative clause or **with** + a noun. So we can say:

*I'm thinking about buying a computer **that has a faster chip**.*
OR *I'd like to buy a computer **with a faster chip**.*

C Use of what

We can use the relative pronoun **what** to replace **the thing(s) that** ... . So we can say:

*I went to buy some some parts, but they didn't have **the things that** we needed.*
OR *I went to buy some some parts, but they didn't have **what** we needed.*

D Non-defining relative clauses

In some relative clauses we must use a relative pronoun, and cannot use the word **that**:

WRONG: *Benetton's latest advertisement, ~~I saw yesterday,~~ is very powerful.*
WRONG: *Benetton's latest advertisement, ~~that I saw yesterday,~~ is very powerful.*
RIGHT: *Benetton's latest advertisement, **which I saw yesterday**, is very powerful.*

Relative clauses like this simply give extra information. They are called non-defining relative clauses, and they begin and end with commas. Look at the difference between the two types:

DEFINING RELATIVE CLAUSE:
*The office **that we work in** is very comfortable.*
(This indicates which office we are talking about.)

NON-DEFINING RELATIVE CLAUSE:
*My father, **who will be 65 next year**, has asked me to take over the family business.*
(The speaker does not need to define my father, and his age is just an extra piece of information.)

Exercise 1
Where

Rewrite the following sentences using **where**.

1 I've got the details of the hotel that you'll be staying in.
   I've got the details of the hotel where you'll be staying.

2 Would you like to visit the factory that we make the cars in?
   _____

3 I recently went back to the town I used to work in.
   _____

4 Ivrea is the town in which Olivetti has its headquarters.
   _____

5 Is this the building that they filmed the Coke advertisement in?
   _____

Exercise 2
With or **that?**

Complete the sentences using **with** or **that** and the phrases in the box.

has a better view	a colour monitor	a bit more experience
has a lot of mistakes	a matching tie	has all the latest information
a £2000 credit limit	a sense of humour	

1 I've got a new credit card *with*   *a £2000 credit limit.*
2 I'll send you a brochure *that*   *has all the latest information.*
3 Have you got a computer _____   _____?
4 We're looking for someone _____   _____
5 I'd prefer a room _____   _____
6 We've received an invoice _____   _____
7 He's bought a Gucci shirt _____   _____
8 I wish I had a boss _____   _____

Exercise 3
Use of **what**

Rewrite these sentences using **what**.

1 He was selling something. I wasn't interested in it.
   I wasn't interested in what he was selling.

2 You asked me to do something. I have done it.
   I have done _____

3 You want a computer to do some things. This computer can do them.
   This computer _____

4 You need something. We can deliver it tomorrow.
   We can _____

5 I'm sorry, you said something. I didn't hear it.
   I'm sorry, I didn't _____

Join the following sentences together using relative clauses and the relative pronoun in brackets.

1 The new accounts program is working very well.
  It cost a great deal of money. (which)
  The new accounts program, which cost a great deal of money, is working very well.

2 The Oriental Hotel is said to be the best in the world.
  Many famous people have stayed in it. (where)
  _____
  _____

3 Richard Branson runs the airline Virgin Atlantic.
  He has now sold his record company to Sony. (who)
  _____
  _____

4 Glaxo is the biggest drug producer in Europe.
  Its products include Zantac. (whose)
  _____
  _____

5 Their new range of cosmetics will be launched next month.
  They have spent £10 million on it. (on which)
  _____
  _____

6 I am writing with reference to my client Mr Warburg.
  I have discussed your proposal with him. (with whom)
  _____
  _____

Correct the mistakes in the following sentences.

1 Yesterday I spoke to your director, that seemed to be very pleasant.
2 The room where we held the meeting in was a little too small.
3 Brazil which is the world's largest exporter of coffee has high inflation.
4 The negotiators finally reached a formula on what everyone could agree.
5 I found it difficult to hear that the speaker was talking about.
6 Tim Lang only joined the company six months ago is going to be promoted.
7 The Rover group its name has been changed several times is now part of BMW.
8 I suggest we have a meeting in Romsey Street, which we rent a few offices.

Task 1

A Read the following text about the history of the trading company Dalgleish & Mackay.

Dalgleish & Mackay, (1) _which is one of Hong Kong's largest trading companies_, was founded in 1832 by Scotsmen Allen Dalgleish and Charles Mackay. They started the business in the Chinese city of Canton (2) _____ . The

_____ trading company exported tea and imported opium (3) _____

_____ .

In 1839 the Chinese authorities (4) _____

_____ seized 7,000 chests of Dalgleish's opium.

The British traders (5) _____ persuaded the British government to go to war to protect 'free trade'. They sent ships to Canton and began the First Opium War (6) _____

_____ .

The Chinese lost, and signed the Treaty of Nanking (7) _____

_____ .

The company moved to Hong Kong (8) _____ and began trading in opium again. In 1860, after the Second Opium War, (9) _____ the company flourished and expanded. It later left the opium business (10) _____ and

_____ expanded into land, brewing, textiles, and many other fields of business.

The company (11) _____ has interests in general trade, insurance, and merchant banking. It announced a strategy of reducing its interests in Hong Kong because of the Chinese takeover in 1997, and now has a 33% share in an international holding company (12) _____

_____ .

B Look through the extra information below. Add this to the text in the spaces provided, using relative clauses.

1 Dalgleish & Mackay is one of Hong Kong's largest trading companies.
2 Canton was an important commercial centre.
3 There was a growing demand for opium.
4 They wanted to stop the opium trade.
5 They had powerful allies in London.
6 The war ended in 1842.
7 Under the treaty, they agreed to give Hong Kong to the British.
8 It opened up new headquarters there.
9 The Second Opium War led to the legalization of opium.
10 The opium business was politically dangerous.
11 The company's legal headquarters are now in Bermuda.
12 The company owns two airlines and a major hotel chain.

35 Countable and uncountable nouns

A Countable nouns

Countable nouns are things like people, animals, plants (**a boss**, **a dog**), concrete objects (**a desk**, **a fax machine**), or units of measurement (**a metre**, **a Deutschmark**).

B Uncountable nouns

Uncountable nouns include things like substances, materials, and commodities (e.g., **water**, **oil**, **money**, **information**), abstract ideas (**profitability**, **progress**), and languages (**English**, **Arabic**). We do not usually talk about 'three informations', 'six monies', 'two waters', etc.

Some other uncountable nouns which sometimes cause difficulty are:

advice	**accommodation**	**baggage**	**cash**
equipment	**furniture**	**information**	**luggage**
machinery	**money**	**news**	**permission**
progress	**room** (=space)	**traffic**	**travel**
trouble	**weather**	**work**	

C Singular or plural?

Countable nouns can be singular or plural. Uncountable nouns are singular:

*The new **brochures** have arrived.* (COUNTABLE)
*The new **furniture** has arrived.* (UNCOUNTABLE)

D A, an, or **some**?

With uncountable nouns we can often use **some** instead of **a** or **an**:

WRONG: *He gave me ~~an advice.~~*
RIGHT: *He gave me **some advice**.*

E Parts of a mass

We can refer to parts of an uncountable mass by using words of measurement, e.g., **a cup of coffee**, **a glass of water**, **a tonne of coal**, **a kilo of sugar**, **a barrel of oil**.

We often use these measurements when talking about the price of something:

*Mineral water is 75p **a bottle**.*
*The price of oil is $17 **a barrel**.*

When we use **a** or **an** with a noun that is usually uncountable (e.g., **wine**, **water**, **beer**), we often refer to a part of a mass:

*'Would you like **a coffee**?'* (one cup of coffee)
*'I'll have **a beer**, please.'* (a glass of beer)

Exercise 1
Countable or uncountable?

In the following pairs of words, one is countable and the other is uncountable. Write **some** or **a** before each word.

1   ___a___ book / _some_ literature
2   _____ report / _____ news
3   _____ desk / _____ furniture
4   _____ accommodation / _____ hotel
5   _____ chance / _____ luck
6   _____ water / _____ litre
7   _____ equipment / _____ machine
8   _____ dollar / _____ money
9   _____ cheque / _____ cash
10 _____ letter / _____ correspondence

Exercise 2
Singular or plural?

Fill in the blanks with **is** or **are**.

1   The equipment that we ordered _____ here.
2   What _____ the weather like at this time of year?
3   There _____ a lot of cars in the car park this morning.
4   The agenda for tomorrow's meeting _____ on your desk.
5   The reports that I have just received from Tokyo _____ not very good.
6   Your Japanese visitors have gone to the hotel, but their luggage _____ still at the office.
7   On the foreign exchanges this morning, the dollar _____ up 0.5 cents against the yen.

Exercise 3
A, an, or some?

In the dialogue, choose the correct option from the words in italics.

HARRY: I've got [(1)] _a problem/some problem_ with Petersens. They owe us [(2)] _a money/some money_ for [(3)] _a work/some work_ we did for them, but they won't pay.

JANET: We've had [(4)] _a trouble/some trouble_ with them before, haven't we?

HARRY: Yes, that's right. Last year they sent us [(5)] _a cheque/some cheque_ for [(6)] _an equipment/some equipment_ we had supplied and the bank returned it. So they haven't got [(7)] _a good record/some good record_.

JANET: May I make [(8)] _a suggestion/some suggestion_? Send them [(9)] _a final demand/some final demand_, saying we want to be paid immediately.

HARRY: And if they still don't pay?

JANET: Go and see [(10)] _a lawyer/some lawyer_ and get [(11)] _an advice/some advice_ about what to do next.

HARRY: All right, I'll send them [(12)] _a letter/some letter_ today.

JANET: Yes, OK. And by the way, there's [(13)] _an information/some information_ about the company and who runs it in the Accounts Department. Have a word with Kerry, because she's got [(14)] _a correspondence/some correspondence_ from them that might be useful.

35 Practice

Exercise 4
Parts of a mass

Use a word from box A and a word from box B to describe the items below.

A

a litre	a pint	a kilo	a tonne
a barrel	a glass	a sheet	

B

paper	oil	wine
coal	beer	sugar	water

1 _____ 2 _____ 3 _____ 4 _____

5 _____ 6 _____ 7 _____

Exercise 5
Prices and quantities

Complete the following items of news with the words from the box.

packet	ounce	barrel	pint	litre	bottle

Petrol and gold rise in Middle East fears

Shell and Texaco have announced that they intend to raise the price of petrol to just over 65 pence (1) _a litre._ They blame the political situation in the Middle East, where shortages of crude have pushed the price of oil up to over $20 (2) _____ . The political worries have also affected the price of gold, which has risen to over $700 (3) _____ in the last few weeks.

Budget misery for smokers and drinkers

In his Budget statement, the Chancellor raised taxes on most alcohol and tobacco. The effect of the changes will mean that the pub price of beer will rise by about ten pence (4) _____ . Supermarket prices for wine will go up by about twenty pence (5) _____ , and cigarettes will increase by over thirty pence (6) _____ .

144

Fill in the blanks with an uncountable noun. Use one word only.

1 A: Would you like to try the salmon? The trout is good as well.
  B: No thanks, I don't really like _fish_.

2 A: Would you like wine, or a beer, or a gin and tonic, or something?
  B: No thank you. I'll just have mineral water. I don't drink _____ .

3 A: Could I have a talk with you about the arrangements for next week?
  B: I'm sorry, could we talk later? I haven't got _____ at the moment.

4 A: It's been raining here for two weeks.
  B: Oh dear. When we were on holiday we had marvellous _____ .

5 A: So your wife handles the accounts, does she?
  B: Yes, it's because I'm no good with _____ .

6 A: Signomi, pou einai o xenodochio Divani Acropolis?
  B: I'm sorry, I don't speak _____ .

7 A: What will you have – chicken, a steak, a hamburger?
  B: Actually, I'm a vegetarian. I don't eat _____ .

8 A: We're going to a couple of department stores to try and buy some clothes.
  B: I think I'll stay here. I hate _____ .

Fortune cookies are biscuits that contain a little piece of paper with a short philosophical message. You have been asked to write some of these messages. Remember that the (ancient Chinese) messages can say anything.

Problems are caterpillars and solutions are butterflies.

Advice is something we like to give but do not like to receive.

Money ... _____

Time ... _____

Meetings ... _____

Work ... _____

Men ... _____

Women ... _____

Experience ... _____

Productivity ... _____

36 Articles: **a/an**, **the**, or **Ø** (no article)?

A **a** vs **an**

We use **a** before consonant sounds, and **an** before vowel sounds:

VOWEL SOUNDS: **an appraisal, an hour, an interview, an office, an MBA**
CONSONANT SOUNDS: **a director, a code, a unit, a question**

B Uses of **a**, **an**

We use **a** or **an** before unspecified singular countable nouns:

*'Could you let me have **an envelope**?'*

We use **a** or **an** to talk about jobs, (but not areas of business):

*Janet's **a Personnel Manager**, and her husband is in Ø **marketing**.*

We use **a** or **an** to talk about frequency:

*We have to submit VAT returns four times **a** year.*

C Uses of **the**

We use **the** with a specific noun we have mentioned before:

*We have bought **a** Mac and **a** PC. **The** Mac cost $2500 and **the** PC cost $2100.*

We use **the** when we add information that defines something:

*Where is **the** file that I gave you this morning?*

We use **the** when it is clear what we are referring to because there is only one:

*Would you like to come in? **The** chairman will see you now.*

We use **the** with superlatives:

*Coca Cola is **the** most famous soft drink in the world.*

We use **the** with adjectives to refer to a group:

***The** rich do not do enough to help **the** poor.*

We use **the** to refer to rivers, mountains, seas, and names of countries that include a noun like **republic**, **kingdom**, **union**, etc.:

***The** Aral Sea in **the** former Soviet Union is very polluted.*

D No article (**Ø**)

We use no article (Ø) to generalize about uncountable or plural nouns:

*Ø Money is **the** root of all evil.* (i.e., money in general, or all money)

We do not use an article (Ø) to refer to companies, cities, roads, single islands, or lakes:

I work for Ø Goldman Sachs in Ø London, and I have a house in Ø Western Road. I also have a holiday home in Ø Crete and another near Ø Lake Garda.

Exercise 1
A vs **an**

Complete the dialogue. Fill in the blanks with **a** or **an**.

A: I had (1) _an_ appraisal with the Personnel Manager the other day, and ...

B: Oh really? How did it go?

A: Fine. We were talking about qualifications and career development, and she said to me that I should consider doing (2) _____ course in Business Administration.

B: That's not (3) _____ bad idea. You've already got (4) _____ university degree, haven't you?

A: Yes, and I'm doing (5) _____ evening course in accounting, but that takes up about (6) _____ hour a week.

B: That sounds like (7) _____ waste of time to me. What you need to do is (8) _____ MBA at (9) _____ institution like Insead, so that you end up with (10) _____ decent qualification.

Exercise 2
Uses of **a**, **an**

Fill in the blanks with **a**, **an**, or Ø (no article).

1 I like to go abroad about three times _____ year.

2 Have you met my brother? He's _____ engineer too.

3 I'm thinking about buying _____ new car. What would you recommend?

4 The *Lloyds Bank Review* is published four times _____ year.

5 _____ computer software is not as expensive as you may think.

6 The government has urged businesses not to give _____ pay rises above inflation.

7 How long have you been in _____ engineering?

8 I go to meetings in London twice _____ month.

Exercise 3
Uses of **the**

Read the following newspaper extract. Fill in the blanks with **a** or **the**.

Coca-Cola has launched (1) _a_ £4 million TV advertising campaign – one of (2) _____ biggest ever seen in Britain – in what will be seen as (3) _____ direct attack on supermarkets' own-brand colas. (4) _____ six-week campaign, which opened last night, is part of an attempt to boost (5) _____ size of the £6 billion (6) _____ year soft drinks market. The advertisements will be aimed mainly at (7) _____ young, but middle-aged drinkers will also be targeted.

(8) _____ drinks giant denied that (9) _____ new advertisements are (10) _____ response to (11) _____ 'cola wars' that raged in supermarkets in (12) _____ summer, but admitted that there was room for improving sales.

Exercise 4
Uses of **the**

In each pair of sentences, fill in one blank with **the**, and the other blank with Ø (no article).

1 A I am not motivated by ____Ø____ money.
   B When are you going to pay back ____the____ money I lent you?
2 A Carbon-dating helps scientists to work out _____ age of fossils.
   B We never refuse to give someone a job on the basis of _____ age.
3 A _____ mistakes you have made cost us a great deal of money.
   B Don't worry. Everybody makes _____ mistakes.
4 A _____ crime in the cities is now at record levels.
   B The police have no idea who committed _____ crime.
5 A This book will give you _____ information you need.
   B CD-ROMs can store large quantities of _____ information.
6 A _____ visitors must be accompanied at all times.
   B _____ visitors are on a fact-finding mission from Japan.
7 A Should _____ unemployed people do more to help themselves?
   B Should the government do more to help _____ unemployed?
8 A _____ Japanese imports are currently at very high levels.
   B It is very difficult to sell to _____ Japanese.

Exercise 5
The vs no article (Ø)

Complete the following passages. In each space, put **the** or Ø (no article).

A

Hi, my name's Todd Sawyer. I'm a financial analyst, and I work for a company called (1)_____ Pacific Investments which is based in (2)_____ Channel Islands. Our offices are in (3)_____ St Helier, (4)_____ capital. (5)_____ Jersey is very popular with financial institutions from (6)_____ England because it is not part of (7)_____ UK for tax purposes, and it is also popular with investors from (8)_____ Europe.

B

I work for a tour operator called (9)_____ Lakeland Travel, and we specialize in bringing people to (10)_____ Lake District, which is in (11)_____ north of (12)_____ England. We run a de luxe hotel in (13)_____ Morrison Road, which is in (14)_____ Ambleside, a small town on the shores of (15)_____ Lake Windermere. Many of our visitors come from Scotland, which is very close, but others come from as far away as (16)_____ New York or (17)____ Far East.

Look at the map. Fill in the blanks with **a**, **an**, **the**, or **Ø** (no article).

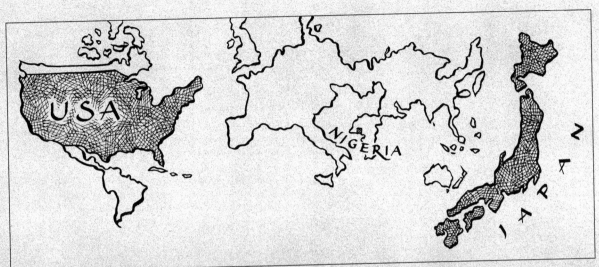

HERE'S WHERE THE MONEY LIVES

USA

(1) _____ richest man in (2) _____ USA is Bill Gates, (3) _____ Chairman of (4) _____ Microsoft. The billionaire, who is known to have a boyish streak, gives 'theme' parties for his employees. One theme was (5) _____ Africa. Party goers tried to fill in names of African countries on (6) _____ giant map and played (7) _____ computer quiz game called 'Jungle Jeopardy'.

NIGERIA

Five ships full of industrial waste were shipped from Italy to Koko in Nigeria, where (1) _____ farmer was paid US$8,750 to store (2) _____ waste on his land. This was a bargain for the Europeans and a fortune for (3) _____ farmer. Local children played in the waste, and took the containers home. However, (4) _____ waste was toxic and radioactive. (5) _____ farmer died from (6) _____ poisoning.

JAPAN

Sanwa Bank, one of (1) _____ world's largest banks, is offering its clients (2) _____ savings accounts for (3) _____ pets. Clients' pets can hold accounts where they can save for special treats, (4) _____ holidays, or visits to the vet. A funeral for (5) _____ cat can cost up to $400, and a gravestone can cost another $2,400.

Choose two other countries. Write two short reports about them (as in the examples above) for the *Benetton Report*.

1 _____

_____

_____

_____

2 _____

_____

_____

_____

37 Some and any

A a/an, some, any

We use **a** or **an** with singular countable nouns. We use **some** and **any** with plural countable nouns and with uncountable nouns:

SINGLE COUNTABLE:	*I've got **an** invoice for you.*
PLURAL COUNTABLE:	*I've got **some** invoices for you.*
UNCOUNTABLE:	*I've got **some** information for you.*

B Some or any

We normally use **any** in questions and negative statements; we use **some** in positive statements:

A *Have you got **any** information about marketing policy?*
B *There are **some** notes in the file on my desk.*

However, we often use **some** in questions if the question is an offer or request, or if we expect the answer to be 'yes':

*Would you like me to send you **some** more information?*
*Could I take **some** samples with me?*

C Something, anything

We can use **something/anything**, **someone/anyone**, **somewhere/anywhere** in a similar way:

***Someone** has used my files, and now I can't find **anything anywhere**!*

D Free choice

We can give people permission to do things using **anything**, **anywhere**, etc.:

A *'Where should I sit?'*   B *'You can sit **anywhere**.'*
A *'What should I tell them?'*   B *'Tell them **anything** you like.'*

E How much and how many

We use **How many, not ... many, only ... a few** with plural countable nouns:

*'**How many** people did you talk to?'*
*'I did**n't** talk to **many** people. I **only** talked to **a few** people.'*

We use **How much, not ... much, only ... a little** with uncountable nouns:

*'**How much** money did you make last month?'*
*'We did**n't** make **much** money. We **only** made **a little** money.'*

In positive answers, we use **a lot of** with both countable and uncountable nouns:

*I met **a lot of people** at the conference. (This is more common than *many people*.)*
*We made **a lot of money** last year. (This is more common than *much money*.)*

Exercise 1
A/an, **some**, **any**

Underline the correct option from the words in italics.

1 I'd like *an/some* advice about the government's latest tax proposals.
2 I've just received *a/some* very nice gift from one of my suppliers.
3 Shall we carry on working, or would you like to go out for *a/some* meal?
4 Do you have *an/any* information about conference facilities in Monaco?
5 I just have to go to the bank to get *a/some* money.
6 Bill wants you to phone him. He says he has *a/some* good news for you.
7 Did you meet *an/any* interesting people at the trade fair?
8 The engineers are having *a/some* problems with the new engine.

Exercise 2
Some or **any**?

A manager is getting the results of some 'upward feedback', and is hearing what his staff think about him. Complete the dialogue with **some** or **any**.

MANAGER: So what did they say? Were there (1) _____ serious problems?
CONSULTANT: Well, we interviewed all the people who work for you, and there are (2) _____ aspects of your management style that are very good.
MANAGER: Did they make (3) _____ complaints? I'd like to start with them first.
CONSULTANT: As you like. There are some people who work for you who feel that you don't listen very much. They say that you don't spend (4) _____ time talking to them and that you seem very busy.
MANAGER: I am. Were there (5) _____ other criticisms?
CONSULTANT: Yes, but I would like to suggest (6) _____ ways of dealing with this particular point before we carry on. I think there should be (7) _____ fixed times when staff can come and see you. If they don't have (8) _____ opportunities to discuss their problems, they will feel nervous about coming to talk to you. The other thing that they mentioned is that you don't give them (9) _____ responsibility, and that they don't make (10) _____ decisions themselves. Now, this is a common problem, and I think it's something you should think about.

Exercise 3
Some or **any**?

Read the following sentences. Put a tick [✔] by the ones that are right, and correct the ones that are wrong.

1 Could you send me some information about your latest range of furniture?   _____✔
2 Did you make any progress in the meeting?   _____
3 I've got any letters for you to sign.   _____
4 Shall I send you some samples of our latest fabrics?   _____
5 We haven't had some major orders for several weeks.   _____
6 Would you like me to get you some money from the bank?   _____
7 I'm having any problems with this new software.   _____
8 Are there any seats left on the BA flight to Tokyo next Tuesday? _____

37 Practice

Exercise 4
Something, anything

Fill in the blanks with the words from the box.

> someone   anyone   something   anything   somewhere   anywhere

1 Did _anyone_ ring when I was out?
2 We've got to find that letter! It must be here _____ !
3 We returned the machines because there was _____ wrong with them.
4 By the way, _____ called in to see you when you were away last week.
5 These plans are secret. You mustn't discuss them with _____ .
6 We are trying to cut down on hotel bills, so now our executives can't stay _____ that costs more than $100 a night.
7 Yes, a meeting next Thursday would be fine. I'm not doing _____ .

Exercise 5
Free choice

Fill in the blanks with **anyone**, **anywhere**, or **anything**.

1 This is not confidential. You can discuss it with _____ you like.
2 If you hire a car, you will be able to go _____ you want.
3 I am now responsible for recruitment, so I can hire _____ I like.
4 George Soros' Quantum Fund has so much money that the company can buy almost _____ it wants.
5 You have to attend the course from 8.00 a.m. to 5.00 p.m., but in the evening you can do _____ you like.
6 Most of the hotels are empty, so you can stay _____ you like.

Exercise 6
Much, many, etc.

Two colleagues are discussing the opening of a new office in Madrid. Fill in the blanks with the words from the box.

> much   many   a lot of   a little   a few

A: How are things in Madrid?
B: We're nearly ready. We didn't have [1] _much_ trouble finding a suitable office. There seem to be [2] _____ empty places at the moment.
A: How [3] _____ work will you need to do on the building?
B: Nothing really. We only need to do [4] _____ painting and decorating and it will be fine.
A: How [5] _____ people are going to be working there?
B: About twenty. We've filled most of the jobs, so it'll only take [6] _____ weeks to find the other people we need. We haven't appointed a sales manager yet, but there has been [7] _____ interest in the job, so we'll get someone soon.
A: How [8] _____ time do you think you will spend there?
B: At the beginning, I'll have to spend [9] _____ time over there, so I have rented an apartment. But I'm hoping that it will only go on for [10] _____ months, and then the office will be able to look after itself.

....

Task 1

Answer the following questions, using the words in brackets.

1   Why do we need to stop at the garage? (any)
    We haven't got any petrol left.

2   Why did you see a lawyer? (some)
    _____

3   Are you sure they have moved offices? (somewhere)
    _____

4   Did you tell staff about the redundancies we are planning? (anything)
    _____

....

Task 2

Reply to the questions using **anyone/anywhere/anything** you like.

1   What is the company policy about hotels?
    You can stay anywhere you like.

2   Is this information confidential?
    _____

3   Are any of these seats reserved?
    _____

4   What sort of information can you store on a CD-ROM disk?
    _____

....

Task 3

Write short paragraphs answering the questions. Use the words in the box.

| not much   a lot of   a little   a few   not many |

I'm sorry to hear your trip wasn't successful. What went wrong?

1   Did you lose a lot of stock in the break-in?
    No. Luckily the burglars didn't have much time, because the alarm went off. They took a lot of cheap pieces of jewellery, and they took a little money as well.

2   I'm sorry to hear your trip wasn't a success. What went wrong?
    _____
    _____
    _____

3   Tell me about your training course in England. Did it go well?
    _____
    _____
    _____

38 Adjectives and adverbs

A Form of adverbs

Most adverbs can be formed by adding **-ly**, **-y**, **-ally**, or **-ily**, depending on the spelling of the adjective or noun on which they are based:

> **expensive/expensively** **full/fully**
> **dramatic/dramatically** **day/daily**

Some adverbs and adjectives have the same form. Common examples of these are:

> **hard**   **early**   **fast**   **late**
> **daily**   **weekly**   **monthly**   **quarterly**

Some words ending in **-ly** are adjectives and have no corresponding adverbs. Common examples are **friendly, elderly, lonely, silly, costly**.

B Adjectives vs adverbs

Adjectives describe nouns and adverbs are used to describe most verbs:

ADJECTIVE: *There has been a **significant** improvement in the economy.*
(Gives more information about the noun ***improvement.***)

ADVERB: *The economy has improved **significantly**.*
(Gives more information about the verb ***has improved**.*)

C Adverbs + adjectives, participles, adverbs

Adverbs can also describe adjectives, past participles, and other adverbs:

ADVERB + ADJECTIVE: *We have had a **relatively good** year.*

ADVERB + PAST PARTICIPLE: *Their products are always **attractively packaged**.*

ADVERB + ADVERB: *She does her job **extremely well**.*

D Verbs and adjectives

Some verbs are qualified by adjectives rather than adverbs. Most of these are verbs of appearance or verbs of the senses:

> **be**   **look**   **seem**   **appear**   **become**
> **get**   **smell**   **taste**   **sound**   **feel**

'You look tired. Are you all right?' (NOT: *look tiredly*)
Honda felt angry about the sale of Rover to BMW. (NOT: *felt angrily*)

E Good and well

Good is an adjective. **Well** is an irregular adverb:

*You ought to go to one of his presentations. He is a very **good** speaker.*
*You ought to go to one of his presentations. He speaks very **well**.*

The word **well** can also be an adjective meaning **in good health**:

*She isn't in the office today because she isn't **well**.*

Exercise 1
Form of adverbs

Fill in the blanks with words from the box. Make any changes to the adjectives necessary to form adverbs.

economic	hard	heavy	late	patient
public	punctual	quarter	safe	silent

1   When you get to New York, give me a ring to let me know you've arrived _safely_.
2   The Economic Review is published _____ , and comes out in March, June, September, and December.
3   Trains in Japan arrive so _____ that you can set your watch by them.
4   The train to the airport arrived _____ , and as a result I very nearly missed the plane.
5   Most stockbrokers will buy and sell shares in _____ -quoted companies.
6   Before privatization, many nationalized industries were _____ subsidized by the government.
7   He was not in a hurry, so he waited _____ until the client was ready to see him.
8   The new motor is very quiet, and at most speeds it operates almost _____ .

Exercise 2
Adjectives vs adverbs

Look at the graph showing the price of Fisons' shares. Rewrite the sentences using verbs and adverbs.

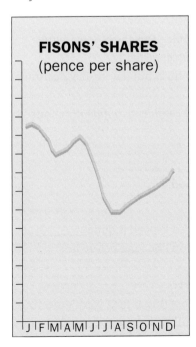

FISONS' SHARES
(pence per share)

J F M A M J J A S O N D

1   There was a sudden fall in March.
In March the shares fell _suddenly_ .

2   There was a brief recovery in April.
In April they recovered _____ .

3   In June there was a dramatic collapse.
In June they collapsed _____ .

4   There was a considerable fall in July.
In July they fell _____ .

5   There was only a slight fall in August.
In August they only fell _____ .

6   There was a steady improvement in September and October.
In September and October they improved _____ .

7   There was a gradual improvement from mid-November.
From mid-November, they improved _____ .

Exercise 3
Adverbs + participles/
adjectives/adverbs

Choose a word from box A and one from box B to complete the sentences.

A | surprisingly badly commercially well totally terribly

B | qualified quickly designed viable good illegal

1 She has a PhD and an MBA so she's certainly very *well qualified*.
2 The results at the end of the year were _____ , and certainly much better than we had thought.
3 The bank decided that the project was not _____ , so they refused to given them a loan.
4 Insider dealing is _____ – if they catch you, you could go to prison.
5 The engine on the XR86 was very _____ , and the car soon gained a reputation for unreliablilty.
6 He spoke _____ , so I couldn't really understand what he was saying.

Exercise 4
Adjective or adverb?

Choose either an adjective or an adverb from the words in italics.

1 Their new offices in the city look very *impressive/impressively*.
2 It's a pity that airline food never tastes as *good/well* as it looks.
3 He reacted *calm/calmly* when I told him the bad news.
4 The new perfume from Dior smells very *expensive/expensively*.
5 We stopped ordering from them, because a lot of their products were *bad/badly* designed.
6 They've changed the clocks, so now it gets *dark/darkly* at about 3.00 in the afternoon.
7 Waiter, could you bring us some more milk – this tastes *sour/sourly*.
8 Your new secretary seems very *competent/competently*.
9 Most policy decisions are taken at head office, but day-to-day decisions are taken *local/locally*.
10 When I spoke to Jeremy, he didn't sound *confident/confidently* about meeting this year's targets.

Exercise 5
Good and **well**

Complete the sentences with either **well** or **good**.

1 Did you have a *good* flight?
2 I've been learning English for three years, so I speak it quite _____ .
3 He's on sick leave at the moment, but it won't be long before he's _____ enough to return to work.
4 The magazine gave their latest fridge-freezers a very _____ review.
5 I think it would be a _____ idea to discuss this at next week's meeting.
6 Jane and I are old friends. We know each other very _____.
7 The new computer system seems to be working _____ .

Task 1

Read this letter from a retailer to a manufacturer of air-conditioners. Choose either the adjective or the adverb in brackets.

Dear Mrs Jones,

I am writing with reference to a (1) (_recent_/recently) shipment of 16 M-113 air-conditioning units which we received on Tuesday 17 May.

Unfortunately three of the units are not working (2)(proper/properly). One of them may have been broken in transit as the packing case was (3) (bad/badly) dented, and I suggest you take this matter up with your insurers. The two others looked (4) (fine/finely), but when we tested them they sounded very (5) (noisy/noisily), and their cooling systems seemed very (6) (ineffective/ineffectively).

I am therefore arranging for the three units to be returned to you (7) (immediate/ immediately). I would be (8) (grateful/gratefully) if you could send us three new units as soon as possible, as the (9) (warm/warmly) weather is approaching and we are expecting a (10) (strong/strongly) demand for air-conditioners in the next few weeks.

I look forward to hearing from you,

Henrietta Watson
Stores Manager

Task 2

Improve the following advertisement for a business handbook by adding adjectives or adverbs of your choice.

Hoover's Handbook is a (1) _revolutionary new_ book that gives a(n) (2)_____ insight into (3)_____ companies. Each (4)_____ profile includes a(n) (5)_____ company description and a resumé of the (6)_____ events in the company's history. Each profile is (7)_____ laid out and provides information about the company's (8)_____ Directors, its (9)_____ products, and its (10)_____ competitors.

'It's (11)_____ amazing that this wealth of information is available at such a(n) (12)_____ price. It's a(n) (13)_____ book for anyone interested in the (14)_____ business scene.'

(_Morgan Directory Reviews_)

Task 3

Write a short extract from a sales letter to a potential customer describing one of the products or services you offer.

I would like to tell you about ... _____

_____

39 Comparison (1): comparing adjectives

A **A** Short adjectives

To make comparisons, adjectives with one syllable add **-er** and **-est**:

	COMPARATIVE	SUPERLATIVE
old	older	the oldest
big	bigger	the biggest

BT is **large**. *NTT is* **larger than** *BT. AT&T is* **the largest** *company in the world.*

Two important exceptions are **good** and **bad**:

good	better	the best
bad	worse	the worst

Adjectives ending in **-y** (e.g., **friendly**, **wealthy**, **easy**) and some two-syllable adjectives (e.g., **clever**, **quiet**, **narrow**) follow this pattern:

friendly/friendlier/friendliest   **clever/cleverer/cleverest**

B Longer adjectives

With most other two-syllable adjectives, and other adjectives with three or more syllables, we use **more/less** and the **most/the least**:

	COMPARATIVE	SUPERLATIVE
modern	more/less modern	the most modern
profitable	more/less profitable	the most profitable

Toyota is **profitable**. *BT is* **more profitable than** *Toyota. The Royal Dutch Shell Group is* **the most profitable** *company in the world.*

C Not as ... as, etc.

We can also make comparisons using **not as ... as**, **as ... as**, and **just as ... as**. In this case the adjective does not change:

BT is not **as large as** *AT&T.*
In America, Toyota is **as well-known as** *Ford.*
Pepsi is **just as popular as** *Coca-Cola.*

D The present perfect and superlatives

The present perfect **ever** is often used with superlatives:

We're having **the best** *year that we* **have ever had**.
He's one of **the most interesting** *people I* **have ever met.**

E Ranking

The superlative can be used with **the second**, **third**, **fourth**, etc. to talk about the position of something in a list:

Siemens is **the largest** *electronics company in Europe.*
Philips is **the second largest** *electronics company in Europe.*

Exercise 1
Form

Complete the table showing the adjectives and their comparative and superlative forms.

valuable	more valuable than	the most valuable
_____	_____	the most expensive
good	_____	_____
_____	wealthier than	_____
_____	_____	the biggest
narrow	_____	_____
_____	cheaper than	_____
_____	_____	the worst
profitable	_____	_____
_____	longer than	_____
_____	_____	the most interesting

Exercise 2
Comparatives

Fill in the blanks by putting the adjectives into the correct form.

Two multinational consumer giants, Sony and Philips, are fighting a fierce war to provide a replacement for the standard cassette tape. Sony has produced the Minidisc, and Philips has backed the Digital Compact Cassette (DCC).

According to Sony, the Minidisc will appeal to a (1) _wider_ (wide) range of consumers than DCC. The minidiscs themselves are (2) _____ (small) and (3) _____ (portable) than DCCs, and the players are (4) _____ (easy) to carry around. Sony claims that its sales figures are much (5) _____ (good) than Philips's, and that it will win the war. Philips points out that Sony's sales of Minidisc players refer to units shipped, not actual sales, and that the real sales figure is much (6) _____ (low). Philips, which has spent £65m in developing DCCs, says that the sound quality of Minidiscs is not as (7) _____ (good) as DCCs, and that DCC players, which are (8) _____ (large) and (9) _____ (sophisticated) than Sony's, will sell to (10) _____ (serious) customers.

According to Philips, there is room for both products. Its spokesperson said, 'The Minidisc will appeal to people who want a tiny, expensive Walkman to show off, and DCC will sell to (11) _____ (quality-conscious) consumers. The minidisc is a much (12) _____ (sexy) idea, sure, but DCC is much (13) _____ (sensible).'

Business Age, February 94

39 Practice

Exercise 3
Superlatives

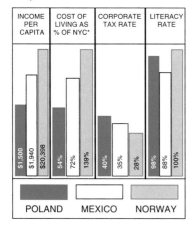

INCOME PER CAPITA	COST OF LIVING AS % OF NYC*	CORPORATE TAX RATE	LITERACY RATE
$1,500 $1,940 $20,398	54% 72% 139%	40% 35% 28%	98% 88% 100%

POLAND　MEXICO　NORWAY

Read the information about Poland, Mexico, and Norway. Using superlatives, write sentences comparing them. (* = New York City)

1 income per capita/high　*Norway has the highest income per capita.*
2 income per capita/low　*Poland has the lowest income per capita.*
3 expensive/to live in　_____
4 cheap/to live in　_____
5 corporate tax rate/high　_____
6 corporate tax rate/low　_____
7 literacy rate/good　_____
8 literacy rate/bad　_____

Exercise 4
Present perfect and superlatives

Rewrite the sentences using the present perfect and a superlative.

1 I have never been to such a long meeting.
　That was the longest meeting I have ever been to.

2 I have never heard such a boring presentation.
　That was_____

3 I have never dealt with such difficult customers.
　They are _____

4 We have never produced a product as good as this.
　This is _____

5 I have never used a program as simple as this.
　This is _____

Exercise 5
Ranking

Read the information and write sentences using the words in brackets.

1 In 1991, British Telecom made profits of $3,557 million.
　It is (no.2/profitable company/world) *the second most profitable company in the world.*

2 Yoshiaki Tsutsumi deals in land, railways, and resorts, and has a personal fortune of $10 billion. He is (no.2/rich/person/world).

　_____

3 Exxon had sales of $103,242 million in 1991.
　It is (no.3/large/industrial corporation/world).

　_____

4 Eviran Haub from Germany owns supermarkets, and is worth $6.9 billion. He is (no.4/wealthy/person/world).

　_____

....
Task 1

Write sentences comparing the following items.

1   The company I work for/the last company I worked for
     (big) _The company I work for is bigger than the last company I worked for._
     (small) _It is not as small as the last company I worked for._

2   The job I do now/my last job
     (hard to do) _____
     (easy to do) _____

3   Inflation this year/it was last year
     (high) _____
     (low) _____

4   Our company/our main competitor
     (large) _____
     (small) _____

....
Task 2

Complete the sentences using the present perfect and a superlative adjective.

1   good meal/have _The best meal I have ever had was in France._

2   interesting course/go on _____

3   good computer/use _____

4   nice country/visit _____

5   expensive hotel/stay in _____

6   fast car/drive _____

7   reasonable boss/work for _____

8   bad job/have _____

....
Task 3

Write a short paragraph comparing one of your products or services with a product or service of one of your competitors. Here is an example.

I work for Darlingtons, a law firm that specializes in commercial property, and our main competitors are Kenworth & Brown. We are not as large as they are, but we have the best taxation department in the City. Because we are smaller, we offer our clients a better service, and our charges are significantly lower.

_____
_____
_____
_____
_____

40 Comparison (2): comparing adverbs and comparing nouns

A Pattern 1: short adverbs

Most adverbs of one syllable, and the adverb **early**, add **-er** and **-est**. These adverbs are usually the ones that have the same form as the adjective:

early	**earlier**	**the earliest**
fast	**faster**	**the fastest**

*He usually arrives **earlier** than I do.*

The most important irregular short adverbs are **well** and **badly**:

well	**better**	**the best**
badly	**worse**	**the worst**

*The company did slightly **worse** than the analysts had expected.*

B Pattern 2: longer adverbs

Adverbs with two or more syllables are compared using **more/less** and **the most/least**:

efficiently	**more/less efficiently**	**the most/least efficiently**
fluently	**more/less fluently**	**the most/least fluently**

*All our manufacturing plants are efficient, but at the moment the one in northern France is operating **the most efficiently**.*

C Adverbs and participles

We often need adverbs when we are comparing present participles (e.g., **growing**) and past participles (e.g., **chosen, given**):

*South East Asia has one of the **fastest growing** economies in the world.*
*She is one of the **best qualified** people in the department.*
*The Engineering Division is much **more efficiently run** than the Plastics Division.*

D Comparing nouns

We can compare quantities and amounts by using **more, less, fewer, not as much as, not as many as**, etc. The correct word depends on whether the noun in question is countable or uncountable (see Unit 35):

COUNTABLE
*The board decided that the company needed **more/fewer** retail outlets.*
*Our Paris office doesn't employ **as many** people **as** our Munich office.*
*The R&D Department has **the most/fewest** people working for it.*

UNCOUNTABLE
*I spent **more/less** time on the project than I had expected.*
*We did**n't** make **as much** money on the deal **as** we had hoped.*
*Of all our surveys, this produced **the most/least** information.*

Exercise 1
Short adverbs

Complete the sentences with the comparative forms of the adverbs in the box.

early	fast	late	well	badly

1 I arrived in New York a little _later_ than I had planned because the plane was delayed by bad weather.
2 PCs with clock speeds of 66 mhz process information much _____ than PCs that run at only 33 mhz.
3 I got to the meeting a few minutes _____ than the others, so I had time to look through my papers before we started.
4 The company did _____ than analysts had been expecting, so their shares fell when they announced their losses for the year.
5 I speak Spanish well, but my assistant speaks it even _____ than I do.

Exercise 2
Longer adverbs

Complete the sentences with the comparative form of adverbs in the box.

carefully	frequently	quietly	slowly	efficiently

1 I don't think Qantas flies to Paris very often. Air France flies there much _more frequently._
2 There were a lot of mistakes in that report you gave me last week. I think you need to check your figures a bit _____ .
3 Could you speak a little _____ , please? I don't understand English very well.
4 The new engine uses fuel _____ than previous models, so it is cheaper to run.
5 We used to have a very noisy dot matrix printer, but the new ink jet prints much _____ .

Exercise 3
Adverbs and participles

Rewrite the sentences using superlatives and present or past participles.

1 In the earthquake, few areas were affected as badly as southern California.
In the earthquake, southern California was one of the _worst affected_ areas.

2 Few drugs on the market have been tested as extensively as this.
This is one of _____ drugs on the market.

3 None of our products is selling as well as this.
This is our _____ product.

4 Few departments in the company are managed as efficiently as this one.
This is one of _____ departments in the company.

5 Few countries in the world are developing as rapidly as Taiwan.
Taiwan is one of _____ countries in the world.

6 Few buildings in London are protected as heavily as the Bank of England.
The Bank of England is one of _____ buildings in London.

40 Practice

Exercise 4a
Comparing countable nouns

Compare the fuel consumption of three 4-wheel drive vehicles, measured in miles per gallon (m/gall), using **more ... than, the most, fewer ... than, the fewest, not as many ... as**.

	4X		V6		Hobo	
	m/gal	gall/100	m/gall	gall/100	m/gall	gall/100
Town driving	21.5	4.65	19.0	5.26	19.5	5.12
Motorway driving	23.0	4.35	21.0	4.76	18.5	5.40
Touring	29.5	3.39	25.0	4.0	26.0	3.85
Average	24.0	4.16	21.5	4.65	21.0	4.76

1 In town, the 4X does _the most_ miles to the gallon.
2 In town, the Hobo does _____ miles to the gallon _____ the V6.
3 On the motorway, the Hobo does _____ miles to the gallon.
4 On the motorway, the V6 does not do _____ miles to the gallon _____ the 4X.
5 Touring, the Hobo does _____ miles to the gallon _____ the 4X.
6 Touring, the V6 does _____ miles to the gallon.
7 On average, the Hobo does _____ miles to the gallon.
8 On average, the 4X does _____ miles to the gallon than the V6.

Exercise 4b
Comparing uncountable nouns

Read the information again. Now compare how much petrol each car uses per 100 miles (gall/100), using **more ... than, less ... than, not as much ... as, the most, the least**.

1 In town, the Hobo uses _more_ petrol _than_ the 4X.
2 In town, the V6 uses _____ petrol of the three models.
3 On the motorway, the Hobo uses _____ petrol _____ the V6.
4 On the motorway, the 4X uses _____ petrol of the three models.
5 When touring, the Hobo does not use _____ petrol _____ the V6.
6 When touring, the Hobo uses _____ petrol _____ the 4X.
7 On average, the V6 uses _____ petrol _____ the Hobo.
8 On average, the Hobo uses _____ petrol of the three models.

Exercise 5
Review: comparing countable and uncountable nouns

Complete the sentences with **more, less, much, many,** or **fewer**.

1 Eurotunnel may never make a profit because the tunnel cost substantially _____ money to build than they had expected.
2 Because of ATMs, banks don't have as _____ branches as they used to.
3 They made 2,000 staff redundant, so now they employ _____ people than they did last year.
4 Now that I'm in management, I don't spend as _____ time at home.

....

Task 1

Write sentences comparing your life now with your life five years ago. Use a comparative adverb (e.g., **more easily**), or **not as ... as**.

1   How early do you get up now?
    I get up earlier than I used to. or *I don't get up as early as I used to.*

2   How regularly do you go abroad now? _____ I used to.

3   How hard do you work now? _____ I used to.

4   How late do you stay at work now? _____ I used to.

5   How well do you speak English now? _____ I used to.

6   How far from work do you live now? _____ I used to.

....

Task 2

Complete the sentences using an adverb of your choice in the superlative.

1   Of the three of us, I would say that I probably drive *the fastest*.

2   Of all the people in the Sales Department, I think Peter works

    _____ .

3   We all go abroad quite often, but Jane goes _____ .

4   Of all the shares I have, the ones I have in ICI have performed

    _____ .

5   Of all the companies we looked at, DHL deliver mail

    _____ .

6   I did not like any of their reps at all, but I thought Henry behaved

    _____ .

....

Task 3

Answer the questions comparing the present with five years ago. Use **more than**, **less than**, **fewer than**, **not as much as**, or **not as many as** in your answers. You can use these phrases without a noun if the context is clear.

1   Do you do a lot of work at the weekends?
    I don't do as much work as I used to. or *I don't do as much as I used to.*

2   Do you have a lot of free time?

    _____

3   Do you go to a lot of parties?

    _____

4   Do you listen to a lot of music?

    _____

5   Do you get a lot of sleep?

    _____

6   Do you buy a lot of books?

    _____

165

41 Degree: **too**, **enough**, **so**, **such**, **such a**

A Too

Notice the position of **too**, **too much**, and **too many** in the sentences:

BEFORE ADJECTIVES:	*We can't afford another photocopier. They're **too expensive**.*
BEFORE ADVERBS:	*I can't understand what he says. He talks **too quickly**.*
BEFORE COUNTABLE NOUNS:	*We've got **too many employees**.*
BEFORE UNCOUNTABLE NOUNS:	*You spent **too much time** on that project.*
AFTER VERBS:	*You **talk too much**.*

B Enough

Notice the position of **enough** in these sentences:

AFTER ADJECTIVES:	*I feel I'm **experienced enough** to apply for promotion.*
AFTER ADVERBS:	*I'll need an interpreter. I don't know English **well enough**.*
BEFORE NOUNS:	*Have you ordered **enough chairs** for the presentation?*
AFTER VERBS:	*I don't think we **advertise enough**.*

C Too/enough (+ for) + infinitive

Too and (**not**) **enough** can be followed by an infinitive or **for** someone/something + infinitive. We do not use a pronoun at the end of a sentence:

The manual was too complicated. I couldn't understand it.
*The manual was **too** complicated (**for me**) **to understand**.* (NOT: *... to understand it.*)

D So and such

So and **such** can be used to add emphasis. **So** is used with adjectives and adverbs, and **such** (**a**) is used with a noun or adjective + noun:

(**so** before adjectives and adverbs)	*You're **so reliable**. You work **so hard**.*
(**such a** with singular countable nouns)	*I've got **such a good accountant**.*
(**such** with plural countable nouns)	*He has **such good ideas**.*
(**such** with uncountable nouns)	*He gives me **such good advice**.*
(**so much** with uncountable nouns)	*I have **so much work** to do.*
(**so many** with plural countable nouns)	*There are **so many people** here!*

E So and such (a) + that

So and **such** with **that** express result. **So** is used with adjectives and adverbs:

*The manual was **so complicated that** I couldn't understand it.*
*The manual was written **so badly that** I couldn't understand it.*

Such (**a**) is used with an adjective + noun:

*They were **such noisy machines that** we couldn't hear her voice.*
*It was **such a bad manual that** I couldn't understand it.*

Exercise 1
Too/enough + adjectives
and verbs

Put either **too** or **enough** in the correct space in each sentence. Put a dash
(–) in the other space.

1   We need new premises. This building isn't ____–____ big _enough_ .
2   We've changed our insurers because we felt the premiums we were
    paying were _____ high _____ .
3   He's not a very good manager – he doesn't communicate his ideas
    _____ clearly _____ .
4   It's never _____ early _____ to start contributing to a pension.
5   You'd better fax them the information. If you post it, it will arrive
    _____ late _____ .
6   You needn't rewrite the report. It's _____ good _____ .

Exercise 2
Too/enough + nouns

The Publicity Manager of a book distribution company is commenting on
the first draft of this year's catalogue. Fill in the blanks with **too much, too
many, too few,** or **too little.**

1   There are _too many_ sections. They make the catalogue confusing.
2   There are _____ printing errors. These must be corrected.
3   There is _____ space given to new titles. They should have a whole page.
4   There is _____ information about each title. It needs to be shorter.
5   There are _____ different text styles. We have to make it more varied.
6   There are _____ entries in the index. This needs to be much shorter.

Exercise 3

Too/enough + infinitive

Combine the following sentences using **too** and **enough.**

1   The exhibition was too far away. We couldn't attend it.
    The exhibition was too far away for us to attend.

2   Your products are too expensive. We can't stock them.

    _____

3   This contract is too complicated. I can't understand it.

    _____

4   My fax wasn't clear enough. He couldn't read it.

    _____

5   Your quotation wasn't low enough. We couldn't accept it.

    _____

6   The project was too risky. They couldn't go ahead with it.

    _____

41 Practice

Exercise 4
So and **such**

Fill in the blanks with **so** or **such**. Then match the words to the things they describe.

1 _so_   entertaining/such marvellous acting/written _so_ well
2 ____   good graphics/ ____ fast/ ____ user-friendly
3 ____   a good idea/ ____ clever/ ____ useful
4 ____   light/decorated ____ beautifully/ ____ modern
5 ____   tasty/presented ____ nicely/ ____ good value
6 ____   nice weather/ ____ friendly people/ ____ lovely beaches
7 ____   illogical/ ____ useful/ ____ easy to learn
8 ____   fair/ ____ a good sense of humour/ ____ supportive

an office	an invention	a language	a colleague	a film
a computer	a meal in a restaurant	a holiday destination		

Exercise 5
So/such + that

Match the sentences in column A with the results in column B. Then re-write them as one sentence, using **so** and **such**.

The meeting went on for such a long time that I missed the train home.

A

1 *The meeting went on for a long time.*
2 The company was in a very bad financial state.
3 Frankfurt was very busy during the book fair.
4 They treat their employees very well.
5 My portable computer is very unreliable.
6 The new drug was very successful.
7 He had a very good CV.

B

A The factory couldn't meet the demand for it.
B Nobody ever wants to leave.
C We decided to interview him.
D They called in the receivers.
E *I missed the train home.*
F We couldn't get a hotel room.
G I don't like to use it.

Reply to these questions using your own ideas and **too** and **enough**.

1   Why are you thinking about moving jobs?
    I've been there too long.

2   Why don't you think we should give him the job?
    _____

3   Why can't we use your office for the meeting?
    _____

4   Why don't you get on with your boss?
    _____

5   Why can't you finish the job by Friday?
    _____

6   Why didn't you go on the course?
    _____

Rewrite the following sentences in two ways, using **too** and **not enough**.

1   Emerging markets are too volatile. You shouldn't invest in them.
    A   (too/volatile) *Emerging markets are too volatile to invest in.*
    B   (enough/stable) *Emerging markets aren't stable enough to invest in.*

2   Their forecasts are always very inaccurate. We never use them.
    A   (too/inaccurate) _____
    B   (enough/accurate)_____

3   Our tax laws are very complicated. Most people can't understand them.
    A   (too/complicated) _____
    B   (enough/simple) _____

4   Rents in the city are very high. We can't have an office there.
    A   (too/high) _____
    B   (enough/low) _____

5   The town is very small. We don't have a branch in it.
    A   (too/small) _____
    B   (enough/big)_____

Add extra comments to these sentences, using **so** or **such**.

1   I'm surprised he is the Managing Director. *He seems so young.*
2   I've got to get to bed early tonight._____
3   I really thought you were English. _____
4   I am amazed that she has resigned _____
5   How can she complain about her salary? _____
6   I always go to his talks. _____

42 Adjective + preposition combinations

A Adjectives + prepositions

Many adjectives are followed by a particular preposition. Here is a list of common adjectives and the prepositions that normally follow them:

accustomed to	afraid of	answerable to
attached to	aware of	capable of
dependent on	different to	doubtful about
enthusiastic about	excited about	famous for
guilty of	interested in	opposed to
pleased with	popular with	proud of
related to	rich in	satisfied with
serious about	similar to	suitable for
suspicious of	used to (= accustomed to)	

B Form

These adjectives and prepositions may be followed by a noun or noun phrase:

*The engineers were very **excited about** the results of the tests.*

When followed by a verb, the **-ing** form must be used:

*Please let me know whether you would be **interested in arranging** a meeting.*

C Adjective + choice of preposition

Some adjectives can be followed by either of two or more prepositions. Look at these common examples and at the differences in meaning:

annoyed about something	*He was **annoyed about** the criticisms in the papers.*
annoyed with someone	*They were **annoyed with** us for charging them extra.*
good/bad at something	*I'm very **bad at** mathematics.*
good/bad for something	*Another cut in interest rates would be **good for** industry.*
good/bad with something	*She should be in Personnel. She's very **good with** people.*
responsible to someone	*The Export Manager is **responsible to** the Sales Director.*
responsible for something	*Who is **responsible for** making conference arrangements?*
sorry about something	*I am sorry about the job. It's a shame you didn't get it.*
sorry for doing something	*He said he was **sorry for** keeping me waiting.*
(feel) sorry for someone	*I feel very **sorry for** Peter. He has been fired.*

Exercise 1
Adjectives + prepositions

Complete the sentences with a suitable preposition or adjective. Then complete the word comb.

1 The Bordeaux region of France is famous _for_ its fine wines. (3 letters)
2 If you are serious _____ going ahead with this, let's have a meeting. (5)
3 The Mini-TV is very popular _____ our younger customers. (4)
4 The NV8 Camcorder is _____ to the NV7 in many ways, but it has some interesting new features. (7)
5 The salesman did not want to sell me the most expensive model he had because he said it would not really be _____ for me. (8)
6 Wage demands are _____ to inflation in a number of important ways. (7)
7 The Finance Director said he was strongly _____ to awarding everyone a 10% pay rise, and explained that the company could not afford it. (7)
8 South Africa is _____ in natural resources like diamonds and gold. (4)
9 I have to travel by car or boat because I am _____ of flying. (6)
10 He has very little experience. I don't think he would be _____ of running such a large project. (7)
11 He was found _____ of fraud and was sent to prison for three years. (6)
12 I would be very _____ in discussing the idea of a joint venture. (10)

1	☐☐☐
2	☐☐☐☐☐
3	☐☐☐☐
4	☐☐☐☐☐☐☐
5	☐☐☐☐☐☐☐☐
6	☐☐☐☐☐☐☐
7	☐☐☐☐☐☐☐
8	☐☐☐☐
9	☐☐☐☐☐☐
10	☐☐☐☐☐☐☐
11	☐☐☐☐☐☐
12	☐☐☐☐☐☐☐☐☐☐

Exercise 2
Form

Fill in the blanks with the verbs from the box, using the **-ing** form.

buy	hire	manufacture	move	run	take

1 I am interested in _buying_ a new computer. Could you tell me a little about the different models you have?
2 Some of the staff are not very enthusiastic about _____ to our new offices.
3 My boss is not afraid of _____ risks.
4 Most politicians know nothing about business, and wouldn't be capable of _____ a small business.
5 Our Personnel Manager is responsible for _____ new staff.
6 Rolls Royce is famous for _____ hand-made luxury cars.

....

Exercise 3
Adjectives + choice of
prepositions

Fill in each blank with a word from box A and a word from box B.

A
annoyed   bad   good responsible   sorry

B
about   at   for to   with

1   I heard him shouting at you. What was he so *annoyed about*?
2   I am _____ your holiday; it must·have been disappointing to have to come home early.
3   The activities of the Insurance Division were _____ a large part of the company's profits.
4   She was _____ her secretary for forgetting to send the letter in time.
5   Sales reps are _____ the Area Manager; her boss is the Export Director.
6   He said he was _____ not calling back, but something had come up.
7   He's _____ his job, but unfortunately he's very _____ customers.
8   Falls in the value of the pound are _____ British exporters.

....

Exercise 4
Review

Complete this letter from a conference centre to a potential customer, using the words in the box.

accustomed   aware   capable   famous   good   interested popular   proud   responsible   rich

Dear Miss Harman,

I was delighted to hear that you may choose Warner Park Hotel as the venue for your next conference, and am writing to introduce myself as the person [1] *responsible* for liaising with potential conference organizers.

We are [2] _____ of the very high level of service we offer and are [3] _____ to organizing conferences of up to two thousand delegates. As you will see from the enclosed brochure, we are [4] _____ of organizing anything from an AGM to a major international conference. Past clients have included BT, ICI, and Hanson, and these firms believe that a successful conference can be very [5] _____ for business in the following year.

The hotel has an excellent range of facilities and no doubt you will be [6] _____ of the fact that the local area is [7] _____ in cultural interest. In addition, our restaurant is [8] _____ for its excellent cuisine, and I am enclosing samples of menus that have been [9] _____ with conference delegates in the past.

Please let me know whether you would be [10] _____ in taking the matter further, and I will be happy to meet you to discuss any special requirements you may have.

I look forward to hearing from you.

Yours sincerely,

Royston.

Lionel Royston
(Managing Director)

Task 1   Rewrite the sentences, using the words in brackets.

1   A lot of executives like the BMW 500 series.
     (popular) _The BMW 500 series is popular with executives._

2   I don't think she can do the work.
     (capable) _____

3   Everyone knows Bordeaux because of its fine wines.
     (famous) _____

4   Janet is the person who hires new staff.
     (responsible) _____

5   The Industrial Society thinks that higher taxes are a bad idea.
     (opposed) _____

6   Would you like to arrange a meeting?
     (interested) _____

Task 2   Answer the following questions, using the words in italics.

1   What are you *responsible* for in your job?
     In my job, I'm responsible for researching into new allergy drugs.

2   Who are you *answerable* to?
     _____

3   What are you *good* at?
     _____

4   What other jobs in the company would you be *capable* of doing?
     _____

5   What sort of salary would you be *satisfied* with?
     _____

Task 3   Using a word from box A, and a word from box B, write sentences about
         yourself.

A

| capable | interested | different |
| afraid | proud | similar |

B

| to | of | of |
| in | of | from |

1   _I think I would be capable of doing what my boss does._
2   _____
3   _____
4   _____
5   _____
6   _____

43 Noun + preposition combinations

A Nouns + prepositions

Here is a list of nouns and the prepositions normally used with them:

advantage of	advice on	alternative to
application for	benefit of	cause of
cheque for	cost of	demand for
difference between	example of	experience of, in
fall in, of	increase/decrease in, of	invitation to
interest in	lack of	matter with
need for	opinion of	order for
price of	reason for	reply to
request for	rise in, of	solution to
tax on	trouble with	

B Nouns followed by a choice of prepositions

Words referring to increases and decreases can be followed by **in** or **of**. **In** refers to something that has risen or fallen; **of** refers to a quantity or amount:

*There has been a large fall **in** unemployment over the last few months.*
*There has been a fall **of** 9.7%.*

C Prepositions + nouns

Here is a list of some common preposition and noun combinations:

at a good price	at a profit/loss	at cost price
at your convenience	at short notice	by post
by hand	by return	by cheque
by law	by car, bus, airmail	by mistake
for sale	for lunch	in advance
in stock	in writing	in general
in the end	in a hurry	in my opinion
in bulk	in charge of	in debt
on application	on sale	on loan
on holiday	on business	on a trip
on hold	on the phone	on television
on the whole	on order	on time
out of order	out of date	to my mind
under pressure	with reference to	

Look at the following examples:

*This matter is urgent. Please reply **by return**.*
*Could you please confirm your order **in writing**.*
*The traffic is so bad I usually get into the centre **by taxi**.* (NOT: *by the taxi*.)

Exercise 1
Noun + preposition

Complete the sentences using a noun from box A and a preposition from box B.

A	
difference	solution
request	invitation
experience	reply
trouble	advantage
cheque	price

B	
of	to
of	for
of	for
to	between
to	with

1   Thank you very much for your _invitation to_ the launch party.
2   At the moment the bank is considering our _____ a larger overdraft, and it will let us have a decision next week.
3   In my opinion, the _____ having a credit card is that you can pay for things over the phone.
4   Have we received a _____ that letter we sent them last week?
5   Yes, they have paid us. We received a _____ £1800 a few days ago.
6   I don't think he would be suitable for the job in Tokyo. He has had very little _____ working overseas.
7   In the long term, inflation is linked to the _____ raw materials.
8   Is there any _____ these two fax machines? They look the same to me.
9   We had a lot of _____ one of our customers who wouldn't pay us, so we took legal advice.
10 Let me know if you can think of a _____ the problem.

Exercise 2
Noun + choice of prepositions

In the newspaper extracts, fill in the blanks with **in** or **of**.

1   There has been an unexpected fall _____ the number of people looking for work. Figures released yesterday showed a fall _____ 28,900 in August, and ministers said that this was a sign that the recovery was going well.

2   The Bundesbank announced yesterday an interest rate rise _____ 0.5%, taking the annual figure to 7.5%. The rise _____ rates had a negative effect on shares, which fell sharply in Frankfurt and London.

3   The increase _____ inflation seem to be slowing down. Figures released this morning showed an increase _____ only 0.15% last month, compared to a rise _____ 0.4% the previous month.

43 Practice

Exercise 3
Preposition + noun
combinations

In the following telephone conversations, fill in the blanks with the missing prepositions.

A A: Hello, Finance.

B: Good morning. I'm calling (1) _____ reference to a cheque I've just had from you. I'm afraid you have put the wrong year on it (2) _____ mistake. The bank have just returned it because it is (3) _____ date.

A: I'm so sorry. It must be because it's January. If you send it back we'll issue a new one (4) _____ return.

B A: Hello, can you put me through to the Marketing Department, please?

B: Yes, of course ... I'm afraid the line's busy, I'll have to put you (1) _____ hold for a moment.

A: OK ...

C: Hello, Marketing.

A: Could I speak to the person who is (2) _____ charge of booking advertising space, please?

C: I'm afraid she's away (3) _____ business at the moment. Can I help you?

A: Well, we are currently offering some attractive discounts for next month's issue of *Face* magazine.

C: Well, (4) _____ the whole we don't book advertising space (5) _____ such short notice, but if you'd like to give us details of your rates (6) _____ writing, we'll look at them and let you know.

Exercise 4
Review

Complete the following advertisement with the missing prepositions.

THE MOST IMPORTANT INVESTMENT YOU'LL EVER MAKE

More and more parents are looking to independent schools to provide an alternative (1) *to* state education.

However, the cost (2) _____ sending a child to boarding school from 7 to 18 can be as much as £150,000, and annual increases (3) _____ school fees are often greater than inflation.

So there is a need (4) _____ specialist advice, and we at Knight Willis have many years of experience (5) _____ helping parents plan for their children's education (6) _____ advance. Early planning can help to achieve reductions (7) _____ over 75%, and (8) _____ the whole, the earlier the school fee plan is started, the greater the savings.

If you would like our advice (9) _____ the best way to plan for your child's future, please fill in the reply-paid form below. We will send you examples (10) _____ different school fee plans, and we can discuss these (11) _____ the phone or at a meeting (12) _____ your own convenience.

Task 1

Complete the following sentences using your own ideas.

1 I don't have much experience *of dealing with difficult customers.*

2 I don't think there is much difference _____

3 I think unemployment is responsible for the rise _____

4 It will be difficult to find a solution _____

5 During the winter months, the demand _____

Task 2

Rewrite the following sentences in a different way, using one of the phrases from page 170, section C (prepositions + nouns).

1 This machine doesn't work. *This machine is out of order.*

2 Quick! I can't wait. _____

3 We lost money when we sold the car. _____

4 I usually drive to work. _____

5 The train did not arrive late. _____

6 My house is on the market. _____

7 He owes money. _____

8 We expect delivery of the goods soon. _____

Task 3

(IDIOMS) **at first, second, etc hand** (used about information that you have received) from sb who was directly/not directly involved: *I have only heard about it at second hand* (= not from sb who was actually there). ☞ Look at **second-hand**.
(close/near) at hand (*formal*) near in space or time: *Help is close at hand.*
be an old hand (at sth) ⟩ OLD
by hand 1 done by a person and not by machine: *I had to do all the sewing by hand.*

in your/sb's hands in your/sb's possession, control or care: *The document is no longer in my hands.* ○ *The matter is in the hands of a solicitor.* ○ *She is in capable hands.*
off your hands not your responsibility any more: *Once the children are off our hands we want to go on a world cruise.*
on hand available to help or to be used: *There is a teacher on hand to help during your private study periods.*
on your hands being your responsibility: *We seem to have a problem on our hands.*
on the one hand... on the other (hand) (used for showing opposite points of view): *On the one hand, of course, cars are very useful. But on the other, they cause a huge amount of pollution.*
out of hand not under control: *Violence at football matches is getting out of hand.* ☞ Look at **in hand**.
out of your/sb's hands not in your/sb's control: *I can't help you, I'm afraid. The matter is out of my hands.*

Look through the extract from a dictionary, which gives a number of different idioms using the word **hand**. Then fill in the blanks with the correct expression.

1 I have a problem *on my hands*, and I'd like your advice about what to do.

2 At first, some of the strikers on the picket line threw stones at the police; then more joined in and soon the demonstration got _____.

3 We don't use machines at all; everything is made _____.

4 When you arrive at your holiday villa, one of our representatives will be _____ to help you with any problems you may have.

5 I can't stop the court case from going ahead. Everything is now _____ of my lawyer, and I can't discuss it with you.

6 On the one hand, a job in England would be a good career move for me. _____, I would miss the people I know here in Milan.

44 Verb + preposition combinations

....

A Verb + preposition

Here is a list of common verbs and the prepositions that normally follow them:

account for	agree on	agree with
apply for	belong to	take care of
complain to	comply with	consist of
depend on	hear about	hear from
look at	look for	pay for
rely on	talk to	think about
think of	wait for	write to

*After several hours, the committee **agreed on** a joint statement.*
*I really like the new design. What do you **think of** it?*
*The new building will have to **comply with** tough planning regulations*

....

B Verb + object + preposition

The following verbs can be followed by an object and a preposition:

ask someone **for**	**blame** someone **for**
borrow something **from**	**congratulate** someone **on**
divide something **into**	**insure** something **against**
invest something **in**	**protect** someone **from**
provide someone **with**	**spend** something **on**
supply someone **with**	**thank** someone **for**

*We **spent** too much **on** advertising last year.*
*Could you **supply** us **with** 200 units a month?*
*Management **blamed** the union **for** provoking the strike.*

....

C Verb + no preposition

These verbs are not usually followed by a preposition:

phone	meet	enter	tell	discuss

*I'll **phone** the company tomorrow morning.* (NOT: *phone to the company*)
*Do you need a visa to **enter** the EU?* (NOT: *enter into the EU*)

NOTE: We can say **have a meeting with** someone, and in American English it is also possible to say **meet with** someone.

Exercise 1
Verb + preposition

Complete the following letter with the correct prepositions.

Dear Mr Hall

Thank you for your letter of 18 May regarding the Kinderbox range of children's paints. The answers to the questions you raised are as follows:

1 All Kinderbox products fully comply (1) *with* European and British safety standards. The paints are non-toxic and washable. Each pack in the Junior range consists (2) _____ a paintbox with eight colours, a paintbrush, and a leaflet in English.

2 The average delivery time for orders to England over DM 5,000 is four days. We do not rely (3) _____ rail transport, so delivery would not be affected by the current train strike. We also take care (4) _____ insurance and export documentation.

3 The level of discount we offer depends (5) _____ the size of orders and their regularity. I would be happy to talk (6) _____ you about this.

4 Goods may be paid (7) _____ in Deutschmarks or sterling, and we offer flexible credit arrangements, so I am confident we could agree (8) _____ suitable credit terms.

Please do not hesitate to contact me if you have any further questions, and I look forward to hearing (9) _____ you.

Yours sincerely,

W. Habisreutinger

Wolfgang Habisreutinger
Sales Manager

Exercise 2
Verb + preposition

Complete the sentences with a word from box A and a word from box B.

A		
agree	hear	look
think	wait	write

B		
about	at	for
of	to	with

1 Mr Langer thinks we should go ahead with this proposal, but I'm afraid that I don't *agree with* him.

2 Did you _____ what happened in the meeting? George resigned.

3 Please _____ me at the above address or phone me on 082 756 4537.

4 How long do you think we will have to _____ a reply to our proposal?

5 I am not sure about these changes. What do you _____ them?

6 If you _____ the small print at the bottom of the insurance form, you will see that we are not covered for accidental damage.

44 Practice

Exercise 3
Verb + object + preposition

Complete the sentences with a suitable verb. Then complete the wordcomb with the missing words to find the name of a famous French company. All the verbs are in section B of the grammar notes on page 179.

1   Who do you _blame_ for the current rail strike? Do you think the management or the unions are responsible? (5 letters)
2   I have asked my former employer to _____ me with a reference. (7)
3   We have had a very good year, and in particular, I would like to _____ David Mason on the excellent results he has achieved in R&D. (12)
4   I've just got to phone Bernard and _____ him for all his help. (5)
5   Many companies will not _____ your car against theft if you live in certain areas of London, because the risk is too high. (6)
6   When you write back, I think you ought to check how many units they will be able to _____ us with each month. (6)
7   A property developer bought the building and decided to _____ it into six separate apartments. (7)
8   The government is planning to _____ about £30 billion on social security payments and unemployment benefit. (5)

1 ▢▢▢▢▢
2 ▢▢▢▢▢▢▢
3 ▢▢▢▢▢▢▢▢▢▢▢▢
4 ▢▢▢▢▢
5 ▢▢▢▢▢▢
6 ▢▢▢▢▢▢
7 ▢▢▢▢▢▢▢
8 ▢▢▢▢▢

Exercise 4
Verb + preposition or no preposition?

Complete the following sentences with a preposition if it is necessary. If it is not necessary, leave a blank (Ø).

1   Rich immigrants find it fairly easy to enter **Ø** the United Kingdom, but people without money do not.
2   When you see the tax inspector, you will have to account _____ all the money you have received over the past six years.
3   If they won't help you, you should complain _____ their Head Office.
4   If you need information about Senegal, phone _____ the embassy.
5   We have offered Helen a job in New York, but she says she needs a few days to think _____ it.
6   I'm looking _____ that letter from Marlino's – have you seen it?
7   Yesterday the Prime Minster met _____ the Head of the European Commission at 10 Downing Street.
8   The next item on the agenda is promotion, and I would like to discuss _____ the plans we have for next year.

....

Task 1

Answer the following questions, using the words in brackets.

What would you do if ...

1   ... you were not satisfied with the service in a restaurant?
(complain) _I would complain to the head waiter._

2   ... you had a serious personal problem?
(talk) _____

3   ... you wanted a copy of a company's annual report?
(write) _____

4   ... you were offered a job in a different city?
(think) _____

5   ... you were asked to sign a contract that you couldn't understand?
(rely) _____

....

Task 2

Using the words in the box, report what the following people said.

blame	congratulate	provide	thank	ask

1   She said to me, 'You caused the accident! It's all your fault!'
_____

2   He said to me, 'Here is the information you wanted.'
_____

3   She said to me, 'Thanks a lot. You've been very helpful.'
_____

4   He said to me, 'What is your opinion?'
_____

5   They said to us, 'Brilliant! Well done! You solved the problem!'
_____

....

Task 3

Give the following people advice using the words in brackets.

1   I have a great business idea, but I have no money.
(borrow ... from) You ought _to borrow what you need from the bank._

2   I have inherited £50,000 from my aunt who died last month.
(invest ... in) You ought to _____

3   What should I do with my £200 clothing allowance?
(spend ... on) You ought to _____

4   Do you think it is safe to keep this valuable painting in my office?
(insure ... against) Yes, but you ought to _____

45 Phrasal verbs

A Meaning changes

Sometimes verbs are followed by a word like **in**, **off**, **at**, etc., and this can change the meaning of the verb. Compare:

1 She **looked through** the window.
2 I'm **looking after** my neighbours' dog. (I'm taking care of it.)

In **1**, the word **through** is a normal preposition and does not change the meaning of the verb **look**. In **2**, the word **after** gives the verb **look** a different meaning. Verbs like this are called phrasal verbs, and they are very common in informal English. **Look after** is one example.

B Separable phrasal verbs

Sometimes it is possible to separate the two parts of a phrasal verb. If the object is a noun, we can put it in two places:

We had to **put the meeting off**. (delay the meeting)
We had to **put off the meeting**.

If the object is a pronoun (i.e., **me**, **you**, **him**, **her**, **it**, etc.), it must come after the verb:

We had to **put it off**. (NOT: put off it)

Here is a list of common separable phrasal verbs:

back ... up	give ... up	put ... off
clear ... up	hold ... up	put ... through
close ... down	keep ... down	ring ... up
cut ... off	look ... up	take ... over
fill ... in	make ... up	throw ... away

C Inseparable phrasal verbs

Some two-part phrasal verbs and all three-part phrasal verbs are inseparable. Many inseparable verbs do not have objects:

We are going to **run out of** money. (NOT: run money out of)
He'll never **get away with** it. (NOT: get it away with)
During the call, she got angry and **hung up**. (put the phone down)

Here is a list of common inseparable phrasal verbs :

back out of	cut down on	look after
break down	do without	look into
call on	get on with	run into
carry on	get over	run out of
come across	go through	take up
come down	hold on	turn up

....

Exercise 1
Meaning changes

In the following sentences, decide whether the verb keeps its ordinary meaning (OM) or whether it is a phrasal verb (PV).

1   What shall we give Amanda for a leaving present?   _OM_
2   His doctor said he was drinking too much and should give it up.   _PV_
3   I was talking to her on the phone, but we were suddenly cut off.   _____
4   The other day I cut my finger with a knife, but it's not serious.   _____
5   I'll take your letter to the Post Office if you like.   _____
6   Hanson PLC took the company over last year.   _____
7   Sorry we're late. We were held up by roadworks on the M25.   _____
8   He held his hand up because he wanted to ask a question.   _____

....

Exercise 2
Separable phrasal verbs

Rewrite each of the following sentences in two ways. In A, change the word order, and in B, use a pronoun.

1   We have got to keep inflation down.
    A _We have got to keep down inflation._   B _We have got to keep it down._
2   Could you pick up James?
    A _____   B _____
3   You must fill the form in.
    A _____   B _____
4   They're going to close the factory down.
    A _____   B _____
5   I have thrown the invoices away.
    A _____   B _____

....

Exercise 3
Common separable phrasal
verbs

In the following conversation, fill in the blanks with a phrasal verb from the box that means the same as the words in brackets.

cut ... off   pick ... up   put ... off   put ... through   ring ... up

A: Could you (connect me) [(1)] _____ to extension 234 again?
B: Certainly. OK, you're through now.
C: Sorry about that. They (disconnected us) [(2)] _____ for some reason.
A: I know. Anyway, I can't make the meeting on the 18th, as I'll still be in Germany, so could we (postpone it) [(3)] _____ until the 24th?
C: Yes, I can't see any problem there.
A: Good, can I have a word with Hugo? He's coming over and I need to know when he wants me to (collect him) [(4)] _____ from the airport.

Exercise 4
Inseparable phrasal verbs

Complete the following memo, using the phrasal verbs from the box which mean the same as the words in brackets.

break down	do without	look into	run out of	take up
call on	check in	hold on	look after	turn up

TO: Amanda

FROM: Brian J.

RE: 1 Service lift   2 Mr Takashi

1. The service lift in the warehouse has (stopped working) [(1)] _broken down_ again. Could you please get the Otis engineer to (investigate) [(2)] _____ what has gone wrong and fix it ASAP? This is urgent, because we really can't (manage) [(3)] _____ it. We're having to move everything upstairs by hand. This is (occupying) [(4)] _____ a great deal of time and soon everyone is going to (have no more) [(5)] _____ patience. Thanks for your help.

2. We are expecting Mr Takashi from Japan some time this afternoon. I have rung the hotel, but he hasn't (registered) [(6)] _____ at the hotel yet, so he may just (arrive unexpectedly) [(7)] _____ at the office. If he does, could you (take care of) [(8)] _____ him and ask him (to wait) [(9)] _____ until I get back? I have to (visit) [(10)] _____ a client at about 2.30, but I should be back by 3.15.

Exercise 5
Review

In the following sentences, choose the best option from the words A–D.

1 Power PCs are expensive, but if you wait, prices will _____ down.
A back   B run   C turn   D come

2 I agree, and if they criticize you at the meeting, I will back you _____ .
A up   B down   C in   D out

3 By the way, I _____ into Jane in York, and she sends you her regards.
A looked   B turned   C came   D ran

4 Could you ring British Airways and find _____ if there are any seats on the flight to Rome?
A up   B in   C over   D out

5 Work is always so much better if you have a boss you _____ on with.
A get   B carry   C take   D hold

Task 1
Study skills

There are a large number of phrasal verbs in English, and it is helpful to keep a note of the ones that you meet. Here is one suggestion about how you can record them.

Write the verb on the left-hand page, and write sample sentences on the right-hand page, showing the phrasal verbs in context. As you meet more phrasal verbs with the same stem, add them to the left-hand page and put examples on the right-hand page.

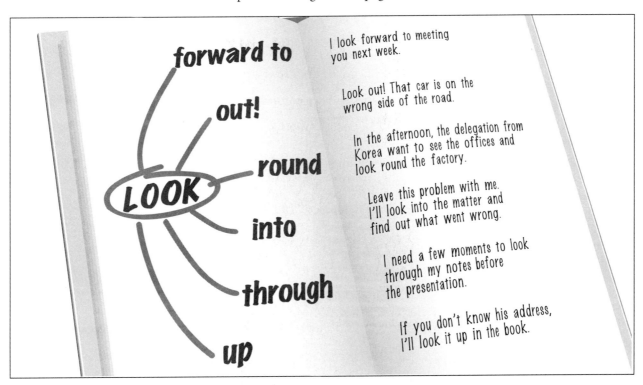

Now complete the following sentences using a phrasal verb with **look**.

1 Could I have the afternoon off? I'd like to look _____ a house that we're thinking of buying.
2 I've forgotten the code for the Dx16 exhaust pipe. Could you look it _____ in the price list?
3 At the moment the accident investigators are looking _____ the cause of the crash.
4 I am really looking _____ to going away on holiday next week.
5 You'd better look _____ – the boss is coming and he is in a bad mood.
6 Could you look _____ this letter quickly and see if there is anything you would like to add to it?

Task 2
Dictionary work

Use your dictionary to make a list of expressions with **write**.

Appendix 1 Spelling of verb forms

1 Present tense, 3rd person form

With most verbs, we add **-s** to the verb in the 3rd person, and make no other changes:

I/you/we/they run   *he/she/it runs*

With verbs that end in **-o**, **-ch**, **-ss**, **-sh**, and **-x**, we add **-es**:

I/you/we/they go	*he/she/it goes*
I/you/we/they teach	*he/she/it teaches*
I/you/we/they miss	*he/she/it misses*
I/you/we/they rush	*he/she/it rushes*
I/you/we/they fix	*he/she/it fixes*

With verbs that end in a consonant + **y**, we remove the **-y** and add **-ies**:

I/you/we/they try   *he/she/it tries*

The same rules apply for adding **-s** to nouns to make plural forms:

quango	*quangoes*
match	*matches*
class	*classes*
dish	*dishes*
box	*boxes*
party	*parties*

2 **-ing** form

With most verbs, we add **-ing** to the verb and make no other changes:

build	*building*
try	*trying*

With one-syllable verbs that have a short vowel sound, and end in a consonant, we double the consonant and add **-ing**:

sit	*sitting*
run	*running*

If the vowel sound is long, we do not double the consonant:

read	*reading*
speak	*speaking*

If the verb ends in a silent **-e**, we delete the **-e** and add **-ing**:

take	*taking*
drive	*driving*

3 Past tense, regular verbs   With most regular verbs, we add **-ed** to form the past tense:

look	*look**ed***
stay	*stay**ed***

If the verb ends in a silent **-e**, we just add **-d**:

like	*lik**ed***
behave	*behav**ed***

If the verb ends in a consonant + **y**, we remove the **-y** and add **-ied**:

try	*tr**ied***
deny	*den**ied***

If the verb has a short vowel sound and ends in a consonant, we double the consonant:

stop	*stop**ped***
ban	*ban**ned***

Appendix 2 Irregular verbs

VERB	PAST TENSE	PAST PARTICIPLE
arise	arose	arisen
be	was, were	been
beat	beat	beaten
become	became	become
begin	began	begun
bend	bent	bent
bet	bet	bet
bind	bound	bound
bite	bit	bitten
bleed	bled	bled
blow	blew	blown
break	broke	broken
bring	brought	brought
broadcast	broadcast	broadcast
build	built	built
burn	burnt	burnt
	burned	burned
burst	burst	burst
buy	bought	bought
catch	caught	caught
choose	chose	chosen
come	came	come
cost	cost	cost
creep	crept	crept
cut	cut	cut
deal	dealt	dealt
dig	dug	dug
do	did	done
draw	drew	drawn
dream	dreamt	dreamt
	dreamed	dreamed
drink	drank	drunk
drive	drove	driven
eat	ate	eaten
fall	fell	fallen
feed	fed	fed
feel	felt	felt
fight	fought	fought
find	found	found
fly	flew	flown
forbid	forbade	forbidden
forget	forgot	forgotten
forgive	forgave	forgiven
freeze	froze	frozen
get	got	got
give	gave	given

VERB	PAST TENSE	PAST PARTICIPLE
go	went	gone
grind	ground	ground
grow	grew	grown
hang	hung	hung
have	had	had
hear	heard	heard
hide	hid	hidden
hit	hit	hit
hold	held	held
hurt	hurt	hurt
keep	kept	kept
know	knew	known
lay	laid	laid
lead	led	led
lean	leant	leant
leap	leapt	leapt
learn	learnt	learnt
	learned	learned
leave	left	left
lend	lent	lent
let	let	let
lie	lay	lain
light	lit	lit
lose	lost	lost
make	made	made
mean	meant	meant
meet	met	met
pay	paid	paid
put	put	put
read	read	read
ride	rode	ridden
ring	rang	rung
rise	rose	risen
run	ran	run
say	said	said
see	saw	seen
seek	sought	sought
sell	sold	sold
send	sent	sent
set	set	set
shake	shook	shaken
shine	shone	shone
show	showed	shown
shrink	shrank	shrunk
shut	shut	shut

VERB	PAST TENSE	PAST PARTICIPLE
sing	sang	sung
sink	sank	sunk
sit	sat	sat
sleep	slept	slept
slide	slid	slid
smell	smelt	smelt
	smelled	smelled
speak	spoke	spoken
speed	sped	sped
	speeded	speeded
spell	spelt	spelt
	spelled	spelled
spend	spent	spent
spill	spilt	spilt
	spilled	spilled
spin	spun	spun
split	split	split
spoil	spoilt	spoilt
	spoiled	spoiled
spread	spread	spread
spring	sprang	sprung
stand	stood	stood
steal	stole	stolen
stick	stuck	stuck
sting	stung	stung
strike	struck	struck
swear	swore	sworn
sweep	swept	swept
swim	swam	swum
swing	swung	swung
take	took	taken
teach	taught	taught
tear	tore	torn
tell	told	told
think	thought	thought
throw	threw	thrown
understand	understood	understood
wake	woke	woken
wear	wore	worn
win	won	won
wind	wound	wound
write	wrote	written

Verbs like this are also irregular when they have a prefix, e.g., mistake – mistook – mistaken, withstand – withstood – withstood.

Answer Key

Unit 1 Present simple

Practice

Exercise 1

1 *do you come*	2 come	3 Do you live
4 don't live	5 live	6 do you do
7 work	8 do you travel	9 don't come

Exercise 2

1 *is*	2 owns	3 operate
4 have	5 produce	6 export
7 does	8 installs	9 manufactures
10 is	11 handles	12 imports
13 consists	14 is	15 sells

Exercise 3

1 *Do you know*	2 doesn't work	3 has
4 does she come	5 comes	6 doesn't stay
7 starts	8 goes	

Exercise 4

1 *have*	2 make	3 goes
4 rise	5 feel	6 spend
7 helps	8 lead	

Exercise 5

1 *is*	2 arrives	3 stops
4 gets	5 is	6 gets
7 does it leave	8 goes	9 Are
10 runs	11 takes	

Production

Task 1 (Sample answers only)
1 *An air steward looks after ...*
2 A stockbroker buys and sells ...
3 An architect designs ...
4 Venture capitalists invest ...
5 Auditors check ...
6 Management consultants advise ...
7 A journalist writes ...
8 Personnel officers arrange ...

Task 2 (Sample answer only)
I work for a large property development company. We employ over 500 people, and we specialize in building retirement homes for the elderly. Our headquarters are in Bristol, but we have regional offices all over the country.

Task 3 (Sample answers only)
1 I come to work by car.
2 It usually takes me about an hour.
3 I deal with the post and contact clients on the phone.
4 I bring sandwiches to the office.
5 In the afternoons I visit the clients I need to see.

6 I usually finish at about 6.30.
7 I visit friends or go to the country.

Unit 2 Present continuous

Practice

Exercise 1

1 *am talking*	2 are having	3 are you doing
4 is expecting	5 isn't working	6 Are you calling
7 am phoning		

Exercise 2

1 f	2 g	3 h	4 b
5 a	6 c	7 e	8 d

Exercise 3

1 *are you doing*	2 am attending
3 are you staying	4 is affecting
5 aren't spending	6 aren't getting
7 is trying	8 are buying
9 isn't doing	10 is managing
11 are looking	

Exercise 4

1 *is coming*	2 are selling	3 are shrinking
4 are spending	5 are turning	6 are taking over
7 are becoming	8 are beginning	

Production

Task 1 (Sample answers only)
1 *He's having a meeting with the auditors.*
2 The photocopier isn't working.
3 Peter's seeing the people from Wal-Mart.
4 She's talking to Rosemary.
5 Someone is coming.

Task 2 (Sample answers only)
1 We're developing a new range of titles on CD-ROM.
2 I'm looking into the technical side of the project.
3 I'm doing a course in design.
4 I'm studying for an advanced programmer's certificate.
5 I'm trying to save enough money to buy a house.

Task 3 (Sample answer only)
There is no public transport, so everyone is travelling to work by bike, or they are walking. Quite a lot of people are staying in hotels near work during the week, and only going home at weekends.

Task 4 (Sample answers only)
1 *On the whole, cars are getting smaller.*
2 Nowadays more and more cars are being fitted with air bags.
3 These days the Japanese are selling more and more cars in Europe.

Answer Key

4 Cars are becoming much more reliable.

5 Electric cars are becoming a little more common.

6 Cars are causing less pollution and are becoming more fuel-efficient.

Unit 3 Present simple vs present continuous

Practice

Exercise 1

1	*do you usually organize*	2	Do the farmers bring
3	we always collect	4	deliver
5	do you have	6	test
7	passes	8	operates
9	isn't working	10	are changing

Exercise 2

1	*manufacture*	2	supply	3	spend
4	are producing	5	is having	6	require

Exercise 3

1	*works*	2	aren't sending	3	am dealing
4	leads	5	aren't doing	6	varies
7	speaks	8	come	9	are spending

Exercise 4A

1	*enjoy*	2	go	3	put
4	run	5	takes	6	is becoming
7	is making	8	is losing	9	is starting

Exercise 4B

1	*is falling*	2	is growing	3	is beginning
4	goes	5	demand	6	makes

Exercise 5

1	*are interviewing, think*	2	are carrying, want
3	are trying, sounds	4	Do you know, is doing
5	am trying, means	6	am applying, depends
7	tastes, is becoming		

Production

Task 1 (Sample answers only)

1 *I come from Austria, but at the moment I'm living in Switzerland.*

2 I speak Spanish and French, and at the moment I'm learning English.

3 I normally like my work, but I'm not enjoying it at the moment.

4 I go on a lot of training courses, and at the moment I'm doing a course in CAD.

5 I usually work from 9 to 5, but at the moment I'm staying late.

6 My boss travels a lot, and at the moment he's visiting Australia.

7 We have several subsidiaries in Europe, and at the moment we are setting up another one in Brussels.

8 We normally export a lot to Greece, but we aren't getting many orders at the moment.

Task 2 (Sample answers only)

1 *Where do you come from?*

2 Who are you writing to?

3 What does he do?

4 How do you get to work?

5 How often does your Sales Director go abroad?

6 Is business going well?

7 Do you know each other?

8 Are you taking on any new staff at the moment?

Unit 4 Simple past

Practice

Exercise 1

1	*didn't realize*	2	Did ... study	3	didn't accept
4	complained	5	Did ... visit	6	placed
7	did ... hire				

Exercise 2A

1	*run*	2	did	3	made	4	go
5	wrote	6	have	7	paid	8	sell

Exercise 2B

1	*ran up ... bill*	2	did business
3	made a profit	4	went abroad
5	wrote a report	6	had problems
7	paid by credit card	8	sold out

Exercise 3

1	*joined*	2	knew	3	used
4	set	5	found	6	were
7	rained	8	had	9	was
10	didn't want	11	decided	12	succeeded
13	didn't have	14	didn't know	15	started
16	tried	17	made	18	cut
19	painted	20	heated	21	worked
22	improved	23	began		

Exercise 4

1 *When did she complete her report? (on)*

2 When did they set up the company? (in)

3 When did you go abroad? (in)

4 When did the meeting finish? (at)

5 When did you order the parts? (on)

6 When did you pay for them? (no preposition needed)

Answer Key

Production

Task 1 (Sample answers only)

1 *They made all the Directors redundant.*
2 They moved to larger premises.
3 They installed new equipment.
4 They changed the hours and improved salaries.
5 They sold the subsidiaries.
6 They increased the number of people in the sales team.
7 They looked for new business in other parts of the country.
8 They improved the design and range of the shoes.
9 They began paying people on time.
10 They equipped the Accounts Department with computers.

Task 2 (Sample answer only)

I left school when I was 18, and joined a major supermarket chain as a trainee. I stayed with them for two years, and then I was promoted. I went on a management training course, and in 1989 I became the Assistant Manager of one of the new stores in Bristol.

Unit 5 Present perfect (1)

Practice

Exercise 1

1 *haven't paid*	2 have fallen
3 Have you written	4 have spent
5 have shut	6 have drawn
7 haven't spoken	8 Have you found
9 has just got	10 have you met

Exercise 2

1 *G and J*	2 I and L	3 A and K
4 C and E	5 B and D	6 F and H

Exercise 3

1 *don't know*	2 *at the weekend*
3 yesterday	4 yesterday
5 yesterday	6 yesterday
7 two years ago	8 during the 1980s
9 don't know	10 don't know

Exercise 4

1 *has just left*	2 have just read
3 have just given	4 have just bought
5 has just arrived	6 have just spoken
7 has just announced	

Exercise 5

1 *has gone*	2 has been	3 have been
4 has gone	5 have (not) been	

Production

Task 1 (Sample answers only)

1 *we have introduced some new product lines.*
2 he has run out.
3 she has just had a baby.
4 we have joined the EU (European Union).
5 it has increased taxes.
6 the weather has been terrible.
7 the price has fallen quite a lot.

Task 2 (Sample answers only)

1 *The new managers have refurbished the building completely and they have put in a new delicatessen section. They have improved their range of fresh foods and have added a cafeteria.*
2 A lot of the people you used to work with have left, and a lot of new staff have arrived. Mr Jackson has been promoted, and they have turned the whole place into a ghastly open-plan office.
3 We have cut our overheads by reducing the workforce, and we have paid off most of our debts. We have brought out a new range of cars which is currently selling very well.

Task 3 (Sample answers only)

1 *She wants to have a word with you.*
2 he has just come back from a marketing trip in Peru.
3 I have just finished it.
4 They have just won an order for 25 new aircraft.
5 has just opened.
6 I have just phoned her, and there was no reply.
7 I have just had one.

Unit 6 Present perfect (2): ever, never, already, yet

Practice

Exercise 1

1 A: *Have you ever worked for yourself?*
  B: *Yes, I have.* or *No, I have never worked for myself.*
2 A: Have you ever worked for a multinational company?
  B: Yes, I have. or No, I have never worked for a multinational company.
3 A: Have you ever had experience of managing people?
  B: Yes, I have. or No, I have never had experience of managing people.
4 A: Have you ever held a position of responsibility?
  B: Yes, I have. or No, I have never held a position of responsibility.
5 A: Have you ever studied economics or accountancy?

Answer Key

B: Yes, I have. or No, I have never studied economics or accountancy.

6 A: Have you ever given a presentation in English?

B: Yes, I have. or No, I have never given a presentation in English.

Exercise 2

1 *Have you ever been, went, did you stay, was*
2 Have you ever been, had, did you go, stayed
3 Have you ever been, went, was it, thought ... was
4 Have you ever heard, did ... was, did you work, didn't stay

Exercise 3

1 *Have you finished it yet?*
2 have already done
3 haven't found any problems yet
4 have already fixed
5 Have you checked
6 have already fixed
7 haven't ordered them yet
8 haven't worked it out yet
9 haven't finished work yet

Exercise 4

1 *has been*
2 have already reached
3 have gone
4 has managed
5 have had
6 have grown
7 have opened

Exercise 5

1 *H*
2 B
3 E
4 G
5 F
6 C
7 D
8 A

Production

Task 1 (Sample answers only)

1 *I have never given a presentation to so many people.*
2 I have never put much money into the stock market.
3 I have never been to the States.
4 I have never read one.
5 it has never given me any trouble.
6 They have never had a strike.

Task 2 (Sample answers only)

1 *We have done a lot of research and we have finalized the design. We have solved the problems we had with the prototype and we have already set up a production unit in Cambridge. We haven't decided who will lead the project yet, but we are interviewing three possible candidates.*

2 I have already written a business plan, and I have already raised the finance that I will need. I have already found a suitable production site, but I haven't recruited any staff yet.

Task 3 (Sample answers only)

1 *I have been late three times this week.*
2 it has sold over 50,000 cars.
3 it has made over 20,000 miners redundant.
4 haven't had any enquiries.

Unit 7 Present perfect (3): for and since

Practice

Exercise 1

1 *Wrong – I have been*
2 Right
3 Wrong – have known
4 Wrong – have you been
5 Right
6 Wrong – has had
7 Wrong – has been
8 Right

Exercise 2

1 *since*
2 since
3 for
4 since
5 Since
6 since
7 since
8 for

Exercise 3

1 A: *How long have you been in charge of the Finance Department?*

B: *I have been in charge of the it for six months.*

2 A: How long have you had a phone line for investors?

B: We have had it for three months.

3 A: How long has the property been on the market?

B: It has been on the market for six months.

4 A: How long have you had an office in Spain?

B: We have had an office in Spain since 1992.

5 A: How long has Jason been in the States?

B: He has been there since the 18th.

Exercise 4

1 *I haven't seen Mr Ng since September.*
2 The company hasn't made a profit for three years.
3 I haven't had a pay rise for two years.
4 We haven't looked at their proposal since July.
5 We haven't raised our prices in real terms since 1992.
6 We haven't played golf together for three months.
7 There hasn't been a fall in unemployment here since 1990.
8 I haven't been on a sales trip abroad since January.

Exercise 5

1 *have been*
2 has risen
3 has increased
4 has gone up
5 have seen
6 have not managed
7 has grown
8 has fallen
9 have enjoyed

Answer Key

Production

Task 1 (Sample answers only)

1 *I met Mr Christiansen in 1988.*
2 I have known Mr Christiansen since 1988.
3 Nissan built a car plant in the UK in 1986.
4 Nissan have had a car plant in the UK since 1986.
5 Greece has been a member of the European Community since 1986.
6 Greece joined the European Community in 1986.

Task 2 (Sample answers only)

1 *I haven't had a statement for several weeks.*
2 I haven't looked at them for some time.
3 I haven't heard from Peter for several days.
4 we haven't had any orders from them since last year.
5 I haven't spoken it since I left Tokyo.

Task 3 (Sample answers only)

1 *Since the new management team took over at Berisford,* the company's financial situation has improved dramatically. Its turnover has risen by 25%, and its profits have doubled. It has signed three new contracts and it has taken on 50 new employees.
2 *Since we adopted Japanese-style working practices* at our factory, productivity has risen by 20%, and absenteeism has fallen by a half. We have only lost one day to strikes, and staff turnover has fallen by 50%.

Unit 8 Present perfect (4): continuous and simple

Practice

Exercise 1

1 *have you been working*
2 have been exporting
3 has been falling
4 haven't been investing
5 haven't been using
6 have been trying
7 have been making
8 have you been sending

Exercise 2

How long have you been running the company?
I have been running the company since 1986.
How long have you been manufacturing equipment for exhibitions?
We have been manufacturing equipment for exhibitions since 1986.
How long have you been exporting to Europe?
We have been exporting to Europe since 1990.
How long have you been organizing exhibitions?
We have been organizing exhibitions since 1992.

How long have you been representing UK publishers in Europe?
We have been representing UK publishers in Europe since 1993.
How long have you been selling books in the USA?
We have been selling books in the USA since 1994.

Exercise 3

1 *have been learning*
2 *have worked*
3 has been looking
4 Have you been waiting
5 has increased
6 have made
7 have been looking
8 have been visiting

Exercise 4

1 *I haven't been feeling well recently.*
2 I haven't had a meeting with them for two weeks.
3 My fax machine hasn't been working properly recently.
4 They haven't given their workers a pay rise for three years.

Exercise 5

1 D 2 F 3 B 4 A
5 C 6 E

Production

Task 1 (Sample answers only)

1 *He has been coming in late and he hasn't been doing any work. He's been spending hours every day talking to his friends on the phone and he's been upsetting the customers.*
2 I've been doing a lot of overtime, and I've been bringing in a lot of new business.
3 I've been listening to the news on the BBC World Service, and I've been improving my grammar.
4 I've been setting up a new outlet in Paris so I've been going there two or three times a week, and I've been recruiting new staff for it.

Task 2 (Sample answers only)

1 *Yes, it's been raining.*
2 I haven't been getting enough sleep.
3 I've been trying to fix the photocopier.
4 I've been playing a lot recently.
5 She's been going to job interviews.
6 I've been having problems with my boss.
7 I've been taking clients out.

Answer Key

Unit 9 Review: simple past, present perfect, and present perfect continuous

Practice

Exercise 1

1 *Right*	2 Wrong – *rose*
3 Wrong – *fell*	4 Right
5 Wrong – *stayed*	6 Right
7 Right	8 Wrong – *was*

Exercise 2

1 *have arrived*	2 have just had
3 have already ordered	4 rang
5 asked	6 hasn't arrived
7 have never needed	8 went
9 took	10 didn't have
11 Have you ever been	12 has been

Exercise 3

1 *been staying*
2 haven't heard
3 has sold
4 have you known
5 have been writing

Exercise 4

1 *haven't been*	2 have been
3 arrived	4 was
5 visited	6 saw
7 was	8 have already received
9 have never had	10 came
11 have been	12 have made
13 had	14 worked
15 set	16 has been acting
17 asked	18 haven't thought
19 have just had	

Production

Task 1 (Sample answers only)

1 *We're going to the Hamburg Book Fair next week. We've reserved a 20 metre stand, so the display will be quite impressive. We have sent most of the stock on ahead, but there are one or two books that haven't come out yet, and we're going to take them with us. We have already arranged a lot of meetings, but there are still a few people that we haven't contacted yet.*

2 We're developing a new range of environmentally-friendly cosmetics, which we hope to launch before Christmas. We have set up a factory in Eastern Europe, and we have already started production, but we haven't received any stock yet. We are finalizing the marketing campaign at the moment. We have chosen the advertising agency, but they haven't finalized all the details of the campaign yet.

Task 2 (Sample answers only)

1 *As you will see from the enclosed CV, I have worked in the financial services sector for several years. I spent two years with Allied Dunbar as a pensions salesman, and then moved to Sun Alliance, where I have been working in the Life Assurance division. I have had considerable managerial experience, and I recently became Area Manager.*

2 I have been in computers for five years now. I did a degree in computing at MIT, and then I joined Honeywell as a programmer. I moved to ICL three years ago, and worked as a systems analyst for 18 months. For the last 18 months, I have been working in the Customer Support Department.

Task 3 (Sample answers only)

1 *I have stayed late three times.*
  I have been working very hard.
2 I have had a couple of interviews.
  I have been looking for a new job.
3 He has fired three people.
  He has been making himself very unpopular.
4 We have already shipped over 20,000 units.
  We have been selling 4,000 units a week.

Unit 10 Past continuous

Practice

Exercise 1

1 *were you talking*	2 was calling
3 was discussing	4 was having
5 was organizing	6 were you doing
7 wasn't working	8 were having

Exercise 2

1 *met*	2 was travelling
3 noticed	4 was standing
5 were waiting	6 realized
7 were having	8 said
9 was coming	10 remembered
11 were having	12 accepted

Exercise 3

1 A *When his car broke down, he was driving to Bonn.*
  B *When his car broke down, he went the rest of the way by taxi.*
2 A When the fire alarm went off, we were having a meeting.
  B When the fire alarm went off, we left the building.
3 A When they took our company over, we were losing a lot of money.
  B When they took our company over, they made a number of people redundant.

Answer Key

4 A When the fax arrived, I was having lunch in the canteen.

B When the fax arrived, my secretary brought it down.

5 A When Mr Yamaichi arrived, the chauffeur was waiting.

B When Mr Yamaichi arrived, he came straight to the office.

Exercise 4
1 *noticed, was walking*
2 met, was going
3 was giving, interrupted
4 was finalizing, rang up
5 noticed, were looking
6 was cleaning, happened
7 dropped, was taking
8 approached, was working

Production

Task 1 (Sample answers only)
1 A *the company driver was waiting for me.*
   B *I went straight to the meeting.*
2 A Peter was talking to the receptionist.
   B I opened my post.
3 A the trainee was cleaning the machine.
   B we had to close the factory down.
4 A they were losing £300,000 a week.
   B they made everyone redundant.

Task 2 (Sample answer only)
1 *because he wasn't feeling well.*
2 because he wasn't making any progress in the company.
3 because she was spending a lot on hire cars.
4 because they were bringing us a lot of business.
5 because the air-conditioning wasn't working.

Task 3 (Sample answer only)
I had a crash a few years ago. I was travelling down to Italy with some friends, and we were driving on the motorway near Paris. It was about 2.00 in the morning, and it was raining lightly. Suddenly, there was a traffic jam ahead of us, but the friend who was driving didn't see it, and we crashed into the car in front of us. Luckily no-one was hurt, but the car was badly damaged and we had to finish our journey by train.

Unit 11 Past perfect

Practice

Exercise 1
1 *had he gone*   2 had left
3 had already chosen   4 had appointed
5 had grown   6 had not studied
7 had put   8 had not signed

Exercise 2
1 *because everyone had gone home.*
  so I locked the doors.
2 so I phoned the police.
  because someone had broken in.
3 because we had won a major contract.
  so we opened a bottle of champagne.
4 because they had not reached an agreement.
  so they got out their diaries.
5 so I called Directory Enquiries.
  because they had moved to new premises.
6 so she went straight home from the airport.
  because there had been a security alert in Tokyo.

Exercise 3
1 I didn't want lunch because I had already eaten.
2 he hadn't had enough experience.
3 a fax had just arrived for her.
4 I hadn't finished work.
5 I had never been to Russia.
6 they had just closed a major deal.

Exercise 4
1 *we had been producing pregnancy test kits for six years.*
2 we had been marketing the kits in the USA for five years.
3 Dr Pierce had been running it for four years.
4 Dr Warner had been the Medical Director for three years.
5 we had been manufacturing thermometers for two years.
6 we had had a production unit in Spain for one year.

Production

Task 1 (Sample answers only)
1 *she had never had a full time job before.*
2 he owed a great deal of money.
3 they had not submitted the correct figures.
4 he had missed the flight.
5 she had already sold her portfolio.

Task 2 (Sample answers only)
1 *The price was the same but the manufacturers had fitted electric windows, air bags, and power steering as standard. They had modified the engine, and they had managed to increase the car's efficiency. There was more room in the back because they had changed the design of the seats, and*

Answer Key

the car was much safer because they had made the side doors stronger.

2 They had appointed a new team of designers, and were busy expanding the range of products. They had fired the old MD, and had appointed a new MD, who had previously been with one of their competitors.

Task 3 (Sample answers only)

1 *he had been working at the VDU all day.*
2 someone had been supplying their competitors with details of their plans.
3 she hadn't been doing well at work.
4 had been phoning his friend in Australia.
5 had been waiting for over nine hours.

Unit 12 The future (1): will

Practice

Exercise 1

1 *G*	2 F	3 H	4 A
5 B	6 D	7 C	8 E

Exercise 2

1 *Unemployment will fall slowly.*
2 Interest rates will fall sharply.
3 Inflation will rise slowly.
4 Consumer prices will remain stable.
5 Industrial production will rise sharply.

Exercise 3

1 *will give, get*		2 will phone, arrives
3 don't receive, will take		4 will show, leave
5 will rise, announces		6 close, will suffer
7 come, will give		8 is, will feel
9 will fall, put up		10 will tidy, gets

Exercise 4

1 *Will anyone collect you from the airport?*
2 I won't be late again.
3 The finance group 3i will loan us £18m for the project.
4 The company will offer a pay rise of 5% in return for a no-strike deal.
5 I won't discuss this information with anyone.
6 They won't increase our discount.
7 The company will pay my relocation expenses.
8 The cash machine won't take my card.
9 I'll give you a hand with those boxes.

Production

Task 1 (Sample answers only)

1 *Really? Then I'll take a train through the tunnel.*
2 Then I'll have a bottle of La Lagune 67.
3 Then I'll pay by credit card.

4 Then I'll cancel the order and go somewhere else.
5 Then I'll go with American Airlines.
6 OK. I'll give her a ring.

Task 2 (Sample answer only)

Technology will allow us to communicate without going into the office. Most people will work from home, and will talk with each other using 'virtual reality' interactive communication systems. We will not need to travel to and from work every day, and companies will be much smaller.

Task 3 (Sample answers only)

1 *before I sign the contract.*
2 we find a replacement.
3 he arrives from the airport.
4 I finish the project under budget.
5 the sales conference is over.
6 there's a suitable vacancy.

Unit 13 The future (2): the present continuous and going to

Practice

Exercise 1

1 *am having*	2 am going
3 am seeing	4 are you coming
5 am not doing	6 am seeing
7 am having	

Exercise 2

1 *They are not going to accept it.*
2 We are going to modernize it.
3 She is going to have a holiday.
4 They are going to build a prototype.
5 We are going to produce it.

Exercise 3

1 *There is going to be a correction soon.*
2 The price is going to rise.
3 It is going to go bankrupt.
4 She is going to leave the company.
5 We are going to be late.

Exercise 4

1 *are leaving*	2 will be	3 are staying
4 will have	5 are seeing	6 Will I need
7 will phone	8 will let	

Exercise 5

1 *will post*	2 are you going to call
3 am going to look	4 won't have
5 are going to cut	6 will take
7 Will you carry	8 will tell

Answer Key

Production

Task 1 (Sample answer only)

The CEO is arriving at Heathrow at 9.00, and he is having a meeting with the Executive Vice Presidents at 10.15. He's having lunch with officials from the DTI, and in the afternoon he is opening the new office in Threadneedle Street. At 7.00 he's giving a speech on 'Financial deregulation in the EU', and he's having dinner at the Guildhall at 8.00. He's flying back to New York on Concorde the following morning at 11.30.

Task 2 (Sample answers only)

1 *I'm going to do a course in business Japanese in September, but I'm not going to take any exams.*
2 We're going to launch a new consultancy service aimed at small businesses.
3 We're going to change our computers to Macintoshes.
4 We're going to make twenty-five people redundant in the next three months.
5 I am going to have a holiday in December.

Task 3 (Sample answers only)

1 *I'm seeing Mr Karlssen in Oslo.*
2 They are going to cut overtime rates.
3 I'll come back later.
4 He's going to buy a Volvo.
5 I'll let you know what I think next week.
6 We're going to open a branch there next year.

Unit 14 The future (3): other future tenses

Practice

Exercise 1

1 *was going to*   2 were going to   3 are going to
4 are going to   5 were going to   6 is going to
7 is going to

Exercise 2

New schedule:

10.00 – 11.30	have meeting with Mr Barber
11.30 – 1.00	see the Finance Director
1.00 – 2.00	lunch at Gee's restaurant
2.00 – 3.30	visit the new warehouse
3.30 – 5.00	give presentation to IT department

1 He was visiting the new warehouse at 10.00, but now he is visiting it at 2.00.
2 He was giving a presentation to the IT department at 11.30, but now he is giving a presentation at 3.30.
3 *He was having lunch at Nelson's, but now he is having lunch at Gee's.*

4 He was having a meeting with Mr Barber at 2.00, but now he is having it at 10.00.
5 He was seeing the Finance Director at 3.30, but now he is seeing him at 11.30.

Exercise 3

1 *we will be demolishing the old building.*
2 *we will have demolished the old building.*
3 we will be building the new factory.
4 we will have built the new factory.
5 we will be installing the equipment.
6 we will have installed the equipment.
7 we will be testing the new machinery,
8 we will have tested the new machinery.
9 we will have started production.

Exercise 4

1 A *will start*
   B will be giving
   C will have finished
2 A will take off
   B will be travelling
   C will have arrived
3 A will start
   B will be having
   C will have finished

Production

Task 1 (Sample answers only)

1 *I was going to accept the job in Qatar …*
2 I was going to go away this weekend …
3 We were going to upgrade our whole IT network …
4 Margaret Thatcher was going to address the convention …
5 We were going to send five people to the sales conference …
6 I was going to get tickets for *Phantom of the Opera* …

Task 2 (Sample answers only)

1 I'll probably be working for a larger company.
2 I'll be the Research Director.
3 I'll be managing large-scale research projects.
4 I'll have already developed several important new drugs.
5 I will have moved to a bigger house, and I will have had three children.

Task 3 (Sample answers only)

1 I will have achieved as much as you have.
2 I'll be lying on a beach in Martinique.
3 It will have started.
4 They will be holding it in Copenhagen instead of Hamburg.
5 I'll be starting my presentation.

Answer Key

Unit 15 The future (4): possibility and probability

Practice

Exercise 1

1 *will definitely*
2 will definitely
3 Maybe ... will
4 will probably
5 probably won't
6 definitely won't

Exercise 2

1 *are unlikely to*
2 is certain to
3 are likely to
4 are unlikely to
5 is likely to
6 is certain to
7 are likely to
8 is unlikely to
9 is certain to

Exercise 3A

definitely: *I'm confident that ...*/I'm quite sure that ...
probably: I should think that .../The chances are that .../I expect that ...
probably not: I doubt if .../I shouldn't think that ...
definitely not: I'm quite sure that ...+ won't .../I doubt very much whether ...

Exercise 3B

1 *H*   2 E   3 A   4 F
5 G   6 B   7 C   8 D

Exercise 4

1 *He is confident that we will get the contract.*
2 Their new store is unlikely to attract many customers.
3 They probably won't give us better terms.
4 I'll probably be busy early next week.
5 I shouldn't think they will deliver the equipment this month.

Production

Task 1 (Sample answers only)

1 *I should think I'll work abroad in the next few years. Perhaps I'll work abroad in the next few years.*
2 I doubt very much whether I'll change jobs. I definitely won't change jobs.
3 I may get rich. Perhaps I will get rich.
4 I will probably get promoted. I should think I'll get promoted.
5 I shouldn't think I'll marry anyone English. I'm unlikely to marry anyone English.
6 I'm very unlikely to take control of the company. I definitely won't take control of the company.
7 I'm unlikely to spend time doing military service. I will definitely spend time doing military service.

Task 2 (Sample answers only)

1 *I should think that the economy will continue to improve in the short term, but the recovery may slow down because of political uncertainty. There will definitely be an election, and taxation is likely to be increased.*
2 The company is likely to expand rapidly over the next few years. I should think we will become market leaders within about five years' time, and we will probably set up offices in Latin America and the Far East.
3 Improved computer graphics are certain to make significant changes to the way we live and work. Virtual reality and interactive conferencing will allow us to take part in meetings even if we are somewhere else.
4 The countries of the Pacific Rim are certain to become more important. They will probably set up a common trade area that will become as important as – if not more important than – Europe or North America.

Unit 16 The passive (1): actions, systems, and processes

Practice

Exercise 1

1 *is not designed*
2 is credited
3 are connected
4 is deducted
5 are told
6 are warned
7 Is it aimed
8 are charged
9 is not put
10 is taken

Exercise 2

1 *are made in China.*
2 are paid weekly.
3 is kept at Fort Knox.
4 are built in South Korea.
5 is grown on the Ivory Coast.
6 is stored underground.
7 are tested extensively.
8 are printed in Hong Kong.

Exercise 3

1 *are programmed*
2 is transferred
3 is collected
4 is used
5 is driven
6 is chosen
7 is checked in
8 is loaded
9 are transmitted
10 is given
11 is cleared
12 is delivered
13 is held

Exercise 4

1 A   2 B   3 A   4 A

Answer Key

Production

Task 1 (Sample answers only)
1   *is advertised in-house.*
2   the vacancy is filled.
3   is advertised in the papers.
4   are asked to send in their CVs.
5   are invited to an interview.
6   is drawn up.
7   are invited back for a second interview.
8   is chosen.
9   are checked.
10   is offered the job.

Task 2 (Sample answer only)
The watches are manufactured in Singapore, and they are shipped to our warehouse in Dresden. Next, they are transported to our distributors. After that, they are sold on to retailers, and finally they are sold to our customers in stores all over the country.

Unit 17 The passive (2): tenses

Practice

Exercise 1A
1   *is working*   2   are being imported
3   are being assembled   4   is planning
5   is growing   6   are being fitted

Exercise 1B
1   *was being transported*   2   was being carried
3   were waiting   4   was being attacked

Exercise 1C
1   *had been awarded*   2   had been sacked
3   had rejected   4   had been dismissed
5   had not done   6   had made
7   had not been treated

Exercise 2
1   *will arrive*   2   will be met
3   will be taken   4   will be
5   will last   6   will be able
7   will not arrive   8   will be kept
9   will not be given

Exercise 3
1   *has been turned*   2   has been set up
3   have made   4   has been promoted
5   have been put   6   Have they sent Ken
7   has been demoted   8   has treated him

Production

Task 1 (Sample answers only)
1   *The Berlin Wall was built in 1961.*

2   The Channel Tunnel was opened in 1994.
3   Radium was discovered by Pierre and Marie Curie.
4   The wireless was invented by Marconi.
5   Fiat SPA was founded in 1899.
6   President Clinton was elected in 1992.

Task 2 (Sample answers only)
1   *It has been sold.*
2   It is being reorganized.
3   He was shouted at by angry shareholders.
4   They have been arrested.
5   It is being put up.
6   It was closed down last week.
7   It has been devalued.

Task 3 (Sample answer only)
The company I work for was founded by two brothers, Jack and Daniel Partridge, back in 1866. They manufactured whiskey, but only on a small scale. However, the whiskey was well produced, and it soon became very popular. They got into difficulties when taxes on liquor were raised, and the company was bought by a major brewer, who still owns it.

Unit 18 The passive (3): passive verbs and infinitives, have something done

Practice

Exercise 1
1   *is said to be*
2   is believed to have
3   is thought to make
4   is believed to own
5   is known to have
6   is said to live
7   *is known to have started*
8   is said to have bought
9   is believed to have purchased
10   is believed to have risen
11   *is thought to be making*
12   is said to be trying
13   is believed to be buying
14   is not thought to be planning

Exercise 2
1   *We have the chips and the motherboards made in the USA.*
2   Then we have them flown to Singapore.
3   We have the other components manufactured in Taiwan.
4   We have them sent to Singapore.
5   We have the computers assembled in Singapore.
6   We have the finished products shipped to the UK every three months.

Answer Key

Exercise 3

1 *I have my suits made in London.*
2 We are going to have 5,000 new catalogues printed.
3 They are having a new office designed.
4 I have had these figures checked.
5 You should have the photocopier mended.
6 We had the new furniture delivered yesterday.

Production

Task 1 (Sample answers only)

1 *He is supposed to be the richest man in the world.*
2 He is believed to be a very heavy drinker.
3 He is thought to earn over $500,000 a year.
4 They are known to be developing a revolutionary new product.
5 They are said to be ruthless.
6 It is supposed to be quite a nice place to live.

Task 2 (Sample answer only)

A lot of the windows were broken, and the carpets and curtains were ruined when the firemen were trying to put the blaze out. Luckily the money in the safe wasn't destroyed, but all the work I had on the computer was lost. One of the firemen got hurt, but luckily it wasn't serious and he didn't need to go to hospital.

Task 3 (Sample answers only)

1 *I had my clothes cleaned and returned within twelve hours.*
2 I had breakfast brought to my room.
3 I had my letters typed out.
4 I had my room cleaned morning and afternoon.
5 I had my presentations prepared for me.
6 I had some business cards made at no extra cost.
7 I had my travel arrangements taken care of.
8 I had all my bills paid by the company.

Unit 19 Conditionals: if you go ...

Practice

Exercise 1

1	D	2	F	3	G	4	B
5	H	6	A	7	C	8	E
9	I						

Exercise 2

1 *finishes, will spend*
   doesn't finish, will catch
2 go, will increase
   don't go, will try to
3 leave, will get
   stay, will be

4 will lose, move
   stay, will be

Exercise 3

1	if	2	when	3	if
4	when	5	if	6	when

Exercise 4

1	*calls*	2	*tell*	3	goes on
4	can	5	may	6	manage
7	must	8	may come	9	is going to

Exercise 5

1 Wrong – *you can go home*
2 Right
3 Wrong – if it is
4 Wrong – if I go
5 Right
6 Wrong – is talking
7 Wrong – if you go

Production

Task 1 (Sample answers only)

1 *If you ring 0800 726354, they'll give you some more information.*
2 If we don't sell them, we'll get our money back from the distributors.
3 If you subscribe now, you'll save 33%.
4 If you don't like it, they'll give you your money back.

Task 2 (Sample answers only)

1 I'll go over to Paris.
2 I'll spend some time in Greece.
3 I'll buy a better car.
4 I'll soon be brilliant at it.
5 I'll go crazy.
6 I'll go to bed early.
7 I'll visit some friends on the way home.
8 I'll get a place that is nearer where I work.

Task 3 (Sample answers only)

1 *I think that interest rates will rise again during the next two or three years. If they do, we will have to try to reduce our costs and the amount we borrow as much as possible, and we will not be able to expand.*
2 I am sure that our market share will increase. At the moment it is under 1%, but that is because Intel is so powerful. However, as our market share increases, there will be a price war.
3 There are a number of other companies who are planning to bring out new chips. If they can produce chips as well as we can, they will affect our market share.
4 In the next two or three years there will be an election. If the current opposition party is elected, there will be a

Answer Key

period of instability, but after a few months, we will all get used to it, and nothing will really change.

Unit 20 Conditionals: if, unless, etc.

Practice

Exercise 1

1 *E*	2 F	3 H	4 A
5 C	6 B	7 G	8 D

Exercise 2

1 *unless something goes wrong.*
2 unless we improve our offer.
3 unless it's an emergency.
4 unless demand increases soon.
5 unless you can cut your overheads.
6 unless I can have my job back when I return.

Exercise 3

1 *in case the hotels are busy.*
2 in case he loses it.
3 in case he wants to hire a car.
4 in case the office needs to phone him.
5 in case he has to see a doctor.
6 in case it is cold.

Exercise 4

1 *I'm going to leave early in case the traffic is heavy.*
2 *If I have a lot of time to spare, I'll read through my notes.*
3 I'm going to inspect the room first in case it is not suitable.
4 If the seating isn't right, I'll see the organizers.
5 I'm going to take extra handouts in case the audience is larger than expected.
6 If the audience is not experienced, I'll keep the talk simple.

Exercise 5

1 *provided that*	2 as long as	3 unless
4 So long as	5 Unless	6 as long as

Exercise 6

1 so that	2 in case	3 so that
4 so that	5 in case	6 in case

Production

Task 1 (Sample answers only)

1 I get a better offer from someone else.
2 the government can keep inflation under control.
3 I can get the day off.
4 they will make substantial profits next year.
5 I'll see you at 6.30.
6 you can maintain the required level of sales.

Task 2 (Sample answers only)

1 A *my boss lets me.*
   B *I get caught up in the traffic.*
   C *I get to the airport on time.*
2 A I can find a bureau de change.
   B I need to get a taxi.
   C I don't have to look for a bank when I arrive.
3 A I go to Bolivia next week.
   B I need to call some contacts.
   C I can write down any new people I meet.
4 A they don't pay tomorrow.
   B the original invoice got lost.
   C they know we are still waiting.
5 A you go to the north of the country.
   B you want to travel outside the main cities.
   C you can be independent.

Unit 21 Conditionals: if you went …

Practice

Exercise 1

1 *got*	2 would have	3 moved
4 would need	5 started	6 wouldn't be

Exercise 2

(In these sentences, the **if** clause can come at the beginning or the end.)

1 *if they weren't so expensive, we would use them.*
2 if I knew their address, I would contact them.
3 if I didn't enjoy my job, I wouldn't work so hard.
4 if we didn't spend so much on R&D, we wouldn't be the market leaders.
5 if I had the authority, I would give you an answer.

Exercise 3

1 *give, applied*	2 were, think
3 change, spoke	4 were*, earn
5 were, produce	

(*was is also possible, but a little less formal)

Exercise 4

1 *contributed, would be*
2 will meet, maintain
3 were, would insist
4 wait, will give
5 comes, let
6 would apply, had
7 would you try to change, were
8 will be, isn't

Exercise 5 (Culture Quiz)

1 Chinese people would find this very offensive. They consider Taiwan to be a part of China, not a separate country.

Answer Key

2 This would be the right thing to do. In most Muslim cultures (and the Malays are Muslims) you should not handle food with the left hand, as it is considered unclean.

3 A Japanese businessman who said this would actually mean, 'No, it is not possible', or 'No, I don't want to'. Sometimes this phrase is used because they consider it rude to refuse a request directly.

4 This would be perfectly acceptable. At most informal social occasions, it is normal to arrive a little late (but not too late). It would be wrong to arrive too early.

5 Your Saudi hosts would appreciate an attempt at speaking Arabic, even if you could only speak a few words such as 'Good morning'.

6 This would be the right thing to do. In many Arab cultures, it would be considered rude to start talking about business immediately.

Production

Task 1 (Sample answers only)

1 *If I invented a new product, I would patent it immediately.*

2 If I lost my job, I would set up my own business.

3 If I were offered a job in Saudi Arabia for five years, I might accept it.

4 If one of my company's main competitors offered me a good job, I would probably turn it down.

5 If I lost all my money and credit cards, I would phone my bank and credit card company immediately.

Task 2 (Sample answers only)

1 *If I were you I'd go to university, because you could join the company later.*

2 If I were you, I would phone them.

3 If I were you, I'd get a Mercedes.

4 If I were you, I'd contact the Personnel Manager.

5 If I were you, I'd go to the Chang Mai Kitchen.

Task 3 (Sample answers only)

1 *If I were the Prime Minister, I would raise taxes and spend more money on education. I would reduce bureaucracy and cut defence spending. I would abolish the monarchy, and move into the palace, which I would make my private home.*

2 If I were Chairman of the company I work for, I would award myself a large pay rise. Then I would start looking at new areas of the world where we could do business, and I would set up operations in the Pacific Rim and Latin America. I would spend much more on new technology, and I would reduce the workforce.

Unit 22 Conditionals: if you had gone …

Practice

Exercise 1

1 *had known*
2 had made
3 would have gone
4 had been
5 had waited
6 would have moved
7 Would (you) have accepted
8 would have stayed

Exercise 2

1 *had brought out, would not have held up*
2 had not had, would have come out
3 had been, would have dropped
4 had not launched, would not have risen
5 had not been, would have cut
6 had not brought out, would not have gone up
7 had won, would have reached

Exercise 3

1 *Wrong – If I had had*
2 Right
3 Wrong – would have made
4 Wrong – wouldn't have received
5 Wrong – hadn't been

Exercise 4

1 C	2 D	3 G	4 F
5 A	6 H	7 E	8 B

Exercise 5

1 *If we had ordered the parts at the end of June, they would be here now.*

2 If we hadn't felt we could trust each other, we wouldn't be partners.

3 If he hadn't lost his driving licence, he wouldn't have to take taxis everywhere.

4 If you had gone/been on the course, you would know how to operate the new equipment.

5 If I hadn't been/gone to school in France, I wouldn't be bilingual.

Production

Task 1 (Sample answers only)

1 *If I had lost my passport the last time I was abroad, I would have gone to the embassy to get a replacement.*

2 If someone had stolen my credit cards and money, I would have gone to the police.

3 If I had needed to contact the office urgently, I would have phoned.

Answer Key

4 If I had fallen seriously ill, I would have been covered by my insurance.

5 If I had missed my return flight, I would have had to buy another ticket.

Task 2 (Sample answers only)

1 *First of all, the company should have done some more market research. If it had looked into potential demand, it would have realized that there was no demand for the product.*

2 They should have made the C5 either much more powerful or much less powerful. If it had been less powerful, it would have been more suitable for children.

3 They should have made the C5 much cheaper. If C5s had been cheaper, parents would have bought them as presents.

4 They should have made the C5 larger. If they had made it larger, it would have seemed safer to use on the road.

Unit 23 Modal verbs (1): suggestions, advice, and criticism – shall, should, ought to

Practice

Exercise 1

| 1 *G* | 2 F | 3 H | 4 D |
| 5 C | 6 E | 7 B | 8 A |

Exercise 2

1 *Why don't we have lunch at Le Manoir?*

2 I suggest that you prepare for the interview carefully.

3 How about waiting until the next financial year?

4 What about organizing a leaving party for Mr Simpson?

5 Why don't you think about it and let me know your decision?

6 Let's share a taxi to the station.

7 I advise you to check her references before offering her the job.

8 Why don't we see if we can sub-contract this work?

Exercise 3

1 *should be met*

2 ought to be accompanied

3 should report

4 ought not to bring

5 should not be left

6 should be deposited

Exercise 4

1 *It shouldn't have offered such valuable air tickets.*

2 There ought to have been more special conditions.

3 The total number of tickets should have been limited.

4 More research ought to have been done.

5 It should not have relied on outdated figures.

Production

Task 1 (Sample answers only)

1 *I think we should increase overtime rates.*

2 I think we should introduce flexitime.

3 I don't think we should have a company crèche.

4 We ought to use more freelance people.

5 Why don't we split the company up into small, independent 'profit centres'.

6 What about getting our products 'placed' on some popular TV shows.

7 I think managers should have a points system and a reward at the end if they reach their targets.

Exercise 2 (Sample answers only)

1 *The builder shouldn't have thrown his bag of tools down from the roof.*

2 She shouldn't have placed all her money in one company.

3 They should have spent some more time on ensuring its reliability.

4 He should have saved it as he was writing it.

5 They shouldn't have raised taxes.

6 They shouldn't have spent so much on the new building.

Unit 24 Modal verbs (2): ability, possibility, and permission – can, could, may

Practice

Exercise 1

| 1 *d* | 2 f | 3 h | 4 g |
| 5 a | 6 c | 7 e | 8 b |

Exercise 2

1 *be able to*	2 can't	3 can
4 can	5 be able to	6 been able to
7 be able to		

Exercise 3

1 *managed to*	2 could	3 managed to
4 managed to	5 could	6 could
7 could	8 managed to	

Exercise 4

1 *G*	2 I	3 E	4 A
5 D	6 H	7 J	8 B
9 C	10 F		

Exercise 5

| 1 *B* | 2 A | 3 B | 4 B |
| 5 A | 6 B | 7 B | 8 A |

Answer Key

Production

Task 1 (Sample answers only)
1 *we can send it first class.*
2 I haven't been able to think of anything.
3 she can speak Japanese and English perfectly.
4 be able to expand.
5 you can order things over the phone.

Task 2 (Sample answers only)
1 I could have gone to work for them.
2 you could both have been killed.
3 she could have become the CEO.
4 could have saved ourselves a lot of money.

Task 3 (Sample answers only)
1 Could I have a drink, please?
2 Could I have a look at your magazine when you've finished with it?
3 Excuse me, could I get past?
4 Could you bring me a vegetarian meal, please?

Unit 25 Modal verbs (3): obligation and necessity – must, have to, needn't, can't, etc.

Practice

Exercise 1

1 *must*	2 can't	3 mustn't
4 needn't	5 can't	6 must
7 don't have to	8 mustn't	9 don't have to
10 must		

Exercise 2
1 a *Airline pilots have to have excellent eyesight.*
  b *They don't have to work office hours.*
2 a Union members have to pay a subscription.
  b They can't work during a strike.
3 a University teachers must be graduates.
  b They don't have to be qualified teachers.
4 a Army officers have to go to training college.
  b They can't go on strike.
5 a Police officers have to be over 1.75m tall.
  b They don't have to carry guns in the UK.

Exercise 3
1 *You must fax them to him immediately.*
2 We needn't discuss the matter any further.
3 You needn't order any more yet.
4 We must make sure we keep our market share.
5 You must give me a ring.
6 I mustn't be late.

Exercise 4

1 *had to*	2 had to	3 had to
4 couldn't	5 couldn't	6 didn't have to
7 didn't have to	8 had to	9 had to

Exercise 5

1 didn't need to	2 needn't have	3 needn't have
4 didn't need to		

Production

Task 1 (Sample answers only)
1 *You mustn't talk to customers like that.*
2 You must have a receipt.
3 You don't have to pay contributions every month.
4 You must prepare what you are going to say.
5 You needn't do this manually, you know.
6 You needn't get insurance, because everyone is covered by the company scheme.

Task 2 (Sample answers only)
I work as a lending officer for a London bank, and I have to discuss loans with clients and decide whether or not to authorize them. I don't have to do the financial analysis of the companies in question because we have a specialized team of analysts for that job. I can authorize loans of up to $500,000, but I can't authorize anything greater than that myself.

I work for a property management company. We have a large number of offices that we rent out, and I have to visit our clients on a regular basis to see if they are OK. I have to authorize repairs, but I don't have to oversee any of the maintenance work that gets carried out. I can't hire builders myself, as that job is done by the Personnel Department.

Unit 26 Modal verbs (4): speculation – may, might, could, must, can't

Practice

Exercise 1

1 *C*	2 E	3 A	4 J
5 I	6 D	7 B	8 G
9 F	10 H		

Exercise 2A

1 might, might, can't	2 must
3 must, might	

Exercise 2B

The finished table should look like this:

Package:	A	B	C
Name:	Mr Green	Mr Brown	Mr Grey
Contents:	photocopier	computer	paper
Weight:	20kg	22kg	18kg

Exercise 3

1 *They must have sent it to the wrong address.*
2 They must have moved to new premises.
3 The meeting must have been cancelled.
4 He might have gone to lunch.
5 She might have been phoning the Sales Department.
6 It can't have been repaired properly.

Exercise 4

1 *might give us the discount we want.*
2 must have been making long international calls.
3 can't have been selling many cars.
4 must have lost a lot of money.
5 may be promoted at the end of the year.
6 can't have been expecting me.
7 can't have heard the announcement.

Production

Task 1 (Sample answers only)

1 *The price of oil might rise.*
2 They might form the next government.
3 It might do really well.
4 There could be a tax rise in the next budget.
5 It may be delayed by several months.

Task 2 (Sample answers only)

1 *She must be out seeing a client.*
2 They must be developing a new model.
3 It must be a fake.
4 He must be at home.
5 She might be able to tell you.

Task 3 (Sample answers only)

A 1 *They can't have sold much Fizzo in July.*
  2 They must have done a lot of advertising during the summer.
  3 They must have increased their market share at the end of the year.
B 1 *They must have made a loss in October.*
  2 They must have spent a lot of money on their advertising campaign.
  3 They might have been selling drinks at a discount.

Unit 27 -ing and infinitive (1): verbs + -ing form or infinitive

Practice

Exercise 1

1 *filming*   2 losing   3 speaking
4 meeting   5 negotiating   6 waiting
7 applying   8 buying

Exercise 2A

1 *to discover*   2 to give   3 to prefer
4 to do

Exercise 2B

1 *to hire*   2 to pay   3 to earn
4 to last

Exercise 3

1 *placing*   2 to supply   3 to go
4 to give   5 to deliver   6 to market
7 changing   8 getting   9 printing
10 sending   11 to be   12 to contact
13 hearing

Exercise 4

1 *to be given*   2 *being interrupted*
3 to be paid   4 being asked
5 to be recruited   6 being taken over
7 to be sent   8 to be disturbed

Production

Task 1 (Sample answers only)

A 1 *I don't mind staying late.*
  2 I really enjoy travelling abroad.
  3 I like taking clients out.
  4 I dislike dealing with difficult customers.
B 1 I really enjoy working on new projects.
  2 I like meeting new people.
  3 I don't like dealing with paperwork.
  4 I can't stand arguing about money.

Task 2 (Sample answers only)

1 *We refused to pay them.*
2 We are planning to expand.
3 He threatened to take them to court.
4 She decided to give in her notice.

Task 3 (Sample answers only)

1 *having a bit more responsibility.*
2 to leave school.
3 seeing all my friends.
4 to go on holiday.
5 starting the course.
6 to be in charge of Production.
7 taking up an offer from ICL.

Answer Key

Unit 28 -ing and infinitive (2): verbs + objects

Practice

Exercise 1

1 *The new law will allow supermarkets to open on Sundays.*
2 They persuaded the bank to finance the project.
3 The court ordered the company to pay compensation.
4 The fall in demand forced us to cut production.
5 They have invited me to speak at the conference.

Exercise 2

1 *He reminded me to post the letter.*
2 He encouraged me to apply for the job.
3 He advised me to make a formal complaint.
4 He asked me to finish the report as soon as possible.
5 He allowed me to leave early.
6 He warned me not to rush into a decision.

Exercise 3

1 *They made us work extremely hard on the training course.*
2 They let us go out at weekends.
3 They made us give a presentation every morning.
4 They made us speak English all the time.
5 They let us watch TV.

Exercise 4

1 *want*	2 *to start*	3 allow
4 to advertise	5 persuade	6 to buy
7 warn	8 not to smoke	9 force
10 to give up		

Exercise 5

1 *make*	2 print	3 make
4 realize	5 let	6 advertise
7 let	8 sponsor	9 help
10 give up	11 let	12 buy

Exercise 6

1 *I heard him talking to someone on the phone.*
2 I smelled something burning.
3 I didn't see her leave.
4 I heard him give a talk on 'Quality Control'.
5 The visitors watched the robots assembling cars.

Production

Task 1 (Sample answers only)
1 to take on another twenty new workers.
2 to work during the holidays when I was young.
3 to learn skills that employers need.
4 to give a talk on Corporation Tax.
5 not to go out alone at night.

Task 2 (Sample answers only)
1 *They will probably make you work fairly hard, but I*

expect they'll let you have the weekends free. They'll make you learn a little Japanese, of course, but it's not very difficult. And you'd better learn some songs too, because they'll definitely take you out to a Karaoke bar and make you sing.
2 It probably won't be as bad as you think. They will make you get up early, and they will make you take regular exercise. They won't let you drink alcohol, of course, and they will probably put you on a special diet. They may let you have the evenings free, but they won't let you leave the grounds of the spa in case you are tempted to go to a restaurant or bar.

Task 3 (Sample answers only)
1 I would ask them to explain what went wrong, and I would tell them to pay the fine.
2 I would encourage her to do what she most enjoys and I would advise her to go to university.

Unit 29 -ing and infinitive (3): changes in meaning

Practice

Exercise 1

1 *E*	2 C	3 H	4 I
5 J	6 D	7 A	8 F
9 B	10 G		

Exercise 2

1 *servicing*	2 to look	3 to send
4 hearing	5 walking	6 to give
7 resigning	8 to say	9 sending
10 to provide		

Exercise 3

1 *going, meeting*	2 to arrange
3 travelling, taking	4 to have
5 working	6 to come

Exercise 4

1 *change*	2 using	3 changing
4 spend	5 convert	6 drinking
7 having		

Production

Task 1 (Sample answers only)
1 *sending them the form myself.*
2 to report back to the head negotiator.
3 seeing her for the first time.
4 to do all my filing at the end of the day.
5 looking after the company payroll, I am in charge of finances for the new building.
6 going away next week.
7 paying such high taxes.

Answer Key

Task 2 (Sample answers only)

A 1 *I prefer having holidays abroad because the weather is much better.*

2 I prefer getting to work early, because the office is much quieter.

3 I prefer working with other people, because I like to discuss work with them.

4 I prefer eating out because the food is much better.

B 1 *I would prefer to be rich because if I was famous, I wouldn't be free.*

2 I would prefer to have a larger house, because I am not interested in cars.

3 I would prefer to work for a woman, because they are much more reasonable.

4 I would prefer to have more time for myself, because I don't see much of my family.

Unit 30 -ing and infinitive (4): other uses

Practice

Exercise 1

1 *to go*   2 to miss   3 to inform

4 to demand   5 to reduce   6 to increase

7 to attract   8 to prevent

Exercise 2

1 *what to do*
   Correct option is C

2 when to arrive
   Correct option is B

3 whether to take
   Correct option is B

4 how close to stand
   Correct option is B

5 how much to give
   Correct option is B

6 how to behave
   Correct option is C

Exercise 3

1 *C*   2 B   3 F   4 E

5 A   6 D

Exercise 4

1 *He left the office without speaking to his boss.*

2 She got a job with Conoco after leaving university.

3 We will give them better credit terms instead of offering them a discount.

4 We managed to expand without increasing our debts.

5 He worked in industry for many years before joining the government.

6 The company became more profitable by making 700 workers redundant.

Exercise 5

1 *leaving*   2 to make   3 to join

4 working   5 to set up   6 seeing

7 buying   8 to expand

Production

Task 1 (Sample answers only)

1 *to ask them for some more information about their charges.*

2 to promote some special product lines.

3 to have a meeting with our main distributor.

4 to organize the move to my new house.

5 to see if she has managed to get me on the flight.

Task 2 (Sample answers only)

1 Trying to keep everyone in the office happy.

2 Dealing with the technical side of the work, but of course, that's quite easy for me.

3 Making my customers happy.

4 Going to international conferences.

5 Keeping up to date with the filing.

Task 3 (Sample answers only)

1 After leaving school, I went straight to university to do a degree in electronic engineering.

2 Before graduating, I spent a few weeks each year with Olivetti in Ivrea.

3 After joining Olivetti, I worked in sales for a while, and I got to know that side of the business well before moving to R&D.

4 After working in research for six years, I was made Head of Product Marketing.

Unit 31 Reported speech (1): statements, thoughts, commands, requests

Practice

Exercise 1

1 *he was thinking about buying a new car.*

2 the new S500 was very good value.

3 he had bought a Mercedes in 1985 and had liked it a lot.

4 he could take it for a test drive.

5 he didn't have any identification, ... the woman in the car was his grandmother.

6 that would be fine.

7 her grandson was taking a long time.

8 he wasn't her grandson ... He had offered to drive her to the shops, but she had never seen him before.

Exercise 2

1 *I am very interested in working for you.*

2 I have been working in the city for three years.

3 I like what I do, but I want more responsibility.

Answer Key

4 I have a degree in Economics and an MBA.

5 I can't leave my job for another month.

6 I will consider your offer, and I will let you have a decision soon.

Exercise 3

1	E	2	D	3	G	4	F
5	A	6	B	7	H	8	C

Exercise 4

1 *He asked me to come to dinner at 8.00.*

2 He told me to send the letter immediately.

3 He asked me not to mention the plans to anyone.

4 He asked me to return the form as soon as possible.

5 He told me not to put any calls through to his office.

Exercise 5

1	*this afternoon*	2	the following day
3	there	4	yesterday
5	here		

Production

Task 1 (Sample answers only)

1 *I told him I was married and that I lived in London.*

2 I told him that the company was very well-managed.

3 I said that I was responsible for buying all the clothes for the stores.

4 I told him I would need at least 20% more.

5 He said that it was a dynamic new company that was expanding fast.

6 He told me that I could almost write my own job description.

7 I told him that I would think about it.

Task 2 (Sample answers only)

1 *it was selling well.*

2 you were that old.

3 it would take so long.

4 he left for Japan last night.

5 it was so expensive.

Task 3 (Sample answers only)

1 *told them to pay at once.*

2 asked her to come back later.

3 told him not to drive home.

4 asked him to pay a cheque into my account.

5 told them to replace it.

6 asked him to give me an estimate.

Unit 32 Reported speech (2): questions and reporting verbs

Practice

Exercise 1

1 *when the new product would be ready.*

2 *how much we were planning to spend on advertising.*

3 where we intended to advertise.

4 what discount we would give our distributors.

5 why it had taken so long to develop.

6 how much market interest there had been in the new product.

7 who the product was aimed at.

8 what sort of problems we had had in developing the product.

Exercise 2

1 *I asked her if she had had a good trip.*

2 I asked her if they had signed the contract.

3 I asked her if she would need to go back again.

4 I asked her if the hotel had been OK.

5 I asked her if she had had any time off.

6 I asked her if she was feeling tired.

7 I asked her if she had had any problems.

8 I asked her if she felt confident about the project.

9 I asked her if they had liked the idea of a joint venture.

Exercise 3

1 *I wonder if the bank has a branch in Geneva.*

2 *Do you know when the plane will get in?*

3 how the negotiations are going.

4 if Peter is coming to the meeting?

5 when the talk is going to start?

6 if I should take the job.

7 where their head office is.

8 if they will accept our offer.

9 if they have sent us an order form?

10 how they got this information.

Exercise 4

1	G	2	J	3	C	4	I
5	E	6	A	7	F	8	H
9	D	10	B				

Production

Task 1 (Sample answers only)

1 *That was Mr Jackson. He asked me if he could change the date of our next meeting to the 15th and I said it would be fine.*

2 That was Miss Lemur. She asked if we could increase our discount, but I explained that we couldn't.

Answer Key

3 That was the Chief Engineer. He was ringing to ask when we could deliver the machinery, and I said he would have it on Wednesday.

4 That was the Production Department. They wanted to know if I had paid the electricity bill, and I said that I had.

5 That was the bank. They wanted to know how much we had lost as a result of their negligence, and I said it was over £16,000.

Task 2 (Sample answers only)

1 *how she is getting on in her new job.*
2 where the station is.
3 whether the price has gone up or not.
4 what flights are available?
5 how to read Greek?

Task 3 (Sample answers only)

1 *I advised her to accept it.*
2 he refused to repair the machine free of charge.
3 they offered to give us better credit terms.
4 apologized for causing so much trouble.

Unit 33 Relative clauses (1): who, that, which, whose, whom

Practice

Exercise 1

1 *which*	2 who	3 which	4 who
5 who	6 which	7 who	8 which
9 which	10 which	11 which	

Exercise 2

1 *that has a 60 number memory.*
2 *that you can use without picking up the handset.*
3 that can store up to 100 messages.
4 that you can call from another phone.
5 that can print at different resolutions.
6 that you can use to copy A4 documents.
7 that has an automatic sheet feeder.
8 that you can program.

You can leave out *that* in 2, 4, 6, and 8.

Exercise 3

1 *whose CVs were very good.*
2 whose mother tongue must be English.
3 whose headquarters are in Helsinki.
4 whose car had broken down.
5 whose key competitors are Sony and Sanyo.
6 whose department was doing well.

Exercise 4

1 *whom, which*	2 who	3 which
4 who	5 whom	6 which

Exercise 5

1 *The man I was talking to is the head of AT&T.*
2 invoice you were looking for.
3 customers I deal with are very pleasant.
4 we wanted to stay in was fully booked.
5 she works for has a very good reputation.
6 we went to wasn't very good.

Production

Task 1

1 *inVoice*
2 cOntract
3 *saLary*
4 banK
5 *subSidiary*
6 laWyer
7 *catAlogue*
8 aGenda
9 *collEague*
10 telephoNe

Answer : VOLKSWAGEN

(Sample answers only)

1 An invoice is a document that asks for payment.
3 A salary is an amount of money that is paid to an employee.
5 A subsidiary is a small organization that belongs to a larger organization.
7 A catalogue is a kind of brochure that lists what a company sells.
9 A colleague is a person that you work with.

Task 2 (Sample answers only)

1 *that manufactures components for aircraft.*
2 who lets me work flexible hours.
3 that consists of twenty people.
4 who need advice on financial planning.
5 that I don't really want to.
6 who are intelligent.
7 who cannot make decisions.
8 that let me relax.

Unit 34 Relative clauses (2): where, with, what, and non-defining clauses

Practice

Exercise 1

1 *I've got the details of the hotel where you will be staying.*
2 Would you like to visit the factory where we make the cars?
3 I recently went back to the town where I used to work.

Answer Key

4   Ivrea is the town where Olivetti has its headquarters.
5   Is this the building where they filmed the Coke advertisement?

Exercise 2

1   *with a £2000 credit limit.*
2   *that has all the latest information.*
3   with a colour monitor?
4   with a bit more experience.
5   that has a better view.
6   that has a lot of mistakes.
7   with a matching tie.
8   with a sense of humour.

Exercise 3

1   *I wasn't interested in what he was selling.*
2   what you asked me to do.
3   does what you want it to.
4   deliver what you need tomorrow.
5   hear what you said.

Exercise 4

1   *The new accounts program, which cost a great deal of money, is working very well.*
2   The Oriental Hotel, where many famous people have stayed, is said to be the best in the world.
3   Richard Branson, who has now sold his record company to Sony, runs the airline Virgin Atlantic.
4   Glaxo, whose products include Zantac, is the biggest drug producer in Europe.
5   Their new range of cosmetics, on which they have spent £10 million, will be launched next month.
6   I am writing with reference to my client Mr Warburg, with whom I have discussed your proposal.

Exercise 5

1   Yesterday I spoke to your director, who seemed to be very pleasant.
2   The room where we held the meeting was a little too small.
3   Brazil, which is the world's largest exporter of coffee, has high inflation.
4   The negotiators finally reached a formula on which everyone could agree.
5   I found it difficult to hear what the speaker was talking about.
6   Tim Lang, who only joined the company six months ago, is going to be promoted.
7   The Rover Group, whose name has been changed several times, is now part of BMW.
8   I suggest we have a meeting in Romsey Street, where we rent a few offices.

Production

Task 1

Dalgleish & Mackay (1), *which is one of Hong Kong's largest trading companies*, was founded in 1832 by Scotsmen Allen Dalgleish and Charles Mackay. They started the business in the Chinese city of Canton (2), which was an important commercial centre.

The trading company exported tea and imported opium (3), for which there was a growing demand.

In 1839 the Chinese authorities (4), who wanted to stop the opium trade, seized 7,000 chests of Dalgleish's opium. The British traders (5), who had powerful allies in London, persuaded the British government to go to war to protect 'free trade'. They sent ships to Canton and began the First Opium War (6), which ended in 1842. The Chinese lost, and signed the Treaty of Nanking (7), under which they agreed to give Hong Kong to the British.

The company moved to Hong Kong (8), where it opened up new headquarters, and began trading in opium again. In 1860, after the Second Opium War (9), which led to the legalization of opium, the company flourished and expanded. It later left the opium business (10), which was politically dangerous, and expanded into land, brewing, textiles, and many other fields of business.

The company (11), whose legal headquarters are now in Bermuda, has interests in general trade, insurance, and merchant banking. It announced a strategy of reducing its interests in Hong Kong because of the Chinese takeover in 1997, and now has a 30% share in an international holding company (12), which owns two airlines and a major hotel chain.

Unit 35 Countable and uncountable nouns

Practice

Exercise 1

1 *a, some*	2 a, some	3 a, some
4 some, a	5 a, some	6 some, a
7 some, a	8 a, some	9 a, some
10 a, some		

Exercise 2

1 is	2 is	3 are	4 is
5 are	6 is	7 is	

Exercise 3

1 *a problem*	2 some money
3 some work	4 some trouble
5 a cheque	6 some equipment
7 a good record	8 a suggestion

Answer Key

9 a final demand   10 a lawyer
11 some advice   12 a letter
13 some information   14 some correspondence

Exercise 4

1 a pint of water   2 a glass of wine
3 a sheet of paper   4 a barrel of oil
5 a tonne of coal   6 a litre of beer
7 a kilo of sugar

Exercise 5

1 *a litre*   2 a barrel   3 an ounce
4 a pint   5 a bottle   6 a packet

Production

Task 1

1 *fish*   2 alcohol   3 time
4 weather   5 money   6 Greek
7 meat   8 shopping

Task 2 (Sample answers only)

1 Money is the root of all evil.
2 Time is money.
3 Meetings are designed to make idle people look busy.
4 Work is the new opium of the people.
5 Men can understand everything except women.
6 Women need men like fish need bicycles.
7 Experience is only valued by the person who has it.
8 Productivity can be measured but satisfaction cannot.

Unit 36 Articles: a/an, the, or Ø (no article)?

Practice

Exercise 1

1 *an*   2 a   3 a   4 a
5 an   6 an   7 a   8 an
9 an   10 a

Exercise 2

1 a   2 an   3 a   4 a
5 Ø   6 Ø   7 Ø   8 a

Exercise 3

1 *a*   2 the   3 a   4 The
5 the   6 a   7 the   8 The
9 the   10 a   11 the   12 the

Exercise 4

1 Ø, *the*   2 the, Ø   3 The, Ø   4 Ø, the
5 the, Ø   6 Ø, the   7 Ø, the   8 Ø, the

Exercise 5

A 1 Ø   2 the   3 Ø   4 the
    5 Ø   6 Ø   7 the   8 Ø

B 9 Ø   10 the   11 the   12 Ø   13 Ø
    14 Ø   15 Ø   16 Ø   17 the

Production

Task 1

	1	2	3	4
USA	The	the	the	Ø
	5 Ø	6 a	7 a	
NIGERIA	1 a	2 the	3 the	4 the
	5 The	6 Ø		
JAPAN	1 the	2 Ø	3 Ø	4 Ø
	5 a			

Task 2 (Sample answers only)

1 The Netherlands has an annual per capita income of $15,000. Recently the Max Havelaar Foundation has set up an organization to import coffee from Nicaragua, Uganda, and Zaire. It only does business with growers who have small, family-run, democratically controlled farms, and pays the growers excellent prices.
2 Sierra Leone is rich in natural resources such as gold, diamonds, and timber. Unfortunately, because of political problems, many of these resources are not being properly used.

Unit 37 Some and any

Practice

Exercise 1

1 *some*   2 a   3 a   4 any
5 some   6 some   7 any   8 some

Exercise 2

1 any   2 some   3 any   4 any
5 any   6 some   7 some   8 any
9 any   10 any

Exercise 3

1 *Right*
2 Right
3 Wrong – some letters
4 Right
5 Wrong – any major orders
6 Right
7 Wrong – some problems
8 Right

Exercise 4

1 *anyone*   2 somewhere   3 something
4 someone   5 anyone   6 anywhere
7 anything

Exercise 5

1 anyone   2 anywhere   3 anyone
4 anything   5 anything   6 anywhere

Answer Key

Exercise 6

1	*much*	2	a lot of	3	much
4	a little	5	many	6	a few
7	a lot of	8	much	9	a lot of
10	a few				

Production

Task 1 (Sample answers only)
1 *We haven't got any petrol left.*
2 I needed some advice.
3 Yes, they've moved to somewhere in West London.
4 No, I didn't tell them anything.

Task 2 (Sample answers only)
1 *You can stay anywhere you like.*
2 No, you can tell anyone you like.
3 No, you can sit anywhere you like.
4 You can store anything you like.

Task 3 (Sample answers only)
1 *No, luckily the burglars didn't have much time, because the alarm went off. They took a lot of cheap pieces of jewellery, and they took a little money as well.*
2 I didn't meet many people because I didn't have much time. It seems that most of our customers haven't got much spare cash at the moment, so we are only getting a few new orders a month.
3 No, I didn't learn much. I spent a lot of time with other Japanese people, but I didn't enjoy myself much. We went out a few times in the evening, but I spent a lot of the time just watching TV.

Unit 38 Adjectives and adverbs

Practice

Exercise 1

1	*safely*	2	quarterly	3	punctually
4	late	5	publicly	6	heavily
7	patiently	8	silently		

Exercise 2

1	*suddenly*	2	briefly	3	dramatically
4	considerably	5	slightly	6	steadily
7	gradually				

Exercise 3

1	*well qualified*	2	surprisingly good
3	commercially viable	4	totally illegal
5	badly designed	6	terribly quickly

Exercise 4

1	*impressive*	2	good	3	calmly
4	expensive	5	badly	6	dark

7	sour	8	competent	9	locally
10	confident				

Exercise 5

1	*good*	2	well	3	well	4	good
5	good	6	well	7	well		

Production

Task 1

1	*recent*	2	properly	3	badly
4	fine	5	noisy	6	ineffective
7	immediately	8	grateful	9	warm
10	strong				

Task 2 (Sample answers only)

1	*revolutionary new*	2	fascinating
3	famous	4	in-depth
5	important	6	main
7	clearly	8	top
9	major	10	key
11	absolutely	12	knock-down
13	extremely useful	14	modern

Task 3 (Sample answer only)
I would like to tell you about a major opportunity that we are currently offering our most valued customers. We are launching a brand new share-dealing service that will let you buy and sell shares instantly. Please read through the enclosed leaflet carefully, and if you would like to know more, phone me on 0188 221 8834.

Unit 39 Comparison (1): comparing adjectives

Practice

Exercise 1

valuable	more valuable than	the most valuable
expensive	more expensive than	the most expensive
good	better than	the best
wealthy	wealthier than	the wealthiest
big	bigger than	the biggest
narrow	narrower than	the narrowest
cheap	cheaper than	the cheapest
bad	worse than	the worst
profitable	more profitable than	the most profitable
long	longer than	the longest
interesting	more interesting than	the most interesting

Exercise 2

1	*wider*	2	smaller
3	more portable	4	easier
5	better	6	lower
7	good	8	larger

Answer Key

9 more sophisticated   10 more serious
11 more quality conscious   12 sexier
13 more sensible

Exercise 3

1 *Norway has the highest income per capita.*
2 *Poland has the lowest income per capita.*
3 Norway is the most expensive to live in.
4 Poland is the cheapest to live in.
5 Poland has the highest corporate tax rate.
6 Norway has the lowest corporate tax rate.
7 Norway has the best/highest literacy rate.
8 Mexico has the worst/lowest literacy rate.

Exercise 4

1 *That was the longest meeting I have ever been to.*
2 That was the most boring presentation I have ever heard.
3 They are the most difficult customers I have ever dealt with.
4 This is the best product we have ever produced.
5 This is the simplest program I have ever used.

Exercise 5

1 *It is the second most profitable company in the world.*
2 He is the second richest person in the world.
3 It is the third largest industrial corporation in the world.
4 He is the fourth wealthiest person in the world.

Production

Task 1 (Sample answers only)

1 *The company I work for is bigger than the last company I worked for.*
   It is not as small as the last company I worked for.
2 The job I do now is harder to do than my last job.
   The job I do now isn't as easy to do as my last job.
3 Inflation this year is higher than it was last year.
   Inflation this year isn't as low as it was last year.
4 Our company isn't as large as our main competitor.
   Our company is smaller than our main competitor.

Task 2 (Sample answers only)

1 *The best meal I have ever had was in France.*
2 The most interesting course I have ever been on was at Insead.
3 The best computer I have ever used was a Power Mac.
4 The nicest country I have ever visited is Argentina.
5 The most expensive hotel I have ever stayed in is the Oriental in Bangkok.
6 The fastest car I have ever driven was a Ferrari.
7 The most reasonable boss I have ever worked for is Robin Vernede.

8 The worst job I have ever had was when I joined the army.

Task 3 (Sample answers only)

I work for Darlington's, a law firm that specializes in commercial property, and our main competitors are Kenworth & Brown. We are not as large as they are, but we have the best taxation department in the City. Because we are smaller, we offer our clients a better service, and our charges are significantly lower.

I work for a local radio station in the south of England, and I sell advertising. Our station is smaller than the main national stations, but our local audiences are larger, so our clients are very interested in our services. Of course it is much cheaper than advertising on TV, and we get a good deal of repeat business because radio ads are more effective than ads in the papers.

Unit 40 Comparison (2): comparing adverbs and comparing nouns

Practice

Exercise 1

1 *later*   2 faster   3 earlier   4 worse
5 better

Exercise 2

1 *more frequently*   2 more carefully
3 more slowly   4 more efficiently
5 more quietly

Exercise 3

1 *the worst affected*
2 the most extensively tested
3 best selling
4 most efficiently managed
5 most rapidly developing
6 the most heavily protected

Exercise 4

a 1 *the most*   2 more ... than
  3 the fewest   4 as many ... as
  5 fewer ... than   6 the fewest
  7 the fewest   8 more
b 1 *more ... than*   2 the most
  3 more ... than   4 the least
  5 as much ... as   6 more ... than
  7 less ... than   8 the most

Exercise 5

1 more   2 many   3 fewer   4 much

Answer Key

Production

Task 1 (Sample answers only)

1 *I get up earlier than I used to.* or *I don't get up as early as I used to.*
2 I don't go abroad as regularly as ...
3 I work harder than ...
4 I stay at work later than ...
5 I speak English better than ...
6 I live further away than ...

Task 2 (Sample answers only)

1 *the fastest* 2 the hardest 3 the most often
4 the best 5 the fastest 6 the worst

Task 3 (Sample answers only)

1 *I don't do as much work as I used to.* or *I don't do as much as I used to.*
2 I don't have as much as I used to.
3 I don't go to as many as I used to.
4 I listen to more than I used to.
5 I get a lot less than I used to.
6 I buy a lot more than I used to.

Unit 41 Degree: too, enough, so, such, such a

Practice

Exercise 1

1 *– enough* 2 *– enough* 3 *– enough*
4 too – 5 too – 6 *– enough*

Exercise 2

1 *too many* 2 too many 3 too little
4 too much 5 too few 6 too many

Exercise 3

1 *The exhibition was too far away for us to attend.*
2 Your products are too expensive for us to stock.
3 This contract is too complicated for me to understand.
4 My fax wasn't clear enough for him to read.
5 Your quotation wasn't low enough for us to accept.
6 The project was too risky for them to go ahead with.

Exercise 4

1 *so entertaining/such marvellous acting/written so well (a film)*
2 such good graphics/so fast/so user-friendly (a computer)
3 such a good idea/so clever/so useful (an invention)
4 so light/decorated so beautifully/so modern (an office)
5 so tasty/presented so nicely/such good value (a meal in a restaurant)
6 such nice weather/such friendly people/such lovely beaches (a holiday destination)

7 so logical/so useful/so easy to learn (a language)
8 so fair/such a good sense of humour/so supportive (a colleague)

Exercise 5

1 *The meeting went on for such a long time that I missed the train home.*
2 The company was in such a bad financial state that they called in the receivers.
3 Frankfurt was so busy during the book fair that we couldn't get a hotel room.
4 They treat their employees so well that nobody ever wants to leave.
5 My portable computer is so unreliable that I don't like to use it.
6 The new drug was so successful that the factory couldn't meet the demand for it.
7 He had such a good CV that we decided to interview him.

Production

Task 1 (Sample answers only)

1 *I've been there too long.*
2 He hasn't got enough experience.
3 It's too small.
4 He is too aggressive.
5 I haven't got enough time.
6 It was too expensive.

Task 2 (Sample answers only)

1 *Emerging markets are too volatile to invest in.*
Emerging markets aren't stable enough to invest in.
2 Their forecasts are too inaccurate for us to use.
Their forecasts aren't accurate enough for us to use.
3 Our tax laws are too complicated for most people to understand.
Our tax laws aren't simple enough for most people to understand.
4 Rents in the city are too high for us to have an office there.
Rents in the city aren't low enough for us to have an office there.
5 The town is too small for us to have a branch in.
The town isn't big enough for us to have a branch in.

Task 3 (Sample answers only)

1 *He seems so young.* 2 I'm so tired.
3 You speak it so well. 4 She had such a good job.
5 She earns so much. 6 He speaks so well.

Answer Key

Unit 42 Adjective + preposition combinations

Practice

Exercise 1

1 *for*	2 about	3 with
4 similar	5 suitable	6 related
7 opposed	8 rich	9 afraid
10 capable	11 guilty	12 interested

Word comb: RAW MATERIALS

Exercise 2

1 *buying*	2 moving	3 taking
4 running	5 hiring	6 manufacturing

Exercise 3

1 *annoyed about*	2 sorry about
3 responsible for	4 annoyed with
5 responsible to	6 sorry for
7 good at, bad with	8 good for

Exercise 4

1 *responsible*	2 proud	3 accustomed
4 capable	5 good	6 aware
7 rich	8 famous	9 popular
10 interested		

Production

Task 1 (Sample answers only)

1 *The BMW 500 series is popular with executives.*
2 I don't think she is capable of doing the work.
3 Bordeaux is famous for its wines.
4 Janet is responsible for hiring new staff.
5 The Industrial Society is opposed to higher taxes.
6 Would you be interested in arranging a meeting?

Task 2 (Sample answers only)

1 *In my job, I am responsible for researching into new allergy drugs.*
2 I am answerable to the Publicity and Promotions Manager.
3 I am good at making visitors feel important.
4 I would be capable of organizing product launches.
5 I would be satisfied with an extra 20%.

Task 3 (Sample answers only)

1 *I think I would be capable of doing what my boss does.*
2 I would be interested in working for a bigger company.
3 My current job is very different from my last one.
4 I am not afraid of taking risks.
5 I am proud of a lot of the things I have achieved.
6 My job is similar to the one my boss does.

Unit 43 Noun + preposition combinations

Practice

Exercise 1

1 *invitation to*	2 request for
3 advantage of	4 reply to
5 cheque for	6 experience of
7 price of	8 difference between
9 trouble with	10 solution to

Exercise 2

1 in, of	2 of, in	3 in, of, of

Exercise 3

A 1 with	2 by	3 out of
4 by		
B 1 on	2 in	3 on
4 on	5 at	6 in

Exercise 4

1 *to*	2 of	3 in
4 for	5 in/of	6 in
7 of	8 on	9 on
10 of	11 over/on	12 at

Production

Task 1 (Sample answers only)

1 *of dealing with difficult customers.*
2 between what you do and what I do.
3 in all kinds of crime.
4 to the political problems in the Middle East.
5 for coal rises dramatically.

Task 2 (Sample answers only)

1 *This machine is out of order.*
2 I'm in a hurry.
3 We sold the car at a loss.
4 I usually go to work by car.
5 The train arrived on time.
6 My house is for sale.
7 He is in debt.
8 The goods are on order.

Task 3

1 *on my hands*	2 out of hand
3 by hand	4 on hand
5 in the hands	6 On the other hand

Answer Key

Unit 44 Verb + preposition combinations

Practice

Exercise 1

1 *with*	2 of	3 on	4 of
5 on	6 to	7 for	8 on
9 from			

Exercise 2

1 *agree with*	2 hear about	3 write to
4 wait for	5 think of	6 look at

Exercise 3

1 *blame*	2 provide	3 congratulate
4 thank	5 insure	6 supply
7 divide	8 spend	

Word comb: MICHELIN

Exercise 4

1 Ø	2 for	3 to	4 Ø
5 about	6 for	7 Ø	8 Ø

Production

Task 1 (Sample answers only)

1 *I would complain to the head waiter.*
2 I would talk to a friend about it.
3 I would write to the Investor Relations Department.
4 I would think about it for a few days.
5 I would rely on my lawyer's advice.

Task 2 (Sample answers only)

1 She blamed me for the accident.
2 He provided me with the information.
3 She thanked me for helping her.
4 He asked me for my opinion.
5 They congratulated us on solving the problem.

Task 3 (Sample answers only)

1 *borrow what you need from the bank.*
2 invest it in the stock market.
3 spend it on a new suit.
4 insure it against theft.

Unit 45 Phrasal verbs

Practice

Exercise 1

1 *OM*	2 *PV*	3 PV	4 OM
5 OM	6 PV	7 PV	8 OM

Exercise 2

1 A *We have got to keep down inflation.*
  B *We have got to keep it down.*
2 A Could you pick James up?
  B Could you pick him up?
3 A You must fill in the form.
  B You must fill it in.
4 A They're going to close down the factory.
  B They're going to close it down.
5 A I have thrown away the invoices.
  B I have thrown them away.

Exercise 3

1 put me through	2 cut us off
3 put it off	4 pick him up

Exercise 4

1 *broken down*	2 look into
3 do without	4 taking up
5 run out of	6 checked in
7 turn up	8 look after
9 hold on	10 call on

Exercise 5

1 D	2 A	3 D	4 D
5 A			

Production

Task 1

1 round	2 up	3 into	4 forward
5 out	6 through		

Task 2 (Sample answers only)

1 Write down – You'll find it easier to remember if you write the number down.
2 Write off – We lost a lot of money on the deal, but we can write it off against tax.
3 Write up – The product had a good write-up in the press.
4 Write out – Get him to write out a cheque when you see him.
5 Write off for – I have written off for a catalogue.

Index

References are to the Glossary (G), Unit numbers (Unit 36, Unit 42), page numbers (54, 55, 59) and Appendices (App. 2).

Index

Index

Index

Oxford University Press,
Great Clarendon Street, Oxford OX2 6DP

Oxford New York
Athens Auckland Bangkok Bogota Bombay
Buenos Aires Calcutta Cape Town Dar es Salaam
Delhi Florence Hong Kong Istanbul Karachi
Kuala Lumpur Madras Madrid Melbourne
Mexico City Nairobi Paris Singapore
Taipei Tokyo Toronto Warsaw

and associated companies in
Berlin Ibadan

OXFORD and OXFORD ENGLISH
are trade marks of Oxford University Press

ISBN 0 19 457068 1

© Oxford University Press

First published 1995

Third impression 1998

Design by Shireen Nathoo Design

Printed in China

Acknowledgements
The author and publisher are grateful to the following for permission
to use extracts from and adaptations of copyright material:

p73 Amstrad plc via Michael Joyce Consultants, company history;
p149 United Colors of Benetton, extracts from *Colors* magazine;
p7 Berli Jucker Public Co. Ltd, company information; p135 British
Telecom, product information; p67 Business Magazines (UK) Ltd,
Business Age Telecom paycard; p28 Compaq Computers Ltd, company
information; p68 DHL International (UK) Ltd, information from
company brochure; p120 *The Economist*, adapted extracts from 'Inch
by inch', from *The Economist* 30.7.94, © *The Economist*, July 1994;
p159 Philips via Mathieu Thomas Ltd, product information;
p124 Specialist Computer Holdings Ltd (SCH) via Harvard Public
Relations, company information; pp20, 59 Sony United Kingdom Ltd,
company history and product information; p147 Times Newspapers
Ltd, extract from 'Coca-Cola launches £4m UK campaign' by John
Ashworth, *The Times* 15.11.94, © Times Newspapers Ltd 1994.

Every effort has been made to trace and contact copyright holders.
However, this has not always been possible. If notified, the publisher
will be pleased to rectify any errors or omissions at the earliest
opportunity.

The author and publisher would like to thank everyone who helped us
by piloting and commenting on the material contained in this book,
particularly the following:

David Allerton, The English Institute, Metz; Catherine Butchart,
Linguarama Spracheninstitut, Hamburg; Robyn Christensen, Schering
AG, Berlin; Kate Cowe, Düsseldorf; Patricia Cook, Formation et
Communication, Paris; Ilse De Kerpel, Silly-Hainault; Joséphine
Ezzarouali and Karen Carnet, LOGOS, Grenoble; Eamonn Fitzgerald,
Munich; Simon Gardner and Katy Ryan, LANSER S.A., Bilbao; Guy
Heath, Aximedia Idiomas, Madrid; Clement Laroy, Nivelles; Kate
Monleón, King's College Business English Programmes, Madrid;
Monica Apraiz Pineda and Juan Antonio Rico, Eurostudy, Bilbao; Beth
Schüth, Tim Hill, and Helmut Hunder, Henkel KGaA, Düsseldorf.

Special thanks to Isobel Fletcher de Téllez.